Foreword by Vinnie Politan, J.D.

AF223981

WOLVES IN SHEEP'S CLOTHING

A Practical Guide for True Crime Enthusiasts

Michael R. King

PROFILING EVIL

Profiling Evil, LLC
www.ProfilingEvil.com
ProfilingEvil@gmail.com
USA

Copyright © 2025 by Profiling Evil, LLC and Michael R. King
Published 2025 • All rights reserved.

Printed in the United States of America.
No part of this book may be used or reproduced in any manner
whatsoever without the express written permission of the author
 and the owner of these rights.

ISBN: 978-1-7362374-9-6 (Paperback)
ISBN: 978-1-7362374-1-0 (Hardback)

DEDICATION

This book is dedicated to the men and women who stand on the front lines of justice—those who have fought, are fighting, and will continue to fight against crime. To the current and next generation of crime fighters, your dedication does not go unnoticed.

My hope is that the sworn police officers, crime and intelligence analysts, forensic experts, support staff, and the mental health and medical professionals who bear witness to the darkest aspects of human nature, may find solace in knowing that your work changes lives and strengthens communities. Your sacrifice and perseverance matters.

And to you, the citizen detectives and true crime enthusiasts, whose relentless curiosity and commitment to uncovering the truth bring new perspectives to unsolved cases—thank you for standing alongside those who protect and serve. Your support and awareness fuel the never-ending pursuit of justice.

This book is for all of you.

CONTENTS

MOTIVATION, JUSTIFCATION & BEHAVIORAL DYNAMICS

UNDERSTANDING VICTIMOLOGY: SELECTION, IMPACT & PREVENTION

DECODING CRIME SCENES: EVIDENCE, PERSONAS & BEHAVIORAL INSIGHTS

UNMASKING PREDATORS: ROOTS, RED FLAGS & COMMUNITY IMPACT

CONCLUSION

ACKNOWLEDGMENTS

I'm grateful to Bonnie. Anything good in my life is because of her. I'm also thankful for our children and their companions who encouraged me to stretch beyond what was familiar. To the many mentors I've had in policing, profiling, business, and faith, you helped shape the course of my life. Your examples left lasting impressions, and your lessons were heard, appreciated, and often followed.

AUTHOR NOTE

Writing *Wolves in Sheep's Clothing* has been a journey of reflection and exploration, a culmination of years dedicated to understanding the darkest corners of human behavior. This book is deeply personal because it is built on the foundations laid by my mentor and dear friend, former FBI Special Agent and profiler Gregory Cooper. Greg not only taught me the art and science of criminal profiling but also inspired me to delve into the bigger questions—*Why are certain crimes committed? What motivates offenders to select certain victims?* Greg's guidance has been instrumental in shaping my approach to criminal investigations.

Together, we traveled the globe, sharing the lesson's we've learned, teaching the intricacies of criminal behavior, and contributing to the field of investigative analysis. One of our proudest achievements was solving what many considered the coldest cold case in history: the murder of the ancient Egyptian pharaoh, Tutankhamun, better known as King Tut. The insights gained from that extraordinary experience reflect the collaborative spirit of our work.

I'd like to express my gratitude to trailblazing profilers who profoundly shaped my education and practical pursuits; John Douglas, with his groundbreaking work in behavioral profiling, and Mark Safarik whose expertise in behavioral analysis has provided invaluable insights into the complexities of the criminal mind. Their contributions have been instrumental in shaping my own perspective on the psychology behind violent crime.

I'd like to acknowledge many others who have influenced and taught me throughout my career—but there are far too many to name. None-the-less, I would be remiss if I didn't mention Dr. Harold J. Bursztajn and Dr. Ann Burgess. Their unwavering dedication to understanding human and criminal motivation has left an indelible mark on me. To all who have paved the way, mentored, and inspired— thank you. I'd like to thank Inge Moore for her assistance in editing this book.

Several years ago, I had the privilege of meeting O. Machelle Morris, an extraordinary attorney from Texas whose deep sense of justice and compassion was shaped by her father's legacy in law enforcement. Her unwavering support, sharp legal mind, and steadfast integrity are deeply appreciated. Thanks Machelle!

I also want to thank to Vinnie Politan, a gifted lawyer, journalist, and lead anchor for Court TV. I have had the privilege of joining him on air to break down some of the most compelling cases in history. Vinnie's ability to balance empathy with razor-sharp legal insight is unmatched, and his dedication to making the legal process accessible to viewers is nothing short of inspiring. I'm honored that he penned the foreword to this book. Whether it's his past work as a New Jersey prosecutor or his Emmy-winning journalism, Vinnie continues to be a trusted voice in American courtrooms and living rooms alike.

And finally, to you the reader, thank you for joining me on this journey. Together, let's shed light on the darkness and uncover the truths hidden in plain sight.

Warm regards,

Michael K King

FOREWORD
by Vinnie Politan, J.D. • Lead Anchor, Court TV

Every night on my television shows on Court TV, I cover the biggest true crime stories and trials in the country. I've been doing this for quite some time, in fact, since the turn of the century. Over these years, I've witnessed the public's interest in true crime grow at an extraordinary rate.

It's brought people from all walks of life into the genre. Go online and you'll see what I mean. You'll find makeup artists talking about fatal love triangles, people sipping wine while dissecting serial killers, film students trying to solve mysteries, and even former mobsters breaking down organized crime. Many of them are captivating storytellers. But for me, true crime is about more than just the story.

It's in the space beyond the facts where you'll find what's most important, the how and the why. Sure, the stories themselves are gripping, often filled with salacious, even seductive details. But if we stop there, we're no better than rubberneckers at a car crash. The real value lies in understanding what caused the wreck, and how to prevent the next one. That level of understanding can expose the problem that caused the carnage and be used to save future victims. The most meaningful discussions on my shows are the ones that go beyond the horrific facts to uncover the how and the why.

While my background is as a former prosecutor, I also recognize the importance of leaning on experts who know how to dig deeper, ask the right questions, and uncover what truly drives criminal behavior. Mike King is one of those experts.

Mike has become a trusted friend and frequent guest on my shows. Over the years, we've developed a strong professional bond that is built upon a shared passion for victims and a deep commitment to justice. That perspective is essential. It gives voice to those who can no longer speak for themselves, and it's something Mike has done throughout his law enforcement career and has carried into his role as an expert. His empathy for those who have fallen prey to the worst in society really provides the strong foundation for his voice and his work in law enforcement. It's not just what he does, it's who he is.

Mike isn't your average "just the facts, ma'am" Joe Friday-style investigator. His insight runs much deeper. He gathers the facts, yes, but he also explores the psychological, behavioral, and environmental factors that impact the conduct of predatory criminals. This type of analysis is crucial for a deeper understanding. Because predatory crimes don't just happen, there's a reason and understanding and exposing those reasons is what he does best.

One of the most powerful examples of his work is the Zion Society case. Mike didn't just help take down a cult leader who abused his power to victimize young girls. He peeled back the layers of how that cult formed, operated, and thrived in secrecy. He studied its origin and its impact. And then, after the arrests he helped the victims navigate their way back into society. That's the kind of compassion and commitment that defines his work. Taking down a predator, while exposing his modus operandi and compassionately helping the survivors are classic Mike moves. It's also the foundation for his new book, *Wolves in Sheep's Clothing*.

The "wolves" in this book are the criminal predators who use charm, influence, or a false appearance of goodness to gain access to their victims. They often manipulate and deceive under the guise of helping. As the title reveals, these "wolves" rely on false perceptions that are disguised to exploit the innocence of the innocent. Mike exposes those deceptive facades and takes us beyond them, revealing the truth and motives behind this dangerous behavior. This is next-level analysis that opens eyes and makes a real impact.

Mike also draws on psychological research to explore the traits that allow these predators to deceive and control others without remorse. He guides us into a very dark place and brings the light we need to see what's really going on. Often, what's happening isn't simple and it comes from a mixture of influences, experiences, and decisions where the answers lie in many different places.

It can begin in childhood. The upbringing of an offender, the conduct of the adults in their lives, their exposure to trauma or twisted ideologies. All these behaviors help shape the predators they become. *Wolves in Sheep's Clothing* examines who these people were before they became offenders. And then, there are the crime scenes themselves. Sure, a fingerprint or strand of DNA might identify an offender, but this book shows us how much more we can learn. Every crime scene tells a story about what happened, but it also exposes who did it and why. That's where Mike takes us beyond traditional forensic analysis and into the mind of the predator.

But what I most appreciate about this book is that it doesn't stop at explaining evil. It goes further by empowering the reader. Mike provides practical tools and insights from these tragedies. He teaches us how to recognize red flags, understand the vulnerabilities predators exploit, and take proactive measures to safeguard ourselves and our communities. That's what makes this book so much more than a retelling of true crime, it's a guidebook and a call to action.

This book doesn't just unravel the complexities of predatory behavior; it instills a sense of responsibility and urgency in those who read it. It challenges us to look beyond the surface, to question what we see, and make informed choices to protect the people we care about. And that, to me, is the real power of this work.

So, as you dive into this book, prepare yourself. You're going to confront some unsettling truths. You're going to learn a lot, and if you're anything like me, you'll walk away with a deeper understanding of how predators think and you'll have a stronger resolve to keep fighting for victims, for justice, and for the truth.
Enjoy the read,

Vinnie Politan, J.D.
Lead Anchor, Court TV

PREFACE

The phrase "wolves in sheep's clothing" has long been emblematic of deception—those who, under the guise of innocence, harbor intentions that are anything but benign. The term originates from a Biblical parable, symbolizing a pervasive threat: individuals who, cloaked in trustworthiness, conceal harmful motives. This book delves into the nature of predators who try to appear harmless. It explores their psychological makeup, behavioral tendencies, and the societal environments that allow them to thrive. In this foreword we'll peek into the tragic and mysterious disappearance of Summer Wells, a five-year-old girl from Hawkins County, Tennessee, whose case epitomizes the uncertainty surrounding such figures. Was Summer's fate a tragic accident, or did she fall prey to a wolf disguised as a sheep?

"Wolves in sheep's clothing" is not merely an idiom; it is a reality in many social, professional, and spiritual contexts. These individuals often possess traits that allow them to seamlessly integrate into trusted spaces. From afar, they appear harmless—even benevolent—but their true nature reveals itself through closer scrutiny. This duality is their most potent weapon, enabling them to exploit trust and manipulate others to achieve their ends.

The psychological profile of a wolf in sheep's clothing often includes traits such as narcissism, immoral manipulation, and, in some cases, psychopathy.

These traits, collectively referred to as the "Dark Triad," equip such individuals with the tools to deceive and harm without remorse. According to studies in psychology, individuals with these traits display superficial charm, a lack of empathy, and an uncanny ability to exploit situations for personal gain.[1]

Dr. Robert Hare's work on psychopathy emphasizes that not all "wolves" are overtly dangerous, some may simply be manipulative—but their potential to harm remains a constant. These individuals often use charm to win trust or feign vulnerability to disarm suspicion. Once embedded within a social or professional circle, they manipulate relationships to create dependency, sow division, or consolidate power.

"Wolves in sheep's clothing" exhibit subtle rebellion against authority, often undermining it while feigning respect. This allows them to challenge norms and assert control without drawing attention. Their methods of control often involve psychological manipulation, such as gaslighting or coercion, designed to maintain dominance. They can display starkly different personas depending on their audience, acting benevolent in public while exploiting or intimidating others in private. Experts like Delroy L. Paulhus and Kevin M. Williams teach us that a common hallmark of a wolf in sheep's clothing is the trail of conflict or harm they leave behind, often excused by a facade of victimhood or righteousness. Talents or spiritual gifts can mask their intentions, as society tends to equate skill with morality, enabling them to exploit others with less suspicion.[2]

The disappearance of Summer Moon-Utah Wells on June 15, 2021, from her family's rural home in Hawkins County, Tennessee, has baffled investigators and captivated public attention. Summer was

last seen playing outside her home, shortly before she reportedly went inside to check on her brothers. Her mother, Candus Bly (Wells), told authorities that Summer was last seen heading to the basement to play, but when Candus tried to locate her, she was gone. The circumstances of her disappearance—in a secluded, heavily wooded area—have led to competing theories and widespread speculation.

From the outset, the case has been fraught with challenges. The rural terrain surrounding the Wells' property made the initial search efforts both exhaustive and perilous, involving hundreds of volunteers and multiple agencies. Despite an Amber Alert and an extensive search, no definitive evidence of Summer's whereabouts has been found. Law enforcement, including the Tennessee Bureau of Investigation (TBI), has stated that all possibilities remain on the table, including abduction, foul play, and an accidental disappearance.

One prevailing theory suggests that Summer may have wandered into the dense woods near her home, became lost and succumbed to the elements. The rugged terrain and wildlife in the area make this a plausible scenario, but the lack of physical evidence—such as clothing or footprints—casts doubt on this explanation. Another theory posits that Summer was abducted by someone familiar with the family, leveraging their trust to commit the crime. Cases of child abduction often involve someone

known to the victim, which aligns with this possibility.

Critics have scrutinized the family's behavior and history, with some questioning the role the parents and their acquaintances may have played in Summer's disappearance. While no charges have been filed, law enforcement has not ruled out foul play, citing inconsistencies in witness accounts and the challenging dynamics within the family. The TBI continues to request credible tips from the public, emphasizing that the investigation is active and ongoing.

The disappearance of Summer Wells is not an isolated incident. It resonates with cases where the perpetrators concealed their intentions behind masks of normalcy. High-profile examples, such as the Jaycee Dugard and Elizabeth Smart cases, reveal similar patterns where abductors posed as trusted figures before committing their crimes. These instances underscore the importance of understanding the behavioral cues that signal danger and the necessity of vigilance in safeguarding trust.

These perpetrators aren't limited to courtroom cases, but they can be found in workplaces, churches, and personal relationships. Their presence reminds us that vigilance is not paranoia; it's a necessary safeguard against exploitation.

Watching how people behave over time can be a great way to spot these predatory imposters. Those who display markedly different personas in public and private should raise concerns. Evaluating how individuals respond to authority can also offer insights, as the "wolf" often resists or undermines it covertly. The Bible's teaching, "by their fruits, you will know them" (Matthew 7:16 KJV), provides a practical framework: a pattern of chaos, harm, or manipulation often indicates deeper issues.

In the frozen wilderness, the Arctic wolf's hunting habits—rooted in survival and instinct—offer a fascinating lens through which to examine the behaviors of serial human predators like serial killers. Despite their profound differences, the parallels and divergences reveal critical insights into the nature of predation.

The Arctic wolf operates on instinctual necessity. When it kills, it does so to secure food, protect its young, or ensure the survival of its pack. Even behaviors like surplus killing occur in specific contexts, such as when conditions favor abundant prey or when the pack's needs require stockpiling resources.[3] In contrast, a human serial predator, like a serial killer, acts not out of necessity but out of intent. Their actions are premeditated, often driven by psychological gratification, control, or a compulsion unrelated to survival.[4]

Wolves are opportunistic hunters. They assess prey based on vulnerability—targeting the weak, injured, or isolated. Their decisions are practical, weighing the effort required against their energy reserves and the risks involved. While human serial predators also target the vulnerable (e.g., individuals isolated from social support or in risky environments), their actions often involve meticulous planning. Serial killers may study their victims, select them based on specific traits, and execute their crimes with calculated precision to fulfill personal motives or avoid detection.[5]

As a wolf matures, its hunting methods grow more sophisticated. Younger wolves may rely on brute force, while older, experienced wolves employ strategy, collaboration, and patience. Serial killers exhibit a similar evolution in their methods. Early crimes may be impulsive and disorganized, but over time, many develop a consistent modus operandi (MO), refining their tactics to maximize success and minimize risk. Unlike the wolf, whose adaptations ensure group survival, a serial killer's evolving behavior serves individual psychological or emotional needs.

Wolves do not kill for sport or thrill. Even when they engage in surplus killing, it is a behavior linked to survival, as the wolves often return to their kills later. Serial killers, on the other hand, frequently report a psychological "thrill" or emotional release from the act of killing. For them, the act transcends physical necessity and becomes a means of exerting control, fulfilling fantasies, or achieving personal gratification.[6]

In their environment, wolves play a vital ecological role. By targeting the weak or diseased, they contribute to the health of prey populations and maintain ecological balance. Their predation is part of a natural system. Conversely, serial killers disrupt social systems, causing widespread fear and distress. Their actions erode trust within communities and leave a trail of psychological, emotional, and societal damage.[7]

For many, the concept of a "wolf in sheep's clothing," carries a spiritual dimension. They are viewed as instruments of deception, not merely in human terms but as part of a larger battle between good and evil. This perspective offers a framework for understanding their motives and for responding to their actions.

The fate of Summer Wells remains unresolved. Was her disappearance the result of an innocent mistake, or did a "wolf" that was hidden in plain sight, take advantage of her family's trust? The answers remain elusive, serving as a stark reminder of the dangers posed by these predators. Whether in personal relationships or broader societal contexts, recognizing and addressing these threats is essential to safeguarding trust and preventing harm.

As we explore *Wolves in Sheep's Clothing*, some of the most dangerous individuals will be those who conceal their true intentions beneath a facade of trust and normalcy. Their manipulative actions are not just calculated but are often driven by a deeper need for control, influence, and the ability to assert power over others. This hunger for dominion does not exist in isolation—it is a thread that weaves through the tapestry of human behavior, particularly in the realm of violent crime.

Transitioning from deception to aggression, we delve into a critical question: What fuels the actions of violent offenders? The answers are often rooted in the same fundamental desires—power, dominion, and control—but pursued through explicitly unlawful and destructive means. Unlike manipulators who operate in shadows, violent criminals manifest these drives through overt acts of harm.

By exploring the psychology and social contexts that lead individuals to commit such crimes, this book hopes to shed light on the mechanisms driving these offenders. Far from being mere agents of chaos, many violent offenders act with purpose, albeit a purpose that is deeply misguided and devastatingly destructive. Let's explore the origins, expressions, and implications of these dark impulses, uncovering the intricate interplay between human nature and criminal behavior.

INTRODUCTION

Violent crimes often stem from a fundamental human desire for power, dominion, and control, but these desires are pursued through illegitimate and destructive means. This perspective highlights that many violent offenders are not motivated solely by chaos or irrationality but by deeply ingrained psychological and social drivers. The difference lies not in the desire itself but in the choice to achieve these ends unlawfully. These high-level examples illustrate how power, dominion, and control play a pivotal role in violent criminal behavior and will serve as the foundational motivations discussed in *Wolves in Sheep's Clothing, A Practical Guide for True Crime Enthusiasts.*

The desire for power is a natural human instinct. When pursued through legitimate means, power leads to roles of responsibility in society, such as political leadership or corporate authority. However, most criminals pursue power through illegal and harmful acts to satisfy their need for dominance.

An example of this is seen in serial killers like Ted Bundy. Bundy's murders were not random acts of violence but a calculated effort to assert control over his victims. His crimes gave him a sense of dominance, as he reduced his victims to objects under his total control. Bundy himself admitted that his acts of violence provided him with the ultimate form of possession—absolute power over life and

Ted Bundy

death. While power in legitimate contexts involves respect and trust, Bundy's illegitimate pursuit of this motivator relied on coercion and violence.

Dominion refers to the need to assert authority or control over others or one's environment. While non-criminal individuals often seek dominion or power through collaboration or leadership, violent offenders impose this control through intimidation, fear, or physical harm. This is especially prevalent in domestic violence cases, where abusers seek to dominate their partners.

Consider the example of abusive relationships, where an offender dominates a partner by controlling their movements, finances, or social interactions. This abusive behavior is rooted in the need to maintain power within the relationship. Unlike healthy partnerships built on mutual respect, this type of dominion involves breaking the will of the victim to maintain superiority and control.

Control is the desire to influence or dictate outcomes in a way that ensures predictability or reinforces a sense of power. Violent crimes motivated by control often involve acts like abduction, stalking, or terrorism, where offenders manipulate others to conform to their desires or beliefs.

Criminal behavior is often seen as deviant and abnormal but understanding its psychological and sociological roots reveals a deeper connection between criminal actions and everyday human desires. By analyzing the motivations behind criminal acts, true crime enthusiasts can gain insights into the complex mechanisms of the criminal mind. This understanding is critical not only for understanding crimes, but also for reducing our own risk of falling victim to such acts.

At the core of criminal motivation lies the pursuit of goals that are often shared by most individuals in society—such as the desire for acknowledgement, security, wealth, or status. However, the pathways to achieving these goals can diverge significantly, with some individuals choosing illegitimate means to achieve what are essentially legitimate desires. Through the lens of criminology, understanding how criminals achieve their desires through illegitimate means can reveal significant similarities between criminal and non-criminal behavior.

In society, the pursuit of power is often considered a legitimate goal. Individuals seek power in various forms: political power, corporate leadership, or even social influence. These are all goals that are widely accepted and celebrated in society, provided they are obtained through legitimate means such as hard work, education, and the establishment of positive relationships.

However, criminals like serial killer Theodore "Ted" Bundy pursue power in illegitimate ways. Bundy's desires weren't centered on financial wealth or material gain, but rather on complete domination over his victims. It wasn't just about controlling another person's life, but more about reducing them to the level of an object, a stage prop he could act out his fantasies with.

While the pursuit of power in legitimate pursuits may involve leadership, influence, and cooperation, Bundy's need for power led him to believe that violence and murder were the only ways to assert this control. His behavior highlights how similar desires for control can manifest in both legitimate and illegitimate forms, depending on the individual's moral framework and psychological makeup.

Between 1974 and 1978, Ted Bundy is believed to have killed at least 30 women, though some estimates suggest the number could be much higher. Bundy's crimes reveal a calculated approach to gaining access to his victims, a method that relied on charm, deception, and predatory cunning. These traits allowed him to lure unsuspecting women into vulnerable positions, where he would abduct, torture, and ultimately murder them. His actions were driven by a need for power and control, which he later admitted were central to his psychological motivations.

Bundy's confessions, including his pivotal interview with Dr. James Dobson shortly before his execution, provide chilling insights into his psyche and the rationalizations he offered for his heinous acts.[8]

Bundy's ability to gain access to his victims was rooted in his disarming charm and calculated deception. A law student with good looks and an articulate demeanor, Bundy did not fit the stereotype of a violent predator. This allowed him to approach women without arousing suspicion. He frequently feigned vulnerability or injury to elicit sympathy, often using props such as a cast, crutches, or a sling. By portraying himself as harmless and in need of help, Bundy exploited the compassion of his victims to lure them into dangerous situations.

Bundy's first confirmed murder occurred in 1974, though he later suggested that he had killed earlier. His earliest known victim was 21-year-old Lynda Ann Healy, a University of Washington student who disappeared from her apartment in January 1974. Bundy broke into her home, bludgeoned her unconscious, and carried her away. This marked the beginning of a string of murders in the Pacific Northwest, targeting young women on or near college campuses.

Over the next several months, Bundy abducted and killed multiple women, including Donna Gail Manson, Susan Elaine Rancourt, and Brenda Carol Ball. He often approached his victims in public spaces, such as university campuses or parks, where he could blend in and observe potential targets. In many cases, Bundy used his injured persona to convince women to help him carry books or load items into his car, a Volkswagen Beetle with its passenger seat removed to facilitate abductions.

One of Bundy's most infamous crimes occurred on July 14, 1974, at Lake Sammamish State Park in Washington. On this single day, Bundy abducted two women, Janice Ott and Denise Naslund, in broad daylight. Witnesses reported seeing a man with his arm in a sling asking women for help. Bundy's ability to convince two separate victims to follow him, despite the crowded environment, underscores his manipulative skills and the effectiveness of his deceptive strategies.[9]

Bundy's methods of torture and murder were as calculated as his abductions. Once he had his victims in his control, Bundy subjected them to unspeakable acts of violence, which often included sexual assault, physical torture, and psychological domination. He later admitted to keeping some victims alive for extended periods to prolong his sense of power over them. Bundy's crimes escalated in brutality over time, with his later murders involving greater physical and sexual violence.[10]

A particularly gruesome aspect of Bundy's crimes was his practice of necrophilia. He confessed to revisiting the bodies of his victims, engaging in sexual acts with their corpses, and even grooming or applying makeup to the remains. Bundy's need to maintain control over his victims extended beyond their deaths, as he sought to preserve his dominance and prolong the sense of power their murders afforded him. Additionally, he kept trophies, such as photographs or personal items, from his victims as mementos of his control.

Bundy's actions were driven by a pathological need for power and control. In interviews, he described his crimes as a desire to assert dominance and fulfill his fantasies of omnipotence. His need for control manifested in various aspects of his crimes, from the way he selected and lured his victims to the brutal methods he used to exert authority over them.

In his final days on death row, Bundy granted an interview to Dr. James Dobson, during which he attempted to explain his behavior. Bundy attributed his violent tendencies to an addiction to violent pornography, claiming that exposure to such material had warped his mind and desensitized him to violence. While this explanation has been met with skepticism, it provides insight into Bundy's attempts to rationalize his actions and deflect responsibility.[11]

More significantly, Bundy acknowledged that his crimes were rooted in a need for control. He described feeling a growing compulsion to dominate and harm others, which eventually culminated in his first murder. Bundy's admission highlights how his desire for control, a trait that can manifest in legitimate contexts such as leadership or personal achievement, took a dark and illegitimate form due to his psychological makeup and lack of moral restraint.

Bundy's behavior underscores a critical distinction between legitimate and illegitimate manifestations of control. The desire for control is not inherently criminal; it is a fundamental aspect of human behavior that drives individuals to succeed, lead, and create order in their lives. However, when this desire is unchecked by ethical boundaries or societal norms, it can lead to destructive outcomes.

In legitimate contexts, the desire for control is expressed through positive avenues such as career success, community leadership, or personal development. For example, an individual might channel their need for control into becoming a manager, entrepreneur, or artist, using their abilities to influence and inspire others constructively.

In contrast, Bundy's pursuit of control took an illegitimate form, driven by a disregard for human life and a willingness to inflict harm. His crimes highlight how a lack of empathy and moral grounding can lead to a warped expression of control, where domination becomes synonymous with violence and dehumanization.

Ted Bundy's ability to manipulate and deceive shows just how easily the pursuit of control can cross from legitimate to dangerous. His case is a chilling reminder of why ethical boundaries and mental health matter when it comes to shaping human behavior. His confessions, especially his interview with Dr. James Dobson, offer a rare glimpse into the mind of a killer. But they also raise bigger questions such as what role do society and psychology play in the making of someone like Bundy? and, what warning signs do we miss?

Understanding Bundy's motivations isn't just about dissecting his crimes—it's about learning how to prevent similar tragedies. When we recognize how normal desires, like power or belonging can take dark and destructive turns, we gain the tools to address the deeper causes of criminal behavior. And in doing so, we take steps toward a safer, more compassionate world.

THE HUMAN DESIRE FOR
SOCIAL BELONGING, WEALTH AND STATUS

A deeply ingrained human need is the desire to be recognized, respected, and valued within society. Status is often gained through traditional markers such as education, professional achievements, and social connections. In contrast, criminals may pursue status through illegitimate means—such as engaging in high-profile, violent acts that attract attention or infamy. A gang member, for example, may engage in illegal activities not just for financial gain, but to gain respect within their social group or criminal network.

Wealth, a universally accepted form of success, is another common goal shared by criminals and non-criminals alike. Most individuals aspire to acquire wealth through education, hard work, and entrepreneurship. These are legitimate avenues available to individuals in a capitalist society. However, wealth is also a primary motivator for many types of crime. Organized criminals, drug dealers, and even corporate criminals commit offenses to gain wealth in ways that bypass legal frameworks. For example, embezzlement, fraud, and robbery all have wealth acquisition as their end goal.

A notable case illustrating the link between legitimate and illegitimate wealth pursuits is the life of notorious crime boss Al Capone. Capone, involved in organized crime during the Prohibition era, built his wealth through bootlegging, gambling, and other illicit activities. The desire for wealth is not inherently criminal, but Capone's choice to break laws to achieve it distinguishes his path from legitimate entrepreneurs. In the

case of Capone and other criminals like him, the pursuit of wealth is still driven by the same desires as that of law-abiding individuals, but the means to achieve it involve manipulation, exploitation, and illegality.

Al Capone became one of America's most infamous gangsters, a symbol of the Prohibition era and organized crime in the early 20th century. His life, from humble beginnings to criminal mastermind, reflects a relentless pursuit of power and fame through illegal means.

He was born Alphonse Gabriel Capone on January 17, 1899, in Brooklyn, New York, to Italian immigrant parents. His upbringing in a rough neighborhood laid the groundwork for his criminal inclinations. Capone dropped out of school at the age of 14 after striking a teacher and subsequently joined several street gangs, including the South Brooklyn Rippers and the Five Points Gang.[12] These affiliations provided Capone with an education in street crime and connected him to Johnny Torrio, a mentor who would significantly influence his criminal career.

Capone's move to Chicago in 1919 marked a turning point. Torrio invited him to join his organization, which was engaged in various illicit activities, including gambling, prostitution, and bootlegging. Capone quickly rose through the ranks, showcasing a talent for orchestrating complex criminal operations and a ruthless willingness to eliminate rivals.

By 1925, Torrio had retired after a near-fatal assassination attempt, leaving Capone in charge of the Chicago Outfit. Under Capone's leadership, the organization expanded its operations, controlling speakeasies, breweries, and distribution networks across the city. Capone bribed law enforcement officials and politicians to ensure the smooth operation of his syndicate.

And while a barroom fight may have given Capone the nickname "Scarface," it was his ruthless consolidation of power that earned him the respect—and fear—of other mobsters. Unlike many crime bosses who relied solely on brute force, Capone combined strategic violence, political maneuvering, and financial influence to establish his dominance.

He eliminated rivals through carefully orchestrated crimes and cemented his reputation as Chicago's undisputed crime boss. He also rewarded loyalty generously, ensuring that those within his inner circle remained fiercely devoted.

At the same time, Capone understood the power of public relations. While he ruled the underworld with an iron fist, he also played the role of a Robin Hood-like figure, funding soup kitchens and presenting himself as a man of the people. This dual image made him not only feared within the Mob but also respected as a savvy businessman and leader who knew how to balance violence with influence—a crucial skill in the world of organized crime.

Capone's empire thrived on violence and intimidation. He orchestrated numerous gangland killings to eliminate competition, the most infamous being the St. Valentine's Day Massacre of 1929. Disguised as police officers, Capone's men executed seven members of the rival North Side Gang in a warehouse. Although Capone was never directly linked to the crime, the massacre cemented his reputation as a ruthless crime boss.[13]

In 2025, the YouTube channel *Profiling Evil* was invited to join actor Laurence Fishburne in Season Six of *History's Greatest Mysteries* episode on Al Capone.

Capone's brutal tactics and strategic eliminations allowed him to dominate Chicago's underworld, but his power wasn't built on violence alone—it was fueled by an empire of illegal alcohol.

During the Prohibition Era (1920–1933), the nationwide ban on alcohol created a lucrative black market, and Capone quickly became one of its most powerful players. Bootlegging—the illegal production, distribution, and sale of alcohol—became the foundation of his criminal enterprise, enabling him to amass immense wealth and influence.

The production of alcohol turned clandestine with illicit

distillation of spirits, often in rural areas, using homemade stills. The end-product was called Moonshine, and it was frequently made in secretive locations, like forests or remote farms. In urban settings, homemade spirits were mixed in small batches called Bathtub Gin. High-quality liquor was imported illegally from Canada, Mexico, and the Caribbean through clandestine routes with vehicles modified to outrun law enforcement. The booze was distributed through Speakeasies, underground bars where alcohol was sold and consumed. Flourishing in urban areas, these hidden dens required passwords or secret signals for entry. The network of distribution was operated by the crime syndicates, and the smugglers who transported the alcohol were referred to as Rum-Runners and Road Transporters. Some suggest that Bootlegging during Prohibition transformed American society, shaping its culture, economy, and criminal landscape, leaving a legacy that still resonates today.

Capone's criminal enterprise included gambling, prostitution, protection rackets, violence, and murder. Capone maintained the gambling operations to launder money and fund other illicit ventures. He and the Chicago Outfit managed brothels, exploiting vulnerable women and profiting from the illegal sex trade. To maintain control and avoid detection, Capone's gang extorted businesses, offering "protection" in exchange for regular payments. Failure to comply often resulted in violence or property destruction. And violence was a key tool for maintaining control and deterring rivals. Capone's men were responsible for hundreds of homicides, often carried out in brutal and public fashion to instill fear.[14]

Al Capone's quest for notoriety was as central to his character as his criminal activities. Unlike other mobsters who sought to remain in the shadows, Capone courted publicity. He appeared at public events, mingled with celebrities, and donated to charitable causes to cultivate an image of a modern-day Robin Hood. This persona endeared him to some members of the public, who viewed him as a rebellious figure defying unjust Prohibition laws.

However, Capone's high-profile antics attracted the attention of law enforcement. Federal agents, led by Agent-in-Charge Eliot Ness and the "Untouchables," began to dismantle his operations. Despite numerous attempts, authorities struggled to convict Capone for his more serious crimes due to his extensive bribery network and lack of direct evidence.

His downfall came not through violence or bootlegging but through tax evasion. In 1931, federal prosecutors charged him with failing to pay income taxes on his illicit earnings. Convicted and sentenced to 11 years in prison, Capone's empire quickly disintegrated. His time in Alcatraz, coupled with declining health due to syphilis, marked the end of his reign. He was released in 1939 and spent his final years in Florida, where he died in 1947.

Somewhat like Capone, Ted Bundy's desire for status was reflected in his ability to manipulate those around him. Both predators presented themselves as a charming, intelligent, and likable person— a strategy that helped them gain trust and social standing among their peers. However, this need for status also played a role in their crimes, although their success in gaining attention and trust allowed them to continue their violent crime sprees for years.

This contrast between legitimate and illegitimate pursuits of status illustrates how individuals seek recognition, but their methods can drastically differ based on their moral compass and willingness to break societal rules. While most people strive for social status through accepted means, criminals may engage in attention-seeking behavior that is destructive and harmful.

These case examples lead us back to a primary question of understanding the fine line between legitimate needs that are pursued through illegitimate means. Theories such as Robert Merton's Strain Theory and Richard Cloward and Lloyd Ohlin's Differential Opportunity Theory provide frameworks for understanding why some individuals resort to illegitimate means to achieve their goals, even when these goals are not inherently criminal. Both theories emphasize the pressures that individuals face when legitimate means to success are inaccessible.

Let's begin with Merton's Strain Theory which posits that individuals in society are expected to achieve certain cultural goals—mainly success, wealth, and social status. However, not everyone has access to the legitimate means to achieve these goals, such as education or stable employment. As a result, those facing strain may turn to illegitimate methods to achieve their desires.

This "strain" occurs when there is a gap between societal expectations and the individual's ability to achieve these expectations legally. The theory explains why, for example, individuals in poverty-stricken neighborhoods may resort to crime—such as drug dealing or theft—to achieve financial success, even if these means are not approved by society.

Merton's Strain Theory suggests that societal structures exert pressure on individuals to achieve culturally prescribed goals, such as wealth and success, but do not always provide equal means to attain them. This mismatch creates "strain," which may lead individuals to resort to deviant means to achieve these goals. Merton identified five modes of adaptation: conformity, innovation, ritualism, retreatism, and rebellion. Each represents a different response to the strain created by the disparity between societal goals and the means to achieve them.

Conformity includes accepting cultural goals and institutionalized means. Innovation includes accepting cultural goals but using unapproved or illegal means to achieve them. Ritualism on the other hand rejects cultural goals but rigidly follows institutionalized means. Retreatism is the rejection of both cultural goals and institutionalized means and often includes withdrawing from society, while rebellion is the rejection and replacement of existing cultural goals and means with alternative ones.

Merton's theory is particularly applicable to understanding criminal behavior that arises from "innovative" adaptations, where individuals pursue success through illegitimate means when legitimate pathways are inaccessible or insufficient.

To better understand this theory, let's apply the principle to both Bundy and Capone. Ted Bundy's criminal behavior aligns with certain aspects of strain theory, particularly in terms of innovative adaptation. Bundy grew up with aspirations of success and was described as charming and intelligent, often conforming outwardly to societal expectations. However, underlying insecurities and feelings of inadequacy, compounded by his failure to achieve personal and professional goals, may have created internalized strain. Unable or unwilling to achieve his desires through legitimate means, Bundy resorted to heinous crimes, including the manipulation and murder of young women.

Bundy's case also illustrates the retreatism dimension of strain, as he abandoned societal norms altogether, retreating into a world of deviance and fantasy. His behavior highlights the extremes to which strain can push an individual, leading to actions that serve his own distorted sense of control and gratification rather than any socially accepted goal.

Al Capone's criminal career offers a stark example of innovation as defined by Merton. Born to immigrant parents in a socioeconomically disadvantaged environment, Capone faced barriers to traditional success. The societal emphasis on wealth and the "American Dream" contrasted with the limited opportunities available to someone of his background.

Capone pursued societal goals of wealth and power through illegal means, most notably during the Prohibition era. He leveraged the demand for alcohol and other illicit services to build a criminal empire, engaging in bootlegging, gambling, and extortion. Capone's syndicate thrived by exploiting the strain experienced by society at large, particularly those unable to obtain alcohol legally. His rise underscores how structural inequalities, and societal pressures can drive individuals toward deviant pathways.

While both Bundy and Capone exemplify innovation, their

motivations diverge. Capone's actions were largely profit-driven, aligning with the societal goal of material success, albeit through illegal means. In contrast, Bundy's crimes were deeply personal, reflecting psychological strain and a distorted response to societal pressures. Capone adapted to external socioeconomic conditions, while Bundy's deviance stemmed more from internalized strain and a rejection of societal norms.

Another theory proffered in Cloward and Ohlin's Differential Opportunity Theory builds on this concept by asserting that some individuals not only face strain due to a lack of legitimate means but also have access to subcultures that offer alternative methods to achieve success. These subcultures provide "illegitimate opportunities" that may be more accessible in certain environments, such as criminal gangs or networks. As a result, individuals living in certain areas may be more likely to engage in criminal behavior, as these groups provide structured, albeit illegal, pathways to success.[15]

Let's examine this theory as it pertains to our criminal examples of Bundy and Capone. Cloward and Ohlin's Differential Opportunity Theory expands upon Robert K. Merton's Strain Theory by focusing on the availability of legitimate and illegitimate opportunities within a given social structure. Developed in the 1960 book *Delinquency and Opportunity: A Theory of Delinquent Gangs*, the theory suggests that access to illegitimate opportunities (just as much as access to legitimate ones) determines whether individuals turn to deviant behavior.

The theory is built upon three key principles, which take into account the Strain and Opportunity Structure where individuals who face barriers to legitimate success may turn to deviance, but only if they have access to an alternative, illegitimate opportunity structure, and it considers Subcultural Adaptations where different neighborhoods and communities fostered different forms of deviance based on the types of illegitimate opportunities available.

The three subcultures of deviance, according to the researchers are Criminal Subcultures where a crime community is already established, Conflict Subcultures described as communities characterized by instability and disorganization, where deviance takes the form of violence or gang-related activities, and Retreatist Subcultures where individuals who "double-fail" by lacking access to both legitimate and illegitimate means may turn to escapism, such as substance abuse.

Ted Bundy's case is somewhat unconventional when viewed through the lens of Differential Opportunity Theory, as he did not engage in deviance for material or social gain. However, elements of the retreatist subculture align with Bundy's behaviors. Bundy "failed" to meet societal expectations of professional success and personal fulfillment, struggling with feelings of inadequacy despite outward appearances of charisma and competence.

Unable to achieve societal goals legitimately or find an alternative opportunity structure for success, Bundy turned inward. His deviance became a retreatist response, manifested in deeply personal, violent crimes. The theory may also highlight the lack of a structured illegitimate pathway for Bundy's ambitions, pushing him toward a more disorganized, isolated form of deviance rather than aligning with any criminal network or conflict-based subculture.

Al Capone provides a textbook example of Differential Opportunity Theory, particularly in relation to the criminal subculture. Capone faced significant barriers to achieving wealth and power through legitimate means. However, he grew up in a neighborhood with a well-established network of organized crime, which provided access to an illegitimate opportunity structure.

His rise through the ranks of this subculture eventually led to a syndicate that capitalized on societal strain during Prohibition, particularly the public demand for alcohol. His success in the criminal subculture underscores the theory's premise that illegitimate opportunities must be present for deviance to occur on a significant scale. Capone's rise was not simply a response to personal or societal strain but also a result of his environment's availability of pathways to deviance.

Bundy and Capone represent contrasting subcultural adaptations within Differential Opportunity Theory. Bundy's deviance aligns more with retreatism, as his crimes stemmed from personal failure and a lack of connection to either legitimate or organized illegitimate networks. In contrast, Capone's deviance is emblematic of the criminal subculture, thriving within an environment that fostered and rewarded organized crime.

Bundy's isolation and psychological motives highlight the limits of opportunity theory in explaining crimes rooted in personal pathology. Capone's case, however, perfectly illustrates how access to a robust illegitimate structure can transform societal strain into organized, profit-driven deviance.

Cloward and Ohlin's Differential Opportunity Theory provides a valuable lens for understanding criminal behavior, emphasizing the role of societal structures and subcultural adaptations. While Bundy and Capone engaged in vastly different forms of deviance, their actions reflect the availability—or lack—of illegitimate opportunity structures in their respective contexts. Capone's rise underscores the impact of organized illegitimate networks, while Bundy's retreat into violent deviance reveals the outcomes of personal strain absent such networks.

Criminal behavior often reflects a distorted pursuit of desires that are universally shared, such as power, wealth, and social status. The fundamental desires behind crime are not inherently criminal but become so when individuals turn to illegitimate means to satisfy them. Analyzing these motivations allows true crime enthusiasts to better understand the factors that lead people to break the law and the psychological frameworks behind their choices.

Through theories like Merton's Strain Theory and Cloward and Ohlin's Differential Opportunity Theory, we can see how individuals in certain situations may resort to crime to achieve goals that they cannot attain through legitimate means. By exploring the similarities between legitimate and illegitimate behavior, society can better address the root causes of criminality, prevent future crimes, and offer rehabilitative solutions to those who have already crossed the line into criminal activity. Understanding the criminal mind is key to creating a safer and more equitable society for everyone.

Criminal behavior is more than just an act of defiance or disregard for the law; it's a complex interplay of psychological, environmental, and sociocultural factors. By defining criminal behavior not merely as unlawful actions but as a manifestation of deeper human tendencies, we unlock the potential to better understand why individuals commit violent acts. What drives someone to cross the line into deviance? What internal and external pressures tip the scales toward a choice that seems incomprehensible to most? These are not just academic questions; they are the key to safer communities and personal empowerment.

Understanding the psychology of criminal deviance holds immense potential for crime prevention. By identifying early warning signs and common pathways leading to violent behavior, we can design interventions that stop crime before it happens. Imagine if schools, workplaces, and communities could work together to defuse conflicts and address risk factors, sparing potential victims and rehabilitating potential offenders before their actions escalate. The more we learn about what motivates violence, the better equipped we are to design systems that prevent it.

For those fascinated by true crime, studying criminal behavior offers a richer, more nuanced lens for sleuthing. True crime stories often hinge on the "why" behind the crime as much as the "how." Equipped with insights into criminal psychology, armchair detectives and professional investigators alike can begin to see patterns that others might overlook. This understanding enhances not only the thrill of solving the puzzle but also the possibility of contributing to a culture of accountability and justice.

Understanding deviant behavior isn't just about solving crimes or preventing them—it's about protecting yourself. Knowledge is power. Awareness of how predators operate, what they look for in a target, and how they rationalize their actions can make you a harder target. It can also inspire vigilance in protecting those who are most vulnerable. By learning the lessons of criminal behavior, you can better arm yourself with the tools to navigate the world with a sharper, more informed perspective.

The first chapter of this book will take you deeper into the heart of criminal psychology as we explore the criminal mind to understand patterns. Doing so is more than just an academic exercise; it's a roadmap to a safer, more informed, and more empathetic world. In your true crime sleuthing, it's not just reading about crime that's interesting: it's learning how to stand resilient against it.

PART ONE

INSIDE THE CRIMINAL PSYCHE: MOTIVATION, JUSTIFICATION & BEHAVIORAL DYNAMICS

Chapter One

Exploring the Criminal Mindset

In the realm of criminal investigations, comprehending the intricacies of how a crime was committed and delving into the mind of a suspect is paramount. This understanding not only aids in apprehending predators but also in preventing future crimes. A critical aspect of this process involves exploring the psychological makeup of violent criminals, particularly focusing on disorders such as psychopathy and sociopathy.

Distinguishing between deviant and criminal behaviors is essential, as the former pertains to actions diverging from societal norms, while the latter involves violations of the law. This chapter will examine these facets in detail, building upon examples from the case of Dennis Rader, infamously known as the BTK Killer (Bind Them, Torture Them, Kill Them), and Richard Ramirez, The Night Stalker.

The process involves the comprehensive study of potential suspects, including their backgrounds, psychological traits, and possible motives. This aids in narrowing down suspect lists and understanding the underlying factors that may drive individuals to commit crimes. By examining aspects such as the suspect's family history, employment records, social interactions, and past behaviors, investigators can identify patterns that align with the crime in question. For instance, in the BTK case, Rader's meticulous planning and his ability to blend into his community and church created challenges for law enforcement in identifying him as a suspect.

This examination of the suspect is coined, "Suspectology" by many serial crime investigators. While the term is not established or universally recognized, it can be interpreted as a nuanced study or systematic examination of any number of individuals who are suspected of engaging in criminal activity. It is particularly relevant in criminology and forensic psychology, where understanding suspects' behaviors, motivations, and actions are crucial to solving crimes and preventing future offenses.

In this framework, Suspectology can include the analysis of demographic and psychological profiles, behavioral patterns and crime sequences before, during, and after the commission of a crime. This approach delves deeper into the why and how of criminal behavior, offering insights that extend beyond traditional investigative techniques.

One critical aspect of Suspectology is deciphering what motivates a suspect to commit crimes. Motivation provides a lens through which investigators can understand why a crime was committed and what the suspect hoped to achieve. For example, the motivation might stem from emotional triggers such as anger or jealousy, financial desperation, ideological beliefs, or even pathological needs like a desire for power or dominance. By identifying these drivers, law enforcement can categorize suspects into behavioral profiles, enhancing their understanding of potential offenders and the risks they pose.

The level of premeditation and planning involved in a crime speaks volumes about the suspect's organizational skills and experience. For instance, a suspect who meticulously plans every detail—choosing the location, timing, and tools for the crime—

demonstrates a high level of organization and forethought. This planning phase often reveals an offender's familiarity with the criminal process and their ability to anticipate challenges.

Patterns in pre-planning behavior can also shed light on the suspect's psychological state. A methodical planner may show traits of compulsiveness or control, while a spur-of-the-moment offender might act on impulse, driven by situational factors. In violent crimes, understanding the extent of planning can help distinguish between crimes of passion and more calculated acts of aggression.

In addition to learning as much about the suspect as possible, the criminal investigator (and true crime enthusiast) must meticulously analyze the method in which the crime occurred. The learned behaviors of experienced offenders can evolve over time or become dynamic in nature. As offenders gain experience or encounter obstacles, they may modify their methods to improve efficiency and reduce the risk of apprehension. An example of this evolution could be a burglar who always enters homes through unlocked windows. This evolution may have occurred because the predator learned this was an easier way to get inside and do so without leaving forensic evidence, or they may have been caught by using certain tools to gain access, only to have those recovered by police in a search warrant.

This process is an examination of the MO and it dissects the methods and patterns an offender uses to execute criminal acts. MO provides insights into the perpetrator's behavior during the buildup stages, the commission of the crime, and the aftermath. It looks closely at the offender's motivation, skills, and possible psychological state. This examination will often reveal the level of planning involved, the selection of victims, and the presence of any ritualistic behaviors, all of which are crucial for building a psychological profile of the suspect.

Modus operandi refers to the specific methods and techniques an offender uses to commit a crime. It includes the tools, strategies, and procedures employed to carry out the criminal act. In almost all cases, the primary purpose of the MO is to successfully complete the crime while avoiding detection and capture. It is often shaped by the offender's experience, knowledge, and the circumstances of the crime. This is extremely important to note. Some offenders are just plain lucky and leave little behind in the way of clues. Most successful predators have a history of criminal experience where they've learned the dos and don'ts along the way, often complimented by stays in a correctional facility.

In criminal investigations and crime scene analysis, "Signature" classifications refer to the distinctive behaviors, actions, or characteristics that an offender consistently exhibits during the commission of a crime, which go beyond what is necessary to complete the offense. These elements are unique to the individual and reflect their psychological or emotional needs, motives, or compulsions. Unlike the MO, which pertains to the techniques and methods used to execute the crime, the Signature remains relatively stable over time and often serves no practical purpose. Instead, it is an expression of the offender's personality or inner drives, providing crucial insights into their psyche and helping to link multiple crimes to a single perpetrator.

A Signature behavior is a unique, personal aspect of the crime that goes beyond what is necessary to commit the crime. It reflects the offender's psychological or emotional needs and is often a consistent and repetitive behavior. Signatures serve to fulfill the offender's psychological or emotional gratification. It is not essential for the completion of the crime but is a manifestation of the offender's fantasies or compulsions. Unlike the MO, the Signature remains relatively stable across different crimes. It is a ritualistic behavior that satisfies the offender's inner desires and is often a key factor in linking multiple crimes to a single perpetrator.

One of the better examples of a Signature and MO is found in study of the case of Richard Ramirez, the "Night Stalker." Ramirez' crimes are among the most chilling and notorious criminal cases in American history. Ramirez terrorized the residents of Los Angeles and

San Francisco between 1984 and 1985, committing a series of brutal murders, sexual assaults, and burglaries.[16] His crimes were marked by extreme violence and a seemingly random selection of victims, which added to the fear and panic he instilled in the communities.

One of the most distinctive aspects of Ramirez's crimes was his use of ritualistic symbols, particularly pentagrams, which he left at several crime scenes. This act served as his "calling card," a "Signature" that was not necessary for the completion of his crimes, but satisfied a deep, symbolic, and personal need. Leaving a drawing of a pentagram was a way for Ramirez to communicate with the police and the public, in effect, taunting them and asserting his identity and beliefs.

Some of the reasons why predators like Ramirez leave Signatures are psychological gratification. For many offenders, the Signature is a way to fulfill psychological or emotional needs. It is often a manifestation of their fantasies or compulsions. In Ramirez's case, the use of this symbol supported his satanic occult fascination, which played a significant role in his identity and motivations.

Another reason for the pentagram was for Ramirez to stake claim on the murders through leaving his unique calling card. It was a way to terrorize the public and taunt police investigators. It was his form of psychological warfare, where he derived satisfaction from the fear and confusion the pentagrams created. While Ramirez was vicariously "marking his territory," he was also exhibiting his sense of power and control while challenging the authorities to catch him.

As Ramirez' crimes progressed, the pentagram became a part of his legacy. He was proud of what he was accomplishing as he racked up murder victim after murder victim. In a personal interview the author conducted with Richard Ramirez inside San Quentin Prison, the killer revealed that drawing the pentagram inside the home of one of his first victims was, "just a reactionary thing," something Ramirez did without thinking. When the public response about the pentagram became so demonstrative, the predator repeated it often, adopted it as his bizarre "calling card." In that same interview, sensing the author's next question of, "Why?" he remarked, "It was good business."

Some offenders have compulsions or rituals that they feel compelled to perform. These actions are not necessary for the commission of the crime but are integral to the offender's psychological state. The repetitive nature of these actions can provide a sense of control and fulfillment. Understanding the reasons behind an offender's Signature is helpful in true crime sleuthing. It provides insights into the offender's psychological state, motivations, and potential future actions. By analyzing these Signatures, we can gain a deeper understanding of the criminal mind and better understand of why the offender did what they chose to do. Most importantly, through analyzing these Signatures, we can often link offenders to multiple crime events.

It's also important to point out that MO and Signature can evolve over time. If we were to break these two designations into three baseline categories, they would look something like this: 1) Functionality vs. Personalization, 2) Adaptability vs. Stability, and 3) Crime Linkage.

When thinking of functionality and personalization, the MO is primarily about the practical aspects of committing the crime, such as how the offender gains entry, what tools are used, and how the crime is executed. The functionality ensures the crime is successfully committed while the personalization allows the offender to symbolically sign off on the criminal act. Thus, the Signature is about the personal and psychological elements being accomplished to satisfy the offender's inner desires.

As criminals learn from past experiences, their MO can change and adapt over time. Adjusting to past experiences requires that the criminal fix errors that increase their risk of arrest or minimize their ability to pursue their fantasy. These fixes are required to continue to be an agent of evil.

The Signature aspects of the criminals' actions usually remain consistent. Signatures represent the offender's unique psychological makeup, and the Signature will rarely change until the driver behind the behavior is satisfied. In short, the MO can be useful in identifying patterns and linkage of crime, but it is not always as reliable as Signature, due to its dynamic nature. The Signature, on the other hand, is a more reliable indicator for linking multiple crimes to a single offender because it is a consistent and unique behavior.

Element	Modus Operandi (MO)	Signature
Definition	The specific methods, techniques, and procedures an offender uses to commit a crime.	A unique, personal aspect of the crime that goes beyond what is necessary to commit it.
Purpose	Ensures the crime is successfully completed while avoiding detection and capture.	Fulfills a psychological or emotional need of the offender; not necessary for the crime itself.
Flexibility	Can change over time as offenders learn from experience and adjust their methods.	Remains relatively stable across different crimes committed by the same offender.
Key Characteristics	Focuses on the practical aspects of the crime, including entry method, tools used, and actions taken to evade law enforcement.	Reflects the offender's personality, compulsions, or rituals; includes symbolic elements left at crime scenes.
Influencing Factors	Shaped by the offender's experience, knowledge, and situational circumstances.	Driven by the offender's inner desires, fantasies, and psychological state.
Evolution Over Time	Highly adaptable; criminals modify their MO to improve efficiency or reduce risks.	Rarely changes; the offender is compelled to repeat signature behaviors.
Examples	A burglar switching from breaking windows to using lock-picking tools after previous arrests.	Richard Ramirez (Night Stalker) leaving pentagrams at crime scenes to express his identity and beliefs.

Understanding these differences is crucial for piecing criminal cases together. By analyzing both aspects, investigators can gain a comprehensive understanding of the offender's behavior, motivations, and psychological profile. This information can be used to predict future actions, identify potential suspects, and ultimately apprehend the offender.

As you study unsolved criminal cases, it's important to understand that the offender's experience also tells us a lot about them. An experienced offender may exhibit calmness, efficiency, and minimal interaction with their surroundings to reduce evidence left at the scene. Conversely, a novice may display erratic or panicked behavior, leading to mistakes such as leaving fingerprints or being caught on surveillance.

As you explore the myriads of unsolved crimes out there, consider the level of control the offender exercised over the victim. This gives you a glimpse into their organizational skills. A well-organized suspect might use restraints, select a remote location, or even clean up the crime scene. Such behaviors suggest not only planning but also a potential history of similar offenses. In contrast, a disorganized crime scene might point to an impulsive, inexperienced, or emotionally overwhelmed individual.

Dig deeply into the suspect's actions after the crime. What was the method of their escape, evasion tactics, or their reaction to the investigation? Evaluating these behaviors can provide you with invaluable clues about the predator's personality and capability. A seasoned criminal might have a pre-planned escape route, use disguises, or have a safe house prepared, indicating a high degree of sophistication and awareness of investigative procedures.

Conversely, an offender who lingers at the scene, seeks attention for their actions, or fails to cover their tracks might exhibit traits of impulsivity, lack of foresight, or even a desire for recognition. These behaviors also hint at their psychological state, such as guilt, arrogance, or detachment. We will discuss these behaviors in Chapter Four, "Order in Chaos: Decoding Organized and Disorganized Crime Scenes."

True crime enthusiasts should also analyze the order in which a suspect carries out pre-planning, the commission of the crime, and the post-crime escape. This is the same process investigators will take to construct a detailed profile of the offender. These elements reveal not only the offender's immediate objectives but also their broader behavioral tendencies.

When considering the offender's level of experience, look for patterns of organization and attention to detail that may indicate whether the suspect has committed similar crimes in the past. As you consider the level of organization, think about the crime and the crime scene. Does it appear that things happened in a methodical way or is the crime scene chaotic? This will help you categorize offenders into organized or disorganized typologies, a distinction central to criminal profiling and something we will explore in later chapters.

Consider the offender's adaptability during the commission of the crime. Did the suspect have to adjust their plans based on unforeseen circumstances? Simple behavioral clues and reactions by the offender can reveal their capacity for strategic thinking and improvisation.

Studying the progression of a suspect's actions across multiple crimes (if applicable) can reveal patterns of escalation, such as increasing violence or complexity in methods. This progression can aid in identifying links between cases, predicting future behavior, and crafting targeted interventions.

Examining the behaviors of the suspect underscores the importance of a comprehensive approach to understanding why they commit crimes. By examining what motivates a suspect and how they act across the evolving phases of a crime—pre-planning, commission, and escape—you, the true crime enthusiast, can glean valuable insights into the offender's psychology, skills, and organizational level. This holistic understanding not only enhances the effectiveness of your crime sleuthing but also contributes to broader efforts in reducing your risk of being victimized.

To help understand a predator, let's explore the mind of the offender through their psychopathy and sociopathy. These categories of behavior are classified under Antisocial Personality Disorder (ASPD) but exhibit distinct characteristics.

Psychopathy is a complex personality disorder marked by a persistent pattern of antisocial behavior, which includes a disregard for social norms and the rights of others. This condition is further characterized by significant impairments in empathy and remorse, meaning that individuals with psychopathy often struggle to understand or care about the emotional experiences of others. These individuals display boldness, a tendency toward uninhibited behavior, and egotistical traits that prioritize their own needs and desires above those of others.[17]

Individuals with psychopathy are often highly manipulative and can appear superficially charming, making them adept at influencing and deceiving others for personal gain.[18] However, this charm is not accompanied by genuine emotional depth, as people with psychopathy typically lack authentic emotional responses, such as guilt, fear, or attachment.[19]

Understanding psychopathy and sociopathy starts with recognizing that while they share some traits, their origins and behaviors are quite different.

Psychopathy has a strong genetic foundation, meaning that some people are simply born with a higher risk of developing it according to online experts. Research suggests that psychopathy runs in families, and brain scans of individuals with psychopathic traits show differences in areas that control emotions and impulses. These neurological differences help explain why psychopaths tend to lack empathy and struggle with impulse control. At its core, psychopathy is a complex mix of biology, psychology, and behavior, making it particularly challenging to understand and treat.

Sociopathy, on the other hand, is believed to be shaped more by life experiences than genetics. Childhood trauma, neglect, or growing up in a toxic environment often contribute to the development of sociopathic traits. Unlike psychopaths, whose traits are deeply rooted in their biology, sociopaths are thought to develop their behaviors as a response to their surroundings.

One key difference between the two is the ability to form emotional attachments. While sociopaths have little regard for rules, laws, or the rights of others, they can still develop bonds with certain people—though these relationships are often inconsistent and self-serving. Psychopaths, by contrast, tend to be emotionally detached and struggle to form genuine connections at all.

Another major distinction is behavioral control. Sociopaths are impulsive, unpredictable, and often act without thinking, making them more prone to violent outbursts or reckless decisions. Their lack of planning and emotional volatility often land them in trouble with the law. Psychopaths, however, tend to be much more calculated, carefully planning their actions to avoid getting caught. This makes sociopaths easier to recognize, as their erratic behavior often leads to more obvious conflicts with society.

Ultimately, sociopathy and psychopathy represent two different paths within the broader category ASPD. While sociopathy is largely shaped by environment and trauma, psychopathy has deeper biological roots. Understanding these differences helps us recognize the warning signs and better address the challenges each condition presents.

Dennis Rader, the BTK killer, exemplifies many psychopathic traits. His ability to lead a seemingly normal life, his complete lack of empathy for his victims, and his compulsive need for control and dominance suggest psychopathy rather than sociopathy. Rader's case demonstrates how predators can disguise their deviance beneath a veneer of normalcy, making them even more dangerous.

Rader presented himself as a responsible family man, a married father of two who actively participated in family activities and seemed to maintain a stable household. He ensured his family viewed him as dependable, often prioritizing their needs and keeping his deviant side hidden. Rader was deeply involved in his local church, serving as the president of the church council. This leadership role reinforced his image as a moral and trustworthy individual and that perception was backed up by his participation in community events and organizations, such as the Boy Scouts, where he volunteered as a scout leader.

In his professional life, Rader worked in compliance and enforcement roles, such as a Park City Compliance Officer, where he was responsible for enforcing city regulations. This position further bolstered his image as a law-abiding, authoritative figure. He maintained a meticulous and professional approach to his work, which masked his darker impulses.

By compartmentalizing his life, he carefully separated his criminal activities from his personal and professional worlds. He planned his murders meticulously, often stalking victims for months and ensuring these activities were not linked to his everyday life. He avoided discussing his crimes or exhibiting any suspicious behavior that might arouse concern among those close to him.

Dennis Rader displayed socially acceptable behavior in public, avoiding overtly deviant or odd conduct that could attract attention. He was polite, composed, and unassuming, qualities that made him blend seamlessly into his community. In addition, the killer capitalized on societal assumptions that a family-oriented, churchgoing, employed man could not be capable of such heinous crimes. His ability to present a facade of normalcy allowed him to evade detection for decades.

By mastering these strategies, Rader was able to lead a double life, concealing his criminal identity and maintaining his reputation as a respectable member of society. This leads our exploration into the differences between deviant and criminal behaviors. Deviant behavior refers to actions that violate societal norms but are not necessarily illegal. These behaviors elicit disapproval from society but do not result in legal sanctions.

WHEN DEVIANT BEHAVIOR BECOMES CRIMINAL

Examples of deviant behavior might include unconventional lifestyles, extreme forms of body modification, or expressions of art that challenge societal norms. Deviance is subjective and culturally specific, often shaped by the moral, religious, and social constructs of a community. What may be considered deviant in one society may be accepted in another.

Criminal behavior, on the other hand, involves conduct that violates codified laws and is punishable by the courts. Criminal acts against persons, such as assault or murder, are universally recognized within a legal framework. While all criminal behavior is deviant because it strays from societal norms, not all deviant behavior is criminal. The distinction lies in the formalization of societal disapproval; deviant acts may provoke outrage or discomfort, but they do not necessarily lead to legal consequences unless codified into law.

One critical distinction between deviant and criminal behavior lies in the potential for escalation. Deviant behaviors, if left unchecked or unaddressed, can evolve into criminal behaviors. This progression is particularly evident in the BTK case. Rader's deviant behaviors—such as his obsession with bondage and the fantasy of domination—initially existed in a private sphere, causing discomfort only to those who might have discovered them. However, as his fantasies became more consuming and unrestrained, Rader transitioned to criminal acts, driven by a need to fulfill these fantasies in increasingly violent and illegal ways.

Understanding the distinction between deviant and criminal behavior is crucial, but equally important is recognizing how that progression can be analyzed and understood through investigative techniques. When deviant behaviors escalate into criminal acts, as seen in cases like BTK, law enforcement must employ specialized methods to track, analyze, and ultimately identify offenders before they can continue their cycle of violence.

This is where criminal investigative analysis, or profiling, becomes an essential tool. By examining an offender's thoughts, emotions, and behaviors—often revealed through their crimes—investigators can systematically narrow the suspect pool and develop strategies to anticipate their next moves. The process of analyzing crime scenes, offender signatures, and behavioral patterns allows law enforcement to uncover critical psychological and motivational elements that drive criminal actions.

Just as we see a psychological evolution from deviance to crime, we also see a methodical investigative response: profiling enables law enforcement to decode the motivations behind an offender's actions, transforming raw behavioral data into actionable intelligence. Let's explore how this process works, and how behavioral analysis helps investigators not only understand the minds of offenders but also predict and prevent further crimes.

Studying behaviors provides invaluable insights into an offender's reasoning and emotional responses. By exploring an individual's thoughts, feelings, and sensory perceptions, investigators can uncover what an offender idealizes or fantasizes about. For example, examining how a criminal responds to stimuli such as touch, sight, or sound can reveal critical details about their personality and motives.

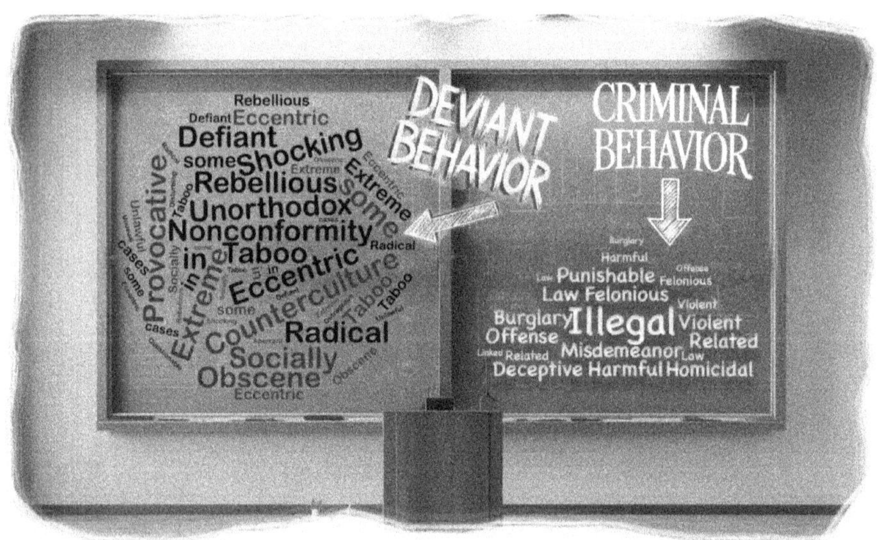

Deviant behaviors, while distressing, are not inherently criminal. These behaviors diverge from societal norms and include actions like excessive drinking, eating disorders, or self-harming. Fantasizing about criminal acts also falls within the realm of deviance rather than crime until such fantasies are acted upon.

Conversely, criminal behavior is defined as any act that violates the law and can involve verbal, nonverbal, or sexual actions.

Consider the case of a government employee who had a fetish for wearing diapers—a deviant but not criminal act. However, when that same individual used government computers to access child pornography, his actions transitioned from deviance to criminality. This example illustrates how deviant behaviors can escalate into criminal acts when boundaries are crossed, and societal norms are blatantly violated.

Dennis Rader's journey from deviant behavior to criminality is a textbook example of how unaddressed psychological issues and deviant fantasies can escalate into violent crime. From an early age, Rader displayed signs of deviance, including torturing animals—a behavior that experts often associate with future violent tendencies. Rader also began experimenting with bondage as a teenager, tying himself up and imagining scenarios of control and domination. These private acts of deviance were accompanied by voyeuristic tendencies and fantasies of inflicting pain on others.

During his early adulthood, Rader's deviant interests intensified. He reportedly developed a fixation on stalking women, fantasizing about abducting and restraining them. Despite these troubling behaviors, Rader's outward appearance remained unremarkable; he was considered a reliable and ordinary member of his community.

The turning point came in 1974, when Rader moved from fantasy to predatory action. On January 15 of that year, he murdered four members of the Otero family in their home. This act marked the culmination of years of deviant behavior and a significant escalation into criminality. Whether these were truly Rader's first murders or not, Rader later admitted that the act of killing provided him with an unparalleled sense of power and fulfillment of his fantasies. The murder of the Otero family was meticulously planned, with Rader breaking into their home and subduing each family member. His methodical approach—binding his victims, torturing them, and finally killing them—exemplified his transition from a deviant fantasist to a cold, calculated killer.

Rader's deviance was further evident in his need to relive his crimes. Over the years and mounting victims, he kept trophies and wrote detailed accounts of the murders, often accompanied by crude drawings. His communication with law enforcement and the media—taunting them with letters and clues—showcased his narcissistic tendencies and desire for control. These behaviors, while deviant, became criminal acts as they directly contributed to his ability to terrorize the community and avoid capture.

Rader's MO involved extensive planning, stalking his victims, and breaking into their homes. Before entering, he would cut the phone cord and once inside, he would bind, torture, and then kill them, deriving sexual gratification from the process. The brutality of the Otero murders pleased Rader and satisfied his uncontrolled fantasies while at the same time, shocked the community.

One of Rader's Signature behaviors was his need for attention. He sent taunting letters to the police and media, detailing his crimes and mocking law enforcement's inability to catch him. These communications showcased his narcissism and desire for recognition. Rader's decision to name himself "BTK" further highlighted his need for notoriety.

The investigation into the BTK killings spanned several decades. Rader's ability to blend into his community and the absence of modern forensic technology in the 1970s and 1980s hindered law enforcement efforts. However, advances in DNA technology and Rader's own arrogance eventually led to his capture.

Rader resumed communication with the media and police in 2004 after years of silence, reigniting interest in the case. He sent letters, photographs, and even a floppy disk to local news outlets, believing he could remain undetected. However, this act of communication became his downfall. Police were able to extract metadata from the floppy disk, which pointed to a computer at Rader's church. This discovery, combined with DNA samples obtained from his daughter, ultimately confirmed his identity as the BTK Killer. Rader was arrested in 2005 and later confessed to his crimes.

Rader's decision to resume communication was driven by a combination of factors. One major motivator was his need for recognition and control. Over the years, the lack of attention surrounding the BTK case likely led to feelings of obscurity, which his narcissistic tendencies could not tolerate. Lieutenant Ken Landwehr, who led the investigation, speculated that media coverage mistakenly attributing the BTK murders to another predator might have been the catalyst for Rader's reemergence. Seeing someone else potentially receive credit for his crimes was likely an affront to his ego, compelling him to reclaim ownership of his actions.

Rader's motivations were deeply rooted in his deviant sexual fantasies and his need for control. He derived pleasure from the suffering of his victims and meticulously relived his crimes through souvenirs and detailed writings. His methodical planning and attention to detail revealed a calculated mind, while his communications with the media and police highlighted his narcissistic and egotistical nature. Ultimately, these traits, combined with his desire to taunt and manipulate authorities, led to his capture and the end of his decades-long evasion of justice.

Understanding the nuances of how crimes are committed, and the psychological profiles of offenders is crucial in criminal investigations. Distinguishing between deviant and criminal behaviors enables law enforcement to identify potential threats and intervene before deviant behaviors escalate into criminal activities. The case of Dennis Rader illustrates the complexities involved in such investigations and highlights the significance of psychological insights in apprehending and understanding serial offenders.

And now, as we delve deeper into the labyrinthine mind of the predator, we'll start to uncover the stark disconnection between their thoughts and the moral compass that governs most individuals. The predator's ability to coldly calculate, manipulate, and execute their desires is chilling, but it's only one piece of the puzzle. Beneath their actions lies a psychological mechanism that allows them to sever the tether of guilt and accountability—a disassociation from the humanity of their victims and an intricate web of justifications that transforms even the most heinous acts into something permissible in their minds.

Your questions may range from, "How does a predator reconcile such acts with their sense of self?" to "How do they construct a narrative in which they are not the villain but, perhaps, the hero—or even the victim?"

It is in this shadowy territory, where morality is reshaped and reality distorted, that we must venture next. For if understanding the mind of the predator is vital, understanding the ways they rationalize and distance themselves from their crimes is the key to unraveling the full portrait of their behavior.

To confront the predator's psyche is to confront the unsettling truth of human nature's capacity for compartmentalization, denial, and moral evasion. In the next chapter, we'll step into the chilling realm where conscience is suspended, and justification reigns supreme. What you discover might not only illuminate the predator's darkest secrets but also challenge your own understanding of right and wrong.

Serial predators often employ psychological strategies to distance themselves from the moral and ethical weight of their actions. This disassociation enables them to commit repeated offenses without the hindrance of guilt or remorse. -MK

Chapter Two

When Predators Disassociate and Justify Their Crimes

The human psyche is a complex tapestry, capable of both profound empathy and unfathomable cruelty. Among the most disturbing manifestations of this duality are the actions of individuals who commit heinous acts yet often lead seemingly ordinary lives. A critical aspect of understanding such individuals lies in examining the psychological mechanisms they employ to disassociate from their victims and justify their crimes.

This chapter delves into the disconnect mechanisms employed by predators and focuses on their rationalization tactics like dehumanization, denial, and minimization. We'll explore the cultural and societal factors that facilitate such disassociation and rely upon illustrations like the case of Gary Ridgway, infamously known as the Green River Killer.

Repeat or serial predators often employ psychological strategies to distance themselves from the moral and ethical weight of their actions. This disassociation enables them to commit repeated offenses without the hindrance of guilt or remorse. Dehumanization is a psychological mechanism that allows individuals to commit acts of violence against others while minimizing feelings of guilt or moral conflict. This process is especially evident in the actions of criminals who commit premeditated offenses. By stripping their victims of an identity or humanity, perpetrators create a mental barrier that justifies their actions and absolves them of responsibility. By examining the psychological, social, and cultural underpinnings that enable individuals to rationalize their violent acts, we'll now explore the process of dehumanization.

At its core, dehumanization is a defense mechanism that suppresses empathy for another individual. Empathy, the ability to understand and share the feelings of another, serves as a natural deterrent to violence. However, criminals who engage in violent acts often develop strategies to override this natural inclination. This process involves perceiving their victims as objects, animals, or entities unworthy of moral consideration.

Criminal psychologists have noted that violent criminals often use language that diminishes the humanity of their victims. Terms like "it," "thing," or derogatory epithets are used to distance the perpetrator from the victim's individuality and humanity. This linguistic distancing reduces the cognitive dissonance associated with harming another human being. In their minds, they are not attacking a person with emotions, dreams, and relationships, but rather an entity devoid of these characteristics.

A chilling illustration of this can be found in the actions of the Nazis during the Holocaust. Prisoners in concentration camps were stripped of their names, referred to by numbers, and categorized in ways that denied their individuality. This systematic dehumanization made it psychologically easier for perpetrators to commit atrocities on a massive scale.

Dehumanization is not solely a psychological phenomenon; it is also shaped by societal and cultural influences. Certain groups are more likely to be dehumanized due to prevailing prejudices, stereotypes, or systemic marginalization. Criminals often exploit these cultural narratives to rationalize their behavior.

Sex workers, homeless individuals, and marginalized racial or ethnic groups are frequently targeted by violent offenders because societal stigmatization makes them appear less valuable or less deserving of empathy. In the homicides committed by Gary Ridgway, the Green River Killer, his victims were often chosen because they belonged to vulnerable and stigmatized populations. Ridgway explicitly stated that he targeted sex workers because he believed they would not be missed, and that law enforcement would not prioritize investigating their disappearances. This belief was reinforced by a societal indifference to the plight of such individuals, effectively enabling his crimes.

The Green River Killer case provides a chilling example of these psychological mechanisms in action. Active primarily during the 1980s and 1990s, Ridgway confessed to murdering 71 women, though he was convicted of 49 counts of murder. His case illustrates how a predator can employ disassociation and rationalization tactics to commit prolonged acts of violence while maintaining a facade of normalcy.

Ridgway predominantly targeted vulnerable women, including sex workers and runaways, whom he perceived as easy targets. By choosing victims from marginalized groups, he could dehumanize them, viewing them as "less than" and thereby justifying his actions in his mind. This dehumanization was evident in his method of approach; he would often show potential victims a picture of his son to gain their trust, only to later betray and murder them.[20]

Ridgway's method of killing—strangulation—allowed for a personal yet detached means of murder. Strangulation is an intimate act, requiring close physical contact, yet it leaves fewer forensic traces compared to other methods. This choice reflects a complex interplay of control and denial; by using his hands or ligatures, Ridgway could maintain a sense of dominance while simultaneously detaching from the brutality of the act. His later confessions revealed a lack of emotional engagement with his crimes, indicating a profound level of denial and compartmentalization.

Ridgway evaded capture for nearly two decades, a feat accomplished through meticulous planning and minimization of his actions. He would often contaminate crime scenes with gum, cigarettes, and written materials belonging to others, deliberately misleading investigators. By minimizing the significance of his crimes and viewing them as mere challenges to overcome, Ridgway could continue his activities without the burden of guilt. His ability to lead a double life—working as a truck painter and other blue-collar jobs, marrying, and maintaining relationships—further exemplifies his skill in compartmentalizing his predatory behavior from his public persona.[21]

Cultural norms surrounding gender roles and power dynamics can also contribute to the dehumanization process. For example, domestic abusers frequently rationalize their violence by adhering to patriarchal beliefs that women are subordinate or should be controlled. In this context, the dehumanization of the victim is bolstered by a broader cultural framework that implicitly supports or excuses such behavior.

Another critical component of the dehumanization process is the use of denial and projection as rationalization tactics. Criminals often deny the severity of their actions or project blame onto their victims. This serves to distance the criminals, in their minds, further from responsibility.

Denial may involve minimizing the impact of the crime or reinterpreting it in a way that reduces guilt. For instance, a perpetrator might claim that the victim "provoked" the violence or that the harm inflicted was "not that bad." In many cases of child sexual assault, predators remarkably say the victim, "encouraged the act" or "enjoyed it." In such cases, denial acts as a psychological shield that prevents the perpetrator from fully confronting the consequences of their actions.

Projection, on the other hand, involves attributing negative traits or intentions to the victim, effectively blaming them for their own victimization. This tactic is commonly employed in cases of sexual violence, where offenders often claim that the victim was "asking for it" through their behavior, clothing, or perceived promiscuity. Such narratives not only dehumanize the victim but also shift the moral burden away from the offender.

Dehumanization is often intertwined with the desire for power and control. By reducing their victims to objects or subhuman entities, criminals assert dominance and reinforce their own sense of superiority. This dynamic is particularly evident in cases of serial killers, who frequently describe their crimes as exercises in control over life and death.

As previously mentioned, serial killer Ted Bundy described his murders as acts of possession, claiming that killing allowed him to own his victims completely. In his view, the victim's humanity was irrelevant; they were simply vessels for his desires. Such an outlook underscores the role of dehumanization in enabling acts of extreme violence.

Similarly, in cases of genocide and mass violence, dehumanization is often a deliberate strategy employed by leaders to mobilize groups against a targeted population. By portraying the victimized group as dangerous, inferior, or non-human, leaders create a moral justification for atrocities. This dynamic was evident in the Rwandan Genocide, where Tutsi individuals were labeled as "cockroaches" by propagandists, paving the way for widespread violence.

The consequences of dehumanization extend beyond the immediate harm inflicted on victims. On an individual level, survivors of dehumanizing violence often experience profound psychological trauma, including feelings of worthlessness, alienation, and a diminished sense of identity. These effects can persist long after the violence has ended, shaping the victim's sense of self and their interactions with others.

On a societal level, dehumanization perpetuates cycles of violence and inequality. When certain groups are consistently dehumanized, it reinforces systemic injustices and normalizes their marginalization. This, in turn, creates an environment where violence against these groups is more likely to occur and less likely to be addressed.

Addressing the process of dehumanization requires a multifaceted approach that targets both individual and societal factors. On an individual level, education and awareness programs can help individuals recognize and challenge dehumanizing attitudes and behaviors. This includes promoting empathy and understanding through storytelling, dialogue, and exposure to diverse perspectives.

On a societal level, combating dehumanization involves addressing systemic inequalities and challenging cultural narratives that marginalize certain groups. This includes advocating for social justice, promoting inclusive policies, and holding perpetrators accountable for their actions. By fostering a culture of empathy and equality, society can reduce the conditions that enable dehumanization and violence.

Dehumanization is a powerful and insidious process that allows criminals to justify their violent acts while minimizing feelings of guilt or accountability. Through psychological mechanisms, social narratives, and cultural biases, perpetrators strip their victims of humanity, creating a mental framework that rationalizes harm. Understanding this process is critical for addressing the root causes of violence and fostering a society that values the dignity and humanity of all individuals. By recognizing and challenging dehumanization, we can work toward a more empathetic and just world.[22]

When criminals use denial to avoid accepting responsibility for their actions, they are employing a critical psychological strategy. Denial serves multiple purposes, enabling offenders to minimize their culpability, preserve a self-image incongruent with their crimes, and shield themselves from the emotional weight of their behavior. Whether it manifests as outright rejection of the facts or as a minimization of the harm caused, denial plays a central role in the mindset of violent predators and other offenders.

One of the most direct forms of denial involves the complete rejection of factual evidence regarding the crime. This denial may manifest in a refusal to acknowledge that the crime occurred at all, or in claims that the offender was not involved. Such outright rejection is particularly common in cases where the perpetrator believes there is insufficient evidence to prove their guilt.

Using Ted Bundy as an example again, the killer repeatedly denied his involvement in a series of brutal murders, even in the face of overwhelming evidence. Bundy maintained his innocence for years, exploiting public fascination and manipulating those around him to garner sympathy and support. By refusing to acknowledge the reality of his actions, Bundy was able to avoid confronting the moral and emotional consequences of his crimes for much of his life.

Psychologists suggest that this type of denial is often a defense mechanism designed to protect the individual's self-concept. For many offenders like Bundy, admitting to the crime would mean acknowledging their capacity for extreme harm and cruelty, which can be psychologically devastating. Instead, denial allows them to maintain a distorted perception of themselves as fundamentally decent or misunderstood individuals.

Another common tactic is the minimization of the severity of the crime, or the harm caused to the victim. This form of denial does not involve outright rejection of the facts but rather a reframing of those facts in a way that diminishes their significance. For instance, domestic abusers frequently downplay the physical or emotional harm inflicted on their victims, describing violent incidents as "not that serious" or as isolated events that do not reflect their true character. Similarly, perpetrators of financial crimes often rationalize their actions by arguing that their victims were not significantly harmed or could afford the loss.

Minimization serves several purposes for the offender. First, it reduces feelings of guilt and shame, allowing the perpetrator to continue their behavior without the psychological burden of remorse. Second, it provides a narrative that can be used to deflect criticism or accountability from others. In some cases, minimization is even used as a legal strategy to secure more lenient sentencing or avoid prosecution altogether.

A closely related strategy involves projecting blame onto the victim or external circumstances. This tactic allows the offender to shift responsibility away from themselves, further reinforcing their denial. In cases of sexual violence, offenders often claim that the victim "led them on" or "provoked" the attack, implying that the crime was a response to the victim's behavior rather than a deliberate act of harm.

Projection of blame is particularly insidious because it not only absolves the offender of responsibility but also exacerbates the suffering of the victim. By framing the victim as complicit in their own victimization, the perpetrator adds an additional layer of psychological trauma and societal stigma. In many instances, this form of denial is rooted in deeply ingrained cultural attitudes that enable such narratives. For example, societal myths about consent and victim behavior often provide fertile ground for offenders to rationalize their actions and avoid accountability.

The psychological phenomenon of cognitive dissonance plays a significant role in enabling denial. Cognitive dissonance occurs when an individual holds two conflicting beliefs or attitudes, creating psychological discomfort. For offenders, the conflict often arises between their self-image as a "good person" and the reality of their harmful actions.

To resolve this dissonance, offenders engage in denial, reframing their behavior in ways that align with their self-concept. This reframing may involve justifying the crime as a necessary or unavoidable action, minimizing the harm caused, or outright rejecting the reality of the crime. By altering their perception of the event, the offender reduces the internal conflict and preserves their self-image.

This dynamic is evident in cases of white-collar crime, where perpetrators often view their actions as justified by the demands of the business world or as a victimless crime. Bernie Madoff, the architect of one of the largest Ponzi schemes in history, rationalized his actions by convincing himself that his investors would eventually benefit from his fraudulent practices. Such justifications allowed him to persist in his criminal behavior for decades.

Denial isn't just a personal defense mechanism; it's often reinforced by the world around us. In many cases, entire communities or societies contribute to the denial of certain crimes, either by ignoring them or minimizing their impact. This is especially true when it comes to crimes against marginalized groups.

Take, for example, crimes against sex workers, homeless individuals, or undocumented immigrants. These cases are often underreported or overlooked, not because they aren't serious, but because societal biases devalue the victims. When law enforcement and the public turn a blind eye, it sends a dangerous message: that some crimes matter less. And when offenders see that certain victims are less likely to receive justice, it only strengthens their ability to justify their actions or deny them altogether.

But denial doesn't just come from society's neglect. Sometimes, it's fueled by the way crime is portrayed in popular media. Serial killers, for instance, are often glorified in movies, books, and documentaries, painted as misunderstood geniuses or even antiheroes. This kind of storytelling, while compelling, can distort the reality of their brutality. It shifts the focus from the suffering of victims to the criminal's own twisted logic, which can reinforce their own denial. If the world sees them as fascinating figures rather than ruthless killers, it becomes easier for them to see themselves the same way.

The consequences of denial are far-reaching. For offenders, refusing to acknowledge the harm they've caused makes rehabilitation almost impossible. If they don't believe they've done anything wrong, or in some wacky way think their crimes were justified, they're far more likely to repeat their behavior.

For victims, denial adds another layer of trauma. When an offender refuses to take responsibility, it invalidates the victim's suffering, making them feel unheard, overlooked, or even blamed for what happened to them. This can deepen their emotional wounds and make healing even harder.

On a larger scale, widespread denial weakens society's ability to address crime effectively. If we allow criminals to evade responsibility—whether through legal loopholes, social bias, or cultural narratives, we create an environment where harm continues unchecked. Addressing denial means challenging these narratives, holding offenders accountable, and ensuring that every crime, no matter the victim, is taken seriously.

At its core, denial is a psychological shield that protects criminals from facing the emotional and moral weight of their actions. Whether they reject the facts, downplay the harm, or shift the blame, it all serves the same purpose: to avoid responsibility. But by understanding how denial works and how society often enables it, we can take steps toward breaking these cycles and fostering true accountability.

Minimization is a common psychological strategy used by criminals to rationalize their actions and reduce personal culpability. By reframing their crimes as less harmful than they objectively are, offenders create a narrative that allows them to evade responsibility and mitigate feelings of guilt. This mechanism is not merely a defense used in the aftermath of crimes but is often an integral part of how offenders justify their actions in the first place. From suggesting that the victim's suffering was minimal or deserved to outright dismissing the harm caused, minimization enables predators to sustain their behavior with reduced psychological stress.

When most people do something that goes against their morals, their brains don't like it. That uncomfortable feeling is called cognitive dissonance, and it's basically the mind's way of saying, "Wait, this doesn't line up with who I think I am."

For criminals who somehow see themselves as good people, this creates a problem. How can they justify hurting others while still believing they're decent human beings? The answer: they rationalize. They come up with excuses, downplay what they did, or shift the blame onto someone else. It's not about facts—it's all about making themselves feel better by convincing themselves that their actions weren't that bad.

White-collar criminals are perfect examples of this phenomenon. These predators often frame their actions as "just business" rather than theft or fraud, suggesting that the harm caused to victims is either negligible or an unavoidable side effect of financial success. Similarly, perpetrators of physical violence may argue that their actions were justified, claiming that the victim provoked the attack or that the injury was minor and temporary. These rationalizations serve to preserve the offender's self-image while deflecting accountability for their behavior.

Research into criminal psychology has shown that this form of self-deception is particularly prevalent among repeat offenders. Studies reveal that individuals who minimize the harm of their actions are less likely to feel remorse and, consequently, less likely to cease their behavior.[23]

One of the most insidious forms of minimization involves suggesting that the victim's suffering was either minimal or deserved. This tactic not only reduces the offender's perceived culpability but also shifts blame onto the victim, reinforcing a narrative that absolves the predator of responsibility.

Sexual offenders often claim that their victims were "asking for it" based on their behavior or appearance. Such narratives exploit cultural myths and stereotypes to dehumanize the victim and justify the perpetrator's actions. By framing the crime as a consensual or mutual interaction, the offender denies the reality of the victim's trauma and minimizes the severity of their own behavior.

Similarly, domestic abusers frequently downplay the impact of their violence, describing incidents as isolated events or claiming that the victim exaggerated their suffering. This type of minimization not only invalidates the victim's experience but also perpetuates a cycle of abuse by enabling the perpetrator to avoid addressing their behavior.

For many offenders, minimizing the severity of their crimes serves a crucial psychological function. Guilt and shame are powerful emotions that can act as barriers to repeated offending. However, by reframing their actions as less harmful, offenders can mitigate these feelings and continue their behavior without significant psychological distress.

Psychologists have noted that such rationalizations are not unique to extreme cases. Even petty offenders frequently employ minimization tactics to reduce guilt and justify their actions. Shoplifters may argue that stealing from large corporations is harmless because the company can absorb the loss. This mindset allows the offender to view their actions as insignificant, reducing the likelihood of self-reflection or change.

Another common minimization tactic involves framing the crime as a necessary evil. Offenders who adopt this mindset argue that their actions were unavoidable or even beneficial in the long run. This strategy is particularly prevalent among white-collar criminals and political offenders, who often claim that their actions were intended to achieve a greater good.

In cases of corporate fraud, perpetrators frequently justify their actions by arguing that they were protecting the company or ensuring its survival.[24] This narrative not only minimizes the harm caused to investors or employees but also recasts the offender as a reluctant hero rather than a criminal. This type of rationalization is also evident in organized crime, where perpetrators may view their actions as part of a broader cultural or familial obligation. By framing their behavior as a duty rather than a choice, offenders create a narrative that absolves them of personal responsibility.

Luigi Mangione, accused of killing a healthcare CEO, might justify his actions by painting himself as a reluctant savior, someone who had no choice but to take drastic action for the greater good. In his mind, he wouldn't see himself as a murderer—he would see himself as a man of principle, standing up against corruption, greed, or betrayal.

He might say something like: "I didn't do this for myself—I did it for the people. The healthcare system is broken, and this man was making it worse. He was cutting corners, putting profits over patients, and destroying lives. No one else had the courage to stop him, so I had to. I didn't want to do this, but he left me no choice. He forced my hand. Someone had to take a stand against the corruption that's ruining our healthcare system. If anything, I did what no one else had the guts to do."

By framing himself as a reluctant hero, Mangione shifts the focus away from his crime and onto a greater cause. Instead of accepting responsibility, he positions himself as a martyr, claiming that his actions weren't about personal gain, but about protecting others. This kind of rationalization allows him to avoid seeing himself as a criminal—he's not the villain, in his mind, he's the one who finally did what needed to be done.

On an individual level, offenders who rationalize their behavior are less likely to seek rehabilitation or acknowledge the need for change. This denial of responsibility perpetuates cycles of harm, increasing the likelihood of reoffending.

For victims, minimization compounds the trauma of the crime by invalidating their experiences and reducing the likelihood of justice. When offenders downplay the severity of their actions, victims are often left feeling silenced and marginalized, exacerbating their emotional and psychological suffering. On a societal level, the normalization of minimization undermines efforts to address systemic issues that contribute to crime. By allowing offenders to evade accountability, society perpetuates a culture of impunity that enables further harm.

Addressing the issue of minimization requires a multifaceted approach that targets both individual and societal factors. On an individual level, interventions should focus on helping offenders recognize and confront the harm caused by their actions. This may involve therapeutic approaches, such as cognitive behavioral therapy (CBT), that challenge distorted thinking patterns and promote empathy for victims.

On a societal level, efforts should be made to challenge cultural narratives that devalue certain groups or normalize harmful behavior. This includes promoting awareness of the impact of crimes on victims, advocating for marginalized populations, and fostering a culture of accountability. By addressing the root causes of minimization and holding offenders accountable, society can work toward breaking cycles of harm and creating a more just and empathetic world.

Societal attitudes and cultural narratives can also play a significant role in facilitating the disassociation employed by serial predators. The portrayal of serial killers in popular media, for instance, often sensationalizes their actions, which can contribute to a cultural fascination that overlooks the victims' humanity. This sensationalism can inadvertently reinforce the dehumanization process, as the focus shifts from the victims to the perpetrators' notoriety.[25]

One of the most unsettling aspects of many criminals, particularly serial predators, is their ability to lead dual lives. These individuals often maintain the veneer of normalcy—stable relationships, careers, and social engagements—while secretly committing heinous acts. This paradox makes their crimes more chilling, as it underscores the disturbing reality that evil can lurk behind the most unsuspecting facades. Serial predators exploit this duality, using their outward appearances to deflect suspicion and maintain anonymity.

This ability to lead a double life is not just a psychological phenomenon—it's a calculated strategy that allows serial predators to operate undetected for years. By seamlessly blending into society, they manipulate those around them, shielding their crimes behind a mask of normalcy.

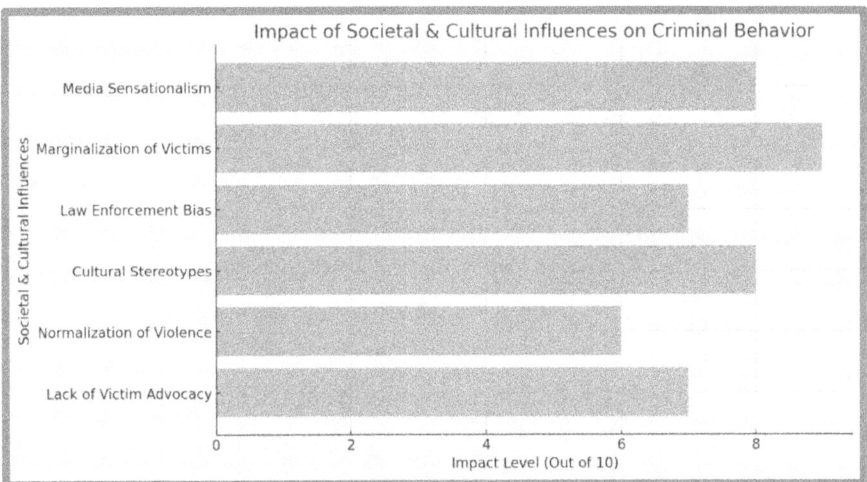

To see this disturbing dynamic in action, let's turn our attention to two recent cases that have captured national and international headlines: accused serial killer Rex Heuermann and convicted dual killer Richard Allen. We will find compelling evidence of how these individuals compartmentalized their lives, deceiving not only law enforcement but also those closest to them. By examining these cases, we can better understand the tactics predators use to evade detection, and the challenges investigators face in uncovering the truth.

Rex Heuermann, who is awaiting his criminal trial for multiple murders, is accused of being the Long Island Serial Killer, exemplifies a chilling case of duality. Heuermann was charged in connection with the murders of several women whose remains were discovered near Gilgo Beach in Long Island, a case that had baffled investigators for years.[26]

To his family, Heuermann was a devoted husband and father. His wife and children were reportedly blindsided by his arrest, expressing shock and disbelief that the man they knew could be capable of such atrocities. This revelation mirrored the experiences of Ridgway's loved ones, who also struggled to reconcile the predator's heinous actions with the persona they had known.

As Heuermann awaits his day in court, his case serves as another disturbing reminder that the most terrifying predators often hide in plain sight.

However, unlike Ridgway, Heuermann's neighbors and acquaintances often found his behavior odd, if not outright suspicious. Reports surfaced of Heuermann exhibiting socially awkward tendencies and displaying an eccentric demeanor.[27] One former client described an encounter that left a lasting impression. It was reported that during a project, Heuermann repeatedly engaged in heated arguments with contractors, particularly a plumber, questioning their work to the point of discomfort. His need for control and insistence on debating even minor details created a tense atmosphere. "It was very odd behavior," the client recalled, noting that Heuermann's demeanor made for an unsettling experience.[28] Neighbors described him as "very quiet" and "not very nice," an individual who kept to himself and exuded an unapproachable presence. His residence, a rundown and neglected home, starkly contrasted the professional image he worked hard to maintain, raising questions about the hidden complexities of his life.[29] Yet, these quirks were not enough to draw serious scrutiny, as his family life and professional status provided a veneer of respectability.

Heuermann's case underscores the importance of understanding how serial predators weaponize their dual lives. While their public personas may occasionally arouse curiosity or mild concern, their ability to compartmentalize their crimes often allows them to evade detection for years, if not decades.

Richard Allen's conviction for the murders of Abigail Williams and Liberty German in Delphi, Indiana, added another haunting example to the annals of criminal duality. In 2017, the two teenagers were found dead near a hiking trail in a case that captivated and horrified the nation. For years, the identity of their killer remained a mystery, with the community growing increasingly anxious as time passed without an arrest.

When Allen was finally charged and convicted years later, the news sent shockwaves through Delphi. Allen, a local pharmacy technician, was well-known in the small community, having interacted with countless residents over the years. Many described him as

friendly and helpful, someone who blended seamlessly into the fabric of daily life.[30]

The revelation of Allen's guilt stunned those who had known him, illustrating how effectively he had maintained his dual life. As with Heuermann, Allen's outward normalcy had shielded him from suspicion, allowing him to navigate within his community without arousing doubt.

Allen's case further demonstrates how predators exploit the trust inherent in close-knit communities. By presenting themselves as ordinary, even helpful individuals, they disarm those around them, creating an environment where their crimes can go undetected.

The ability of serial predators to lead dual lives is not accidental; it is a deliberate strategy that is rooted in psychological compartmentalization. This process allows them to separate their violent impulses from their public personas, enabling them to engage in horrific acts without disrupting the facade of normalcy. This compartmentalization helps them avoid detection by deflecting suspicion. Predators often cultivate trustworthy and unremarkable images, knowing that society is less likely to suspect individuals who conform to conventional norms. Second, maintaining a dual life allows predators to manage their own cognitive dissonance. By creating a clear divide between their public and private selves, they can suppress guilt and avoid confronting the moral implications of their actions.

This psychological duality also reflects a broader societal failure to recognize and address red flags. Predators exploit cultural assumptions that evil is overt and easily recognizable. By presenting themselves as ordinary or even upstanding citizens, they capitalize on society's reluctance to question appearances, ensuring that their crimes remain hidden for as long as possible.

The discovery of a predator's dual life has devastating consequences for their families and communities. Loved ones often grapple with feelings of betrayal and disbelief, struggling to reconcile the person they knew with the person capable of committing such atrocities. Communities, too, are left reeling in the aftermath of such revelations. In Delphi, Richard Allen's conviction shattered the sense of safety and trust that had defined the small town. Residents struggled to comprehend how someone so familiar could harbor such darkness, underscoring the profound impact of these cases on the collective psyche.

The dual lives of predators are only one piece of the puzzle in understanding the complex dynamics of crime. To fully comprehend how these individuals operate, it is essential to examine the victims they target and the factors that make certain individuals more vulnerable.

As predators navigate their shadowed worlds of disassociation and justification, they construct intricate psychological frameworks to excuse their actions. They compartmentalize their deviant behaviors, convincing themselves that their crimes are inevitable, necessary, or even deserved by their victims. But this rationalization is only one piece of a larger puzzle. Beneath the surface lies a much deeper force driving their actions: fantasy.

Fantasy is the seed from which their criminal behavior grows—a rich, distorted world where they are all-powerful, unchallenged, and free from consequence. For predators, these fantasies often begin innocently enough, but over time, they evolve into elaborate scripts of control and domination. They refine every detail, immersing themselves in a reality of their own making, one that fulfills their darkest desires.

The problem, however, is that fantasy is perfect—untainted by the messy, unpredictable realities of life. The execution of these fantasies in the real world often falls short, leaving predators unfulfilled, yet hungrier for control. The gap between what they imagine and what they experience fuels a vicious cycle, pushing them to escalate their actions in a desperate attempt to bridge the divide.

In the next chapter, we will delve into the power of fantasy as both the origin and the driver of predatory behavior. We will examine how these imagined worlds not only shape a predator's actions but also trap them in a dangerous loop where satisfaction is perpetually out of reach, leading to a relentless pursuit of their prey.

When predators attempt to actualize their fantasies, they often encounter the inherent unpredictability of real-life situations. Victims may not respond as envisioned; and the anticipated feelings of omnipotence may be diluted by the flawed reality. This is the predator's psychological cycle. -MK

Chapter Three

The Elusive High: Chasing Fulfillment in the Shadow of Fantasy

Predatory individuals often harbor elaborate fantasies of victimization, constructing intricate mental scenarios where they exert absolute control over their victims. These fantasies serve as a psychological sanctuary, allowing predators to indulge in their deviant desires without the constraints of reality.

When these dark fantasies are translated into reality, the resulting experience often fails to live up to the imagined perfection that fueled them. The disconnect that occurs between expectation and reality frequently carries devastating psychological consequences—not only for the victim, who suffers immeasurable harm, but also for the predator, whose actions plunge them further into moral and emotional turmoil.

The predator, in attempting to actualize their malevolent desires, is forced to confront the grim reality of their deeds, often finding themselves ensnared in a cycle of failure and escalating depravity. Each attempt to achieve their distorted goals requires a recalibration of their methods, driving them to pursue their objectives repeatedly. Tragically, this cycle is perpetuated at the grievous expense of innocent lives, with each new victim bearing the cost of the predator's insidious pursuit.

This pattern underscores the profound and far-reaching damage caused by such actions, leaving lasting scars on the victims who lay in the wake of this destruction.

Fantasy is central to the psyche of predators, particularly those who commit serial or sexually motivated crimes. These fantasies typically develop over time, starting with vague, often innocuous scenarios in childhood that progressively become more elaborate, violent, or sexually deviant in adulthood. Psychologists have identified fantasy as a "blueprint" for offending behavior, serving as a rehearsal space where predators script scenarios to achieve maximum gratification. Over time, these fantasies intensify, reinforcing the predator's deviant desires and desensitizing them to the moral implications of their actions.

Fantasy's role in predatory behavior has been well-documented in criminal psychology. The Behavioral Analysis Unit (BAU) of the FBI has noted that serial offenders often immerse themselves in a progressively intensifying loop of fantasy that acts as both a coping mechanism and a source of arousal.[31] This loop can begin with seemingly harmless daydreams but evolve into highly specific and meticulously detailed narratives that predators replay in their minds repeatedly. These mental rehearsals increase the likelihood of offenders acting on their fantasies, as they build confidence and desensitization through repeated visualization.

The journey from fantasy to criminal action often unfolds along a disturbingly predictable trajectory, rooted in psychological processes that escalate over time. It begins with a triggering event—an external occurrence that stirs deep feelings of inadequacy, rejection, humiliation, or frustration. This event might be a perceived slight, an interpersonal conflict, or a moment of profound disappointment in the predator's personal or professional life. Whatever the nature of the trigger, it ignites an inner turmoil, heightening the predator's need to assert control and reclaim a sense of validation that feels irrevocably lost.

In response to this perceived destabilization, the predator retreats into an internal world of fantasy. This imagined realm serves as both a sanctuary and a stage, allowing them to construct scenarios that provide an illusion of power and dominance. The fantasies often become increasingly elaborate and detailed, offering a psychological escape where the predator reigns supreme, unchallenged by the complexities and failures of real life. This mental space becomes a potent source of both comfort and empowerment, momentarily soothing the predator's insecurities and fulfilling their craving for superiority.

The act of refining these fantasies serves a dual purpose: it deepens the predator's detachment from reality while solidifying the blueprint for potential future actions. As the predator immerses themselves in these imagined scenarios, their sense of invincibility and entitlement grows. They may rehearse the fantasy repeatedly in their mind, perfecting every aspect of the narrative to heighten the thrill and perceived success. This psychological rehearsal not only intensifies their fixation but also diminishes their internal resistance to acting out these thoughts in the real world.

During this stage, the predator feels a sense of satisfaction, albeit temporarily. The fantasy world provides an illusory sense of resolution and triumph, which can create a deceptive calm. However, this sense of fulfillment is fleeting, as the gap between the imagined and the actual eventually becomes too great to ignore. The predator begins to feel that only real-world action can validate and bring their fantasies to life, setting the stage for the dangerous escalation from thought to deed. Over time, mere visualization becomes insufficient. The predator begins to experience a "tolerance" for the fantasy, much like an addiction. The scenes they once found arousing or satisfying lose their potency, driving them to create increasingly extreme or violent scenarios to achieve the same psychological effect.[32] Eventually, this tolerance propels the predator to seek real-world outlets for their fantasies, as they become convinced that only reality can deliver the fulfillment they crave.

When predators attempt to actualize their fantasies, they often encounter the inherent unpredictability of real-life. Victims may not  respond as envisioned; external circumstances, such as the presence of witnesses or any unexpected resistance, can interfere with the fantasy and the anticipated feelings of omnipotence may be diluted by any logistical complications. This conflict between the idealized fantasy and the flawed reality is a critical moment in the predator's psychological cycle.

The frustration stemming from this disparity often manifests as increased aggression and a compulsion to "perfect" the act through repetition. Serial killers, for example, frequently report that their initial murders did not meet their expectations. As a result, they commit further killings in hopes of achieving the satisfaction they anticipated. Ted Bundy described his first murder as "disorganized and clumsy," which drove him to refine his methods in subsequent crimes.[33]

Predators may also irrationally attribute the shortcomings of their real-world experiences to their victims. If the victim resists, shows fear in an unexpected way, or fails to behave according to the predator's script, the predator may blame them for "ruining" the scenario. This misattribution can result in the predator inflicting additional harm on the victim, both to punish them and to attempt to salvage the fantasy.[34]

The failure to achieve the fulfillment promised by fantasy often leaves predators feeling empty, frustrated, and enraged. This psychological void can trigger a cycle of escalating violence, as they attempt to close the gap between their imagined and real experiences. For some, this frustration also leads to a sense of alienation and detachment, as they come to view the world and the people in it as obstacles to their gratification.[35]

Additionally, the repeated failure to actualize their fantasies can drive predators to experiment with new methods or victims. This "experimentation phase" is often characterized by increased risk-taking, as the predator's desperation to achieve their ideal scenario overrides their fear of detection or capture.[36]

For victims, the consequences of a predator's unmet expectations are often dire. The initial victimization is compounded by the predator's subsequent frustration and rage, which may lead to increased violence, prolonged suffering, or even fatal outcomes. The unpredictable nature of the predator's behavior in these situations significantly diminishes the victim's chances of survival.

Victims who survived often report that the predator's anger seemed disproportionate or irrational, reflecting the predator's internal struggle with their unmet fantasies. This dynamic illustrates the profound dangers posed by predators whose imagined realities clash with the imperfections of real-life victimization.[37]

Historical analyses of serial offenders reveal patterns consistent with this dynamic. Jeffrey Dahmer's fantasies of creating a "compliant" companion through murder and manipulation provide a particularly illustrative example. From an early age, Dahmer harbored fantasies of absolute control over another person, imagining scenarios where his victim would be entirely submissive to his will.[38]

To realize these fantasies, Dahmer experimented with increasingly grotesque methods, including drugging, strangulation, and even attempts at lobotomization. However, the reality of his actions rarely lived up to the idealized scenarios he envisioned. The resistance of his victims, the logistical difficulties of disposing of bodies, and the fleeting nature of his gratification all contributed to his profound sense of dissatisfaction. This frustration drove Dahmer to escalate his crimes, ultimately leading to the murder of 17 victims.[39]

Dahmer's case also highlights the paradox of his fantasy: while he sought connection and control, his actions ensured isolation and chaos. His inability to reconcile his imagined world with reality underscores the destructive power of fantasy when it becomes a driving force for criminal behavior.

Jeffrey Dahmer's crimes weren't just random acts of violence, they were painstakingly scripted performances, acted out to bring his long-held fantasies to life. Like a playwright crafting the perfect scene, he envisioned absolute control over another human being: someone who would never leave, never resist, and never challenge his authority. But in reality, no one willingly stepped into the role Dahmer had written. So, he forced them into it and his evil script played out the same way, time and time again.

Act One: The Lure. Dahmer approached young men with charm and promises of things like money for photos, a drink, or just some company. He often hunted in places like Shaker's Cigar Bar in Milwaukee, Wisconsin, where he carefully chose his victims, ensuring they fit the role he had imagined. But once they left the bar and stepped inside Dahmer's apartment, the illusion of free will vanished.

Bob Weiss, the owner of Shaker's Cigar Bar, had a front-row seat to the eerie presence of Jeffrey Dahmer before the world knew what he was capable of. He remembers Dahmer as an odd, non-communicative figure who stood out from the usual crowd. While other patrons engaged in conversation, Dahmer kept to himself, making a point to only be served by male bartenders, avoiding any interaction with the bar's predominantly female staff.

What left the most unsettling impression on Weiss, though, was Dahmer's peculiar preference for one specific barstool. Among dozens of identical seats in the establishment, Dahmer always chose the one stool that sat slightly higher than the rest. It wasn't an accident. Weiss believes Dahmer wanted to elevate himself, literally and symbolically above those around him, a quiet assertion of dominance. He would sit there, slowly sipping a gin and tonic through a straw, watching people in the bar as if they were prey.

This seemingly small detail offers a chilling look into Dahmer's fantasy world, where control was everything. Just as he manipulated his victims into playing the roles he had scripted, he curated his own presence in the places he frequented, subtly reinforcing his delusions of superiority. He was rehearsing, refining and preparing, just like a wolf in the wild, crouching and creeping until he found the perfect moment to act.

Weiss's encounter with Dahmer fits perfectly into the patterns explored earlier in this book, fantasy as rehearsal. Serial predators often test the waters, playing out elements of their fantasies in everyday life before escalating to violence. For Dahmer, sitting above the crowd, watching without being watched, was just another step in a deeply disturbing performance that would only end when his double life was finally exposed.

Act Two: Submission. To strip them of autonomy, Dahmer drugged his victim's drinks, rendering them powerless. In his mind, this wasn't just about control—it was about eliminating rejection. He didn't want to kill his target for the sake of violence; he wanted to freeze them in a moment in time, creating a compliant companion who would never leave. His attempts at lobotomizing his victims included the horrific act of drilling holes into his victims' skulls and injecting acid. These were Dahmer's desperate attempts to manufacture obedience by stripping his victims of anything that made them resist.

But fantasy rarely translates into reality the way predators imagine. His perfect, compliant companion never materialized. One by one, his victims died, and their bodies became both trophies and complications for the killer. The illusion shattered, leaving Dahmer frustrated, empty, and forced to start over. That led to problem-solving that included ways to dispose of the remains.

And so, **Act Three:** Escalation. Each failed attempt led to darker, more desperate measures. Dahmer continued to take personal trophies by keeping body parts or taking photographs, not just to satisfy his morbid fascination, but to fulfill his delusions. Yet with all his attempts at accomplishing his fantasies, his reality failed to cooperate.

But even Dahmer, the so-called director of his own twisted play, couldn't control everything. His script was always doomed to fail because human beings aren't props. His final act came when one of his intended victims escaped and ran for help. Dahmer's fantasy collapsed and his murderous rampage was exposed. His attempt at architecting his perfect world collapsed around him and the reality of arrest defined him.

Dahmer's story reinforces an earlier truth in this book that fantasy is the rehearsal for crime. Predators refine their fantasies, justify them, and when they fail to match reality, the violence escalates. The danger lies not just in the fantasy itself, but in the predator's relentless need to force their world to conform to it, regardless the cost.

The interplay between fantasy and reality in predatory behavior highlights a critical aspect of criminal psychology. Predators' relentless pursuit of their idealized fantasies, coupled with the inevitable shortcomings of real-world enactments, fosters a cycle of frustration, anger, and escalating violence. Understanding this dynamic is essential for developing effective intervention strategies and enhancing victim protection measures.

As we have explored, fantasy serves as the engine driving a predator's actions, a meticulously crafted mental escape that fuels their need for power and control. Yet, as these fantasies collide with the harsh realities of criminal acts, they often unravel in ways that leave the predator unsatisfied, and the victim deeply scarred. This dissonance between imagined perfection and real-world execution traps the predator in a vicious cycle, prompting repeated attempts to refine their actions to achieve the unattainable.

But what happens when we shift our lens from the predator's internal world to the external traces left behind at the crime scene? Here, the interplay between fantasy and reality becomes strikingly visible. The act of victimization—rooted in the predator's constructed illusion—leaves behind clues not only about the crime itself but also about the predator's psyche. These clues manifest in the degree of organization or disorganization at the scene, offering profound insight into their level of planning, control, and emotional state during the act.

In the next chapter, we will delve into this critical junction where the predator's imagined world meets the stark evidence of their actions. How does the chaos or precision of a crime scene illuminate the predator's mental state? What do the inconsistencies between fantasy and execution reveal about their methods, motives, and compulsions? These questions guide us deeper into the intricate workings of the predatory mind, as we uncover how the principles of fantasy and reality merge to shape both their internal motivations and external behaviors.

Every crime scene tells a story—organized offenders leave calculated precision, while disorganized offenders reveal chaos and impulse. Both expose the predator's mind in chilling detail. -MK

Chapter Four

Order in Chaos:
Decoding Organized and Disorganized Crime Scenes

The meticulous nature of criminals is not confined to their personalities; it permeates the very fabric of their criminal acts and the scenes they leave behind. Predators exhibit specific behavioral traits and deliberate actions that reflect a calculating, methodical approach to crime or the opposite. An organized crime scene is a chilling testament to the offender's personality, revealing an intricate balance of planning, control, and emotional detachment. The disorganized crime scene teaches us about the mind of the criminal. This interplay between personality traits and crime scene characteristics offers invaluable insights into the offender's psyche, motivations, and methods.

Understanding the mind of a criminal begins with the scene they leave behind. For some, every detail is deliberate and planned with precision, executed with control, and erased with calculated detachment. These are the hallmarks of the organized offender. Their crimes are not acts of impulse but carefully orchestrated events that reflect a chilling mastery over both their victims and their surroundings. To truly grasp their psychology, we must first examine the intricate balance of planning, control, and manipulation that defines their every move.

THE ORGANIZED OFFENDER

Organized offenders are characterized by a distinctive set of personality traits that facilitate their deviant behavior. Among these traits are manipulativeness, cunning, and an almost complete disregard for societal norms. They are adept at blending into the social fabric, often assuming roles that mask their intentions. This chameleon-like quality allows them to navigate their environments undetected, adapting their appearance and demeanor to project an air of normalcy.

Their interpersonal skills can be disarming, enabling them to establish relationships with potential victims or gain their trust. This veneer of normalcy conceals a core personality marked by narcissism, a superiority complex, and a tendency to externalize blame. Organized offenders often rationalize their actions as justified responses to perceived slights or injustices, further demonstrating their detachment from societal and moral norms.

The development of antisocial traits is often marked by early behaviors indicative of a disregard for others, such as cruelty to animals, fire-setting, or theft. These behaviors are commonly associated with potential future criminality, as individuals may gradually refine their methods and escalate into more sophisticated offenses. This progression is frequently examined in psychological and criminological studies on antisocial behavior.

A widely known concept related to this is the Macdonald Triad, proposed by psychiatrist J.M. Macdonald in 1963. Many people know the theory from the more slang term of the homicidal triangle, which suggests that childhood behaviors like animal cruelty, fire-setting, and persistent bedwetting are linked to violent tendencies in adulthood.

Although influential in discussions about early warning signs, the Triad has faced criticism, with experts arguing that not everyone displaying these behaviors becomes violent, implying that additional factors are at play.

Further research in forensic psychology links early symptoms of conduct disorder—such as aggression, deceit, and rule-breaking—to the development of antisocial personality disorder (ASPD) in adulthood. Individuals with ASPD often display persistent disregard for social norms and the rights of others, with some refining their antisocial behaviors over time. Longitudinal studies, like the Dunedin Multidisciplinary Health and Development Study, have shown that early behavioral issues can predict later criminal activity, especially in the absence of effective intervention.

However, it is crucial to understand that this pathway is not deterministic. While early warning signs are significant, many individuals exhibiting such behaviors do not become criminals. Outcomes are influenced by genetic predispositions, environmental factors, and social interventions.

Critics also argue that the Macdonald Triad is less predictive than initially believed, noting that many children who engage in isolated animal cruelty or minor delinquency do not escalate to severe criminal behavior. The nature-versus-nurture debate reveals the complex interplay of biological, psychological, and social factors in shaping behavior, suggesting that early signs of antisocial behavior, while noteworthy, are not definitive predictors of future criminality.

For criminals like Richard Ramirez, early signs of deviance were evident in his teenage years, where he developed an interest in violence and the occult, setting the stage for his later crimes. Similarly, Jeffrey Dahmer exhibited troubling behavior during adolescence, as described earlier.

Organized offenders approach their crimes with a level of preparation that underscores their methodical nature. Crime scenes orchestrated by such individuals reflect careful planning and execution. Each detail—from the choice of location to the disposal of evidence—demonstrates an effort to minimize risk and maintain control over the situation.

Richard Ramirez is infamously known as the "Night Stalker," exemplified the traits of an organized offender. During his 1984–1985 crime spree, Ramirez meticulously planned his attacks, targeting

homes that were easily accessible and choosing times when victims were most vulnerable. He carried tools such as a crowbar to aid in breaking and entering and brought weapons to the scene, ensuring he was prepared for any resistance. Ramirez also demonstrated adaptability, selecting a variety of weapons—including knives, guns, and blunt objects—making it difficult for investigators to establish a consistent MO.

Jeffrey Dahmer, on the other hand, showcased organization through his calculated approach to luring victims and disposing of evidence. Dahmer often frequented gay bars, targeting young men who he believed would be less likely to be reported missing immediately. He employed charm and persuasion to entice victims to his apartment, where he had already prepared the setting for his crimes.

A hallmark of organized offenders is their propensity to collect trophies or souvenirs from their victims. These items, often insignificant in monetary value, serve as psychological tokens that allow the offender to relive the crime. For the organized offender, these trophies are symbols of power and dominance, providing a means to revisit their perceived triumphs.

Richard Ramirez demonstrated this behavior by taking items from his victims, such as jewelry or personal belongings, which he later gifted to acquaintances. This act of integrating trophies into his daily life allowed him to relive the thrill of his crimes while maintaining his anonymity. Ramirez's choice to distribute these items also underscored his confidence in evading capture, as he believed the items would not link him to his victims.

Jeffrey Dahmer took this practice to a darker level, preserving body parts such as skulls and bones as mementos. Dahmer's collection served multiple purposes: it allowed him to relive the crimes, satisfied his obsession with control over his victims even in death, and reflected his deep-seated psychological disturbances. These trophies were often stored in his apartment in plain sight, demonstrating his belief that he could maintain secrecy despite the gruesome nature of his actions.

Despite the calculated nature of their crimes, organized offenders exhibit a remarkable ability to adapt when faced with unforeseen challenges. For instance, Richard Ramirez occasionally altered his methods when encountering resistance, such as switching from stealth to brute force to overpower his victims. This adaptability extended to his use of various escape routes and his ability to leave crime scenes with minimal evidence, complicating law enforcement efforts.[40]

Similarly, Jeffrey Dahmer adapted his methods when necessary, such as employing different techniques to subdue his victims, including the use of drugs to incapacitate them. Dahmer's ability to maintain control over his environment—despite the presence of decomposing remains—further highlights his organizational skills.

Organized offenders represent a chilling subset of criminal behavior, characterized by their calculated methods, meticulous crime scenes, and psychological complexity. These individuals do not act on impulse; their crimes are driven by a blend of dominance, control, and a deep-seated desire for recognition. Each element of their behavior—from the selection of victims to the precision of their actions and the rituals they engage in after the crime reflects a deliberate, methodical approach. In many instances, the organized offender learns from their mistakes, to evolve and get better at being bad.

The cases of Richard Ramirez and Jeffrey Dahmer vividly illustrate this profound organizational prowess. By studying such offenders, investigators gain invaluable insights into their motivations and methods, which not only aid in solving crimes but also contribute to the broader understanding of criminal psychology.

But not all criminals operate with such precision. In stark contrast to the cold, calculating nature of organized offenders are their counterparts, disorganized offenders, whose chaotic and impulsive crimes leave behind a very different trail. Where organized offenders thrive on control, disorganized offenders often descend into chaos, marked by panic, confusion, and an inability to conceal their actions. What drives these offenders to act in such a frenzied and uncalculated manner? And what can their fragmented crime scenes reveal about their psychology?

As we turn our focus to disorganized offenders, we step into a world of impulsivity, emotional outbursts, and disorder—a reflection of an entirely different psychological profile. Understanding these differences not only sharpens the investigative lens but also deepens our comprehension of the vast spectrum of criminal behavior. As we progress in this next section, pay close attention to the often-unpredictable minds of disorganized offenders, where chaos reigns and the evidence they leave behind tells its own tragic story.

While organized offenders are known for their meticulous planning and calculated approach to crime, their ability to maintain this level of control is not always sustainable. Over time, various factors such as increased pressure from law enforcement, escalating psychological turmoil, substance abuse, or a growing sense of invincibility can erode their structured methods. As a result, some organized offenders begin to display disorganized tendencies, making impulsive mistakes, leaving behind critical evidence, or acting out in frenzied, erratic ways.

This decline into chaos is often seen toward the later stages of an offender's criminal career. The longer they evade capture, the more emboldened they may become, leading them to take unnecessary risks. The same control that once defined their crimes can unravel under the weight of stress, overconfidence, or addiction. Richard Ramirez became sloppier as his crimes progressed, leaving behind footprints, fingerprints, and even witnesses who survived his attacks. Similarly, Jeffrey Dahmer's carefully structured methods collapsed toward the end, as his apartment became a gruesome collection of evidence, making it increasingly difficult to conceal his crimes.

However, the inverse of this transition is rarely observed. A truly disorganized offender, someone who acts on impulse, lacks control over their actions, and is driven by emotional instability is unlikely to develop the structured, methodical traits of an organized offender. Their crimes remain chaotic, unplanned, and often leave behind an abundance of evidence, making them easier to identify and apprehend. While organized offenders may deteriorate into disorder due to external pressures, the deeply rooted impulsivity and lack of foresight in disorganized offenders typically prevent them from evolving into more strategic criminals.

In stark contrast to their methodical counterparts, disorganized offenders act without premeditation, driven by raw emotion, psychological distress, or overpowering urges. Their crime scenes tell a different kind of story—one of chaos, impulsivity, and a complete lack of control.

The disorganized crime scene reflects the offender's fractured psyche. Their violent outbursts often appear frenzied and excessive, with victims suffering. There is no calculated attempt to stage the crime scene, dispose of evidence, or select victims with a specific pattern in mind. Instead, their actions are dictated by the chaos within, leading to crime scenes that offer immediate and obvious clues to law enforcement.

To fully grasp the mindset of the disorganized offender, we must explore their erratic behaviors, their psychological vulnerabilities, and the critical mistakes that often lead to their downfall.

THE DISORGANIZED OFFENDER

Disorganized offenders represent a stark contrast to their organized counterparts, exhibiting a range of chaotic, impulsive, and emotionally charged behaviors that manifest both in their personalities and in the crime scenes they leave behind. While organized offenders meticulously plan their actions and exercise control over every aspect of their crimes, disorganized offenders act on impulse, driven by psychological turmoil and emotional instability. By exploring the defining characteristics of disorganized offenders, their behavioral tendencies, and notable case studies that illustrate the disturbing nature of their crimes, we are better positioned to understand more about this type of offender's personality, their criminal experience, and what motivates them.

Disorganized offenders typically lack the forethought and planning that characterize organized criminals. Their actions are impulsive, often driven by strong emotions or psychological triggers, and their crime scenes reflect this chaos. Unlike organized offenders who carefully select their victims and meticulously control the environment, disorganized offenders often act spontaneously, targeting victims of opportunity. Their crimes are often messy, unplanned, and frequently leave behind an abundance of physical evidence.

Some of the key behavioral and psychological traits that are commonly associated with disorganized offenders might include social isolation. Some disorganized offenders are socially marginalized individuals who struggle to form meaningful relationships. They are typically described as loners who feel rejected by society and internalize anger, frustration, and fear. This social isolation contributes to their lack of experience in dealing with others, which is reflected in the chaotic nature of their crimes.[41]

Due to their lack of planning and personal security, disorganized offenders often commit crimes close to their homes or places of employment. The crime scene is usually the same location where the victim was attacked, as these offenders lack the resources or foresight to transport the victim or conceal their actions.

If they are carrying a weapon, it is usually a weapon of opportunity. Disorganized offenders rarely carry weapons or tools specifically intended for their crimes. Instead, they use objects readily available at the scene, such as knives, blunt objects, or household items. These weapons are often left behind, providing crucial evidence for investigators.[42]

The crime scene for the Delphi, Indiana double murder of Abigail "Abby" Williams and Liberty "Libby" German has been the subject of intense scrutiny, not just because of the brutality of the crime but because of the strange mix of organized and disorganized elements it presents. Looking at what's been reported, it suggests that now convicted killer Richard Allen may have had a murderous plan in place as he approached the girls, but he either lost control, got sloppy, or was dealing with a psychological unraveling that made his actions more erratic.

One of the biggest indicators of a disorganized crime scene, and criminal is the unspent round (bullet) found on the ground. Typically, an organized offender who brings a firearm would make sure that evidence like shell casings or bullets wouldn't be left behind. The fact that an unspent round was found suggests either fumbling under stress, mechanical failure, or an unexpected development in the attack. If Allen chambered a round, but it ejected onto the ground, it might mean he was trying to intimidate the victims or that his initial control over the situation slipped in some way.

Then there's the placement of objects on the victims' bodies, another key indicator of disorganization. Reports suggest that specific items were placed or staged in a deliberate manner, which could suggest some sort of ritualistic behavior or an attempt to send a message. This isn't something an offender typically does if they're strictly trying to evade capture. Staging often reflects an emotional need or a psychological compulsion rather than calculated strategy. If Allen took the time to position objects or make alterations to the scene, it could mean that his crime was more personal or fueled by a deep-seated fantasy.

Another strange detail is the markings found on the trees in and around the crime scene. If they were freshly made and related to the attack, it could suggest a moment of impulse, possibly a post-crime ritual where the killer left a mark symbolizing something significant to him. It could also indicate that the offender was losing control of himself in the aftermath, lashing out in a way that wasn't necessary for the crime itself.

The is speculation, more likely proof based on forensics, about the use of both a handgun and a knife. This suggests an escalation of violence and potentially a loss of control. If the gun was initially used to corral or intimidate the victims, but then a knife was introduced, it could mean a few things like the gun may have malfunctioned, forcing the killer to switch weapons. Most likely, the attack didn't go as the predator had planned, leading to an escalation of violence, or there was a psychological component to the killing where the use of a knife was always part of the fantasy.

Typically, though, offenders who use a combination of weapons aren't operating under a strict, pre-planned script. Instead, they may be adapting to unexpected resistance or indulging in an impulse-driven need for overkill, both hallmarks of a disorganized offender. This draws our attention to the crime itself, a mixture of opportunity and familiarity. The Monon High Bridge trail isn't the most isolated area in the world, but it's just secluded enough that an offender could feel emboldened to act. If Allen was familiar with the location, which appears likely given his residence in Delphi, it might have given him a sense of control, knowing the best places to escape or stay hidden. However, the fact that it was broad daylight, and in an area where other people frequent, suggests a level of recklessness, which again leans toward a disorganized mindset, at least when the crime occurs.

The killer could have come into the area in a very organized and methodical way but when things didn't work out like the fantasy, something as simple as a phone recording him walking across the bridge, things fell apart. And that leads us to ask why Abby and Libby were chosen as his victims, were they victims of opportunity? That's highly likely. It doesn't appear that the killer stalked them for days or planned this attack far in advance. Instead, it seems more like he saw an opportunity and took it. If this was a fantasy-driven crime, the victims may have simply fit the moment, rather than being specifically targeted ahead of time.

Richard Allen has been found guilty of murder and he's in prison for life (unless he's granted a retrial). His crime scene along the Monan High Bridge Trail paints a picture of someone with a loose plan, that fell apart when he couldn't adequately control the victims, the crime scene and his response to a disintegrating situation. The presence of the bullet, the potential staging, and the possible weapon-switching all point to someone who was impulsive, sloppy, and possibly unraveling psychologically. This isn't the work of a criminal mastermind; it's the work of someone whose inner chaos spilled out into reality. And that chaos, in part, led to his conviction.

When disorganized offenders attack, it is usually in a frenzied and ritualistic way. These attacks are often characterized by extreme violence, such as uncontrolled stabbing, slashing, or mutilation. These actions may include biting, dismemberment, or the insertion of foreign objects, reflecting the offender's psychological distress and inability to control their impulses. Ritualistic elements, such as staging the victim's body or leaving symbolic objects, are not uncommon and often provide insight into the offender's fantasies or psychological needs.[43]

Unlike organized offenders who strive to leave minimal evidence, disorganized offenders frequently leave behind abundant physical evidence, including DNA, fingerprints, and personal belongings. This lack of caution stems from their impulsivity and inexperience. Disorganized offenders often suffer from mental health issues, such as schizophrenia, depression, or other psychological disorders. They may have a history of trauma, neglect, or abuse, which contributes to their feelings of inadequacy and social alienation.[44] This type of offender will often prey on individuals who are physically or socially vulnerable, such as children, the elderly, or those who are isolated. This targeting reflects their desire for power and control over victims they perceive as weaker.

The chaotic nature of disorganized offenders is most evident at the crime scene, which is often a direct reflection of their psychological state. These scenes are typically messy, disorganized, and located near the offender's residence or place of work. Key elements of disorganized crime scenes include a lack of concealment. Unlike organized offenders who go to great lengths to hide their crimes, disorganized offenders make little to no effort to conceal the body or evidence. Victims are often left in plain sight, and the crime scene may exhibit signs of panic or haste.[45] They may arrange the victim's body or objects at the scene in a symbolic or ritualistic manner. These actions are driven by fantasy or psychological compulsion rather than logic or strategy.[46] The level of violence at the scene is often excessive, reflecting the offender's emotional state. Acts of mutilation, dismemberment, or overkill are common, with the violence sometimes continuing post-mortem.

To highlight the principles of the disorganized offender, let's revisit the murder of a 26-year-old woman in a Bronx, New York, apartment. On October 12, 1979, Carmine Colabro brutally murdered the woman and left her body on the stair landing of her building, with no attempt to conceal it. Ritualistic elements included the positioning of the body to resemble a Jewish religious medal and the placement of personal items, such as earrings and a comb, in symbolic arrangements. The offender used the victim's pen to write a vulgar message on her body and left the pen inserted in the victim's body.[47]

Evidence of excessive violence, such as bite marks and the severing of body parts, underscored the frenzied nature of the attack. Colabro's psychological profile matched the disorganized offender archetype. He was socially isolated, unemployed, and had a history of mental health issues. The forensic evidence and behavioral analysis provided critical leads that ultimately led to his arrest and conviction.

Fantasy frequently plays a significant role in the behavior of both organized and disorganized offenders. Their crimes often serve as a means of acting out deep-seated fantasies that they are unable to fulfill in real life. This is evident in the ritualistic elements of their crimes, such as staging the body, collecting trophies, or inflicting post-mortem injuries. These actions provide the offender with a sense of control and satisfaction, albeit fleeting. Trophies or souvenirs taken from the victim often serve as tangible reminders of the crime, allowing the offender to relive the experience. In some cases, offenders may return to the crime scene or grave site, further underscoring their fixation on the act.[48]

Some of the factors that contribute to disorganized behavior are mental illness, substance abuse, lack of criminal experience, and environmental triggers. Many disorganized offenders suffer from untreated mental health conditions that impair their ability to plan or control their actions. Drugs and alcohol can exacerbate impulsive behavior and reduce inhibitions, increasing the likelihood of disorganized crimes. Inexperienced offenders are more likely to leave evidence and act impulsively, as they lack the knowledge or skill to cover their tracks,[49] and stressful life events, such as job loss, the death of a loved one, or rejection, can serve as triggers for disorganized behavior.

Disorganized offenders present unique challenges for investigators. The chaotic nature of their crimes can make it difficult to discern patterns or motives. However, the abundance of physical evidence left at the scene often provides crucial leads. Behavioral profiling can also play a key role in narrowing down potential suspects by identifying psychological traits and social characteristics common to disorganized offenders.[50]

The disorganized offender represents a profoundly disturbing subset of criminal behavior. Their impulsive actions, chaotic crime scenes, and psychological instability make them both dangerous and unpredictable.

Characteristic	Organized Crime Scenes	Disorganized Crime Scenes
Planning	Meticulous planning, little evidence left behind	Impulsive, chaotic, disorganized
Victim Selection	Targeted victims, often stalked before assault	Opportunistic victims, random selection
Crime Scene Control	Clean and controlled, minimal signs of struggle	Messy, signs of struggle and evidence of unplanned
Use of Weapon, Type Weapon	Brought by offender and usually removed after the assault	Weapon originates at the scene, i.e., rock, blunt instrument, signs of improvisation
Evidence Left at Scene	Minimal, attempts to conceal	Abundant, no effort to clean up
Disposal Site	Victim (or body) may be moved or hidden to delay discovery	Victim (or body) may be left at the scene, exposed.
Location of Crime Scene	Remote, controlled settings, pre-determined	Public area, familiar to suspect and evidence of unplanned selection
Offender Characteristics	Intelligent, socially adept, blends in. Chameleon	Lower intelligence, socially awkward, impulsive

By studying the behavioral and psychological traits of these offenders, law enforcement and forensic psychologists can gain valuable insights that aid in apprehension and prevention. Understanding the disorganized offender not only sheds light on the darker aspects of human behavior but also underscores the importance of addressing mental health and social isolation as critical factors in preventing violent crime.

Understanding the predator—their disassociation, justifications, and the interplay of fantasy and reality—offers critical insight into their psychology and behavior. The distinction between organized and disorganized crime scenes provides a window into the predator's inner chaos or control, but this focus only tells half the story. While these elements help unravel the "why" behind their actions, they do not answer the "who."

Crime does not exist in a vacuum; every act of violence leaves behind someone who bears the physical, emotional, and psychological scars—if they survive at all. The victim is not just an endpoint in the predator's narrative but a central figure whose experiences and vulnerabilities may reveal as much about the crime as the perpetrator's motives.

To truly understand the nature of criminal behavior, we must now shift our lens. It's time to move beyond the predator's mind and examine the victim's world: who they are, why they were targeted, and what their stories can teach us about prevention, justice, and healing.

PART TWO

UNDERSTANDING VICTIMOLOGY: SELECTION, IMPACT & PREVENTION

Victims of violent crime often share certain psychological and situational characteristics that predators exploit. -MK

Chapter Five

Through the Victim's Eyes: The Art & Science of Victimology

The lens of human curiosity often fixates on a singular question when confronted with a heinous crime: "Who did this?" It is a natural reaction, a primal instinct embedded in our psyche to seek out the perpetrator and deliver justice. But in our fervor to uncover the identity of the villain, we overlook an equally important question: "Who is the victim, and why did they become a victim?" This shift in focus is not a mere academic exercise; it is the cornerstone of effective investigation. By understanding the victim, their lifestyle, behaviors, and vulnerabilities, we not only humanize their story but also narrow the field of potential suspects. It's a perspective that transforms chaos into clarity and speculation into strategy.

Victimology, the study of victims, delves into these critical questions. It unveils patterns, relationships, and circumstances that help investigators paint a fuller picture of the crime. By focusing on the victim's life and its intersection with danger, we begin to piece together the intricate puzzle of "why them, why now?" This chapter unpacks how victimology serves as an indispensable tool in modern crime-solving and highlights real-world applications that have brought resolution to otherwise baffling cases.

Victimology examines the victim's role within the broader context of a crime. It evaluates their lifestyle, routine activities, and interactions to identify risk factors and potential triggers. According to Dr. Marvin Wolfgang, one of the pioneers of victimology, the concept often explores "victim precipitation," where the victim's actions, albeit unintentionally, may have contributed to the crime. This does not imply blame but rather an understanding of the dynamics that made the victim a target.[51]

For instance, in a study published by the Journal of Interpersonal Violence, researchers identified that victims who exhibited predictable routines or frequented high-risk areas were more likely to encounter danger. These findings suggest that criminals often exploit patterns and perceived vulnerabilities. Thus, an investigator who understands these elements can better predict the offender's behavior and refine the search for suspects.[52]

A powerful example of victimology's utility can be seen in the investigation of the "Green River Killer." Gary Ridgway, who

confessed to murdering at least 49 women, targeted sex workers and vulnerable individuals who lived on society's margins. By studying the victims' lives, investigators began to see patterns such as the transient nature of their existence, their social isolation, and their occupations and how these pointed toward a predator exploiting systemic vulnerabilities. This understanding not only helped detectives focused investigative efforts but also highlighted the societal structures that allowed these crimes to persist.

Similarly, in the case of Ted Bundy, investigators noted that many of his victims shared physical characteristics: they were young, brunette women with long hair parted down the middle. Bundy's fixation on this archetype offered critical insight into his psyche and helped narrow investigative leads. Understanding the victims' shared traits provided a framework for profiling the killer and predicting his next move.

In the early stages of a criminal investigation, the pool of potential suspects can be vast and overwhelming. Victimology acts as a filter, systematically eliminating improbabilities by homing in on the "why" and "how" of the victim's selection. For example, in domestic homicide cases, victimology often reveals intimate connections between the victim and the perpetrator. Studies have consistently shown that in over 70 percent of such cases, the offender is someone known to the victim.[53] For domestic violence homicides not involving intimate partners, offenders are typically classified as other family members or household members. This includes individuals such as parents, siblings, children, or extended family members who reside with or have a close relationship with the victim.

By studying the victim's relationships, investigators can identify potential motives and link them to specific suspects. Conversely, in random or opportunistic crimes, victimology highlights situational factors—such as location or timing—that may have contributed to the crime. This dual approach ensures that investigators are equipped with a roadmap, reducing reliance on conjecture.

Understanding a victim's background can provide crucial insights in an investigation, but it's important to approach this with care. Too often, victim-blaming creeps into discussions, shifting the focus away from the offender and onto the person who suffered the crime. This not only distorts the investigation but also adds unnecessary pain to the victim and those who care about them. The key is to differentiate between analyzing circumstances and assigning blame. As one expert put it in a Psychology Today article titled, *Effective Victimology Seeks to Empower, Not Stigmatize*, good victimology should help us understand, not judge. It's about uncovering the truth while respecting the dignity of those affected.

The study of victimology is more than a method; it is a paradigm shift in how we approach crime-solving. By asking, "Who is the victim, and why did they become a victim?" we uncover truths that propel investigations forward. Victimology transforms the victim's story from a static portrait to a dynamic narrative, rich with clues and insights. In the pursuit of justice, understanding the victim is not merely an option—it is an obligation.

Victimology is central to the analysis of criminal behavior and the successful resolution of investigations. It provides critical insights into the victim, their circumstances, and the dynamics surrounding the crime. By unraveling the complexities of a victim's life and situation, investigators can eliminate unfounded leads and focus on the most probable suspects. As highlighted by the FBI's Crime Classification Manual, victimology is "one of the most beneficial investigative tools in classifying and solving violent crimes." It not only helps investigators understand why a victim was targeted but also helps reveal motives that can point investigators toward potential offenders. This investigative approach underscores the necessity of creating a thorough and comprehensive victim profile to guide the inquiry effectively.

Victimology involves assessing numerous characteristics to form a detailed understanding of the victim. These characteristics include, but are not limited to, demographics, lifestyle, behavioral patterns, environmental and situational factors, and risk factors. These elements not only provide a baseline for understanding the victim's life but also facilitate the investigation by revealing potential motives and identifying risk levels. For instance, if the victim was a low-risk individual (e.g., someone with a stable and routine lifestyle), this might suggest a targeted crime rather than a random act of violence. Conversely, high-risk individuals (e.g., those involved in criminal activities or transient lifestyles) are often victims of opportunity.

One of the core aspects of victimology is assessing the victim's risk level, which serves as a diagnostic tool to understand the potential relationship between the victim and the offender. Key factors influencing risk assessment include situational elements like the physical location and the victim's mental or emotional state at the time of the crime. Circumstantial influences must be considered to better understand the surrounding conditions or events that contributed to the victim's vulnerability, including environmental contexts that include the broader social, cultural, and geographical settings of the crime scene.

The risk level of becoming a victim of crime is often closely tied to the nature of the relationship between the victim and the offender. Research on various victim-related crimes suggests that individuals categorized as low-risk victims typically share some form of prior connection with the offender, even if this connection is subtle or goes unnoticed by the victim. This association might stem from acquaintanceships, professional interactions, or even fleeting encounters.

On the other hand, high-risk victims are generally individuals whose lifestyle choices, behaviors, or environmental circumstances significantly increase their exposure to potential harm. These factors often place them in situations where they are more likely to encounter and be targeted by strangers. For example, frequenting high-crime areas, engaging in high-risk activities, or having a lack of protective measures can elevate one's likelihood of victimization by an unknown assailant. Understanding these distinctions is crucial for assessing vulnerability and implementing effective preventive measures.

The cornerstone of effective victimology lies in asking the right diagnostic questions. These questions focus on the "why" of victimization and help uncover the offender's motivations and methods. Essential inquiries include questions about why the victim was chosen by a particular predator. Why was the crime committed in the location and way it occurred? And what was the offender's behavior towards the victim during and after the crime?

In the book *Analyzing Criminal Behavior* by Cooper and King, the victimology continuum was explained further by four guiding principles that align risk levels with offender characteristics. The principles teach that the lower the victim's risk level, the higher the likelihood of pre-association with the offender. For instance, a low-risk individual's situational displacement—such as traveling alone on a remote highway—can elevate their risk level, exposing them to opportunistic offenders. Low-risk victims are more likely to be specifically targeted by offenders aware of their routines or vulnerabilities. A predator who is familiar with a victim's daily schedule may exploit this predictability to commit the crime.

When considering victims who are engaged in or living a higher-risk lifestyle, the victim is frequently a stranger to the offender. High-risk individuals, such as runaways or substance abusers, encounter elevated vulnerability due to their exposure to unsafe environments and individuals. High-risk victims are more likely to fall prey to crimes of opportunity by predators who often seek out high-risk individuals, capitalizing on their frequent exposure to dangerous settings.

The insights gleaned from victimology extend beyond the investigation phase, benefiting true crime enthusiasts in their pursuit for answers, but these insights also benefit law enforcement and investigators, prosecutors, mental health professionals, and correctional officers who deal with the results of violent crimes. Understanding victimology fosters empathy and respect for the victim, ensuring that their experiences and suffering are given due recognition and justice.

Victimology is not just an analytical tool but the foundation of understanding the intricate dynamics of a crime. By systematically examining the victim's life, choices, and circumstances, investigators can shift from possibilities to probabilities, unveiling the offender's identity and motivations. This approach ensures that investigations are thorough, justice is served, and victims are honored in their adversity.

The phenomenon of victimization has long been a focal point of criminological studies exploring the dynamics between victims and violent predators. One compelling book on this topic is Gavin de Becker's *The Gift of Fear: Survival Signals That Protect Us from Violence*. De Becker's work provides profound insights into the patterns and characteristics of victims, as well as their interactions with offenders before, during, and after a crime event.

Victims of violent crime often share certain psychological and situational characteristics that predators exploit. De Becker argues that one of the most significant factors is a tendency to ignore intuition and early warning signals. Individuals raised in environments where they are conditioned to suppress fear or comply with authority are particularly vulnerable. This learned behavior often manifests as a reluctance to assert boundaries, leaving potential victims exposed to manipulation.

Whether through physical isolation (being alone in a secluded area) or emotional isolation (exhibiting signs of low self-esteem or distress), this vulnerability increases the likelihood of being singled out. De Becker's emphasis on contextual vulnerability highlights how situational factors, such as time of day, location, and perceived distractions, such as using a mobile phone, play a critical role in predatory selection.

The pre-crime phase often involves a "testing" period, during which predators assess the vulnerability of their target. This may include behaviors such as engaging in seemingly innocuous conversations to gauge compliance or employing charm and flattery to disarm suspicion. De Becker describes these tactics as part of the "interview" process, wherein predators test boundaries and exploit any signs of submission or naivete.

Victims who are unaware of these strategies may inadvertently enable the predator's progression. For example, predators often use "forced teaming," a tactic that creates a false sense of partnership to lower a victim's guard. Recognizing these manipulative behaviors is critical for potential victims to disrupt the offender's strategy before it escalates to violence.

The dynamics between victim and offender during a violent crime are shaped by power, fear, and survival instincts. Victims often experience a "freeze" response, wherein their ability to think critically and act decisively is impaired. This reaction is rooted in the brain's fight-or-flight response, which, when overwhelmed, can lead to paralysis. Violent predators exploit this response by asserting dominance through verbal threats, physical force, or psychological manipulation.

De Becker emphasizes the importance of understanding the predator's objectives during the crime. For instance, compliance may reduce immediate physical harm in some scenarios, but resistance or escape could be a safer option in others. Each situation is unique, and victims must rely on intuition and environmental cues to make split-second decisions.

Post-crime interactions often involve continued manipulation, particularly in cases of stalking or domestic violence. Predators may attempt to reassert control through intimidation, coercion, or emotional appeals. Victims frequently experience feelings of guilt, shame, or self-blame, which can hinder their recovery and make them susceptible to further victimization.

Support systems and psychological counseling are crucial in this phase to help victims regain a sense of autonomy and security. De Becker underscores the importance of empowering victims to trust their instincts and recognize that responsibility for the crime lies solely with the offender.

As we close this chapter on the intricate interplay between victims and predators, we see how the threads of awareness, intuition, and preparedness form a protective shield—empowering individuals to recognize danger and reclaim their sense of control. Yet, one lingering question remains: why do predators choose the victims they do?

It is no accident. Behind every encounter lies a web of calculated decisions, often invisible to the untrained eye. What traits draw the predator's gaze? What behaviors mark someone as a target—or act as a deterrent? Understanding the predator's perspective not only completes the picture, but arms potential victims with the insight to disrupt the predator's plans before they can begin.

In the next chapter, we step into the predator's shadowed mind, illuminating the methods and motivations behind their victim selection process. The answers will surprise, disturb, and, most importantly, prepare you to see what others might miss.

The stage is set for an unsettling but vital exploration. Turn the page—and take the first step into unraveling the secrets of choice and chance in the predator's hunt.

Criminal predators often follow a distinct pattern when selecting and victimizing individuals. The process begins with identifying potential victims, followed by a subtle test of boundaries to gauge how the victim might react to the predator's advances. -MK

Chapter Six

The Hunter's Gaze: How Predators Choose Their Prey

In the intricate dance between predator and prey, understanding the factors that influence a predator's choice of victim is paramount. By delving into the vulnerabilities that predators exploit—such as age, environment, lifestyle, and situational awareness—we can equip ourselves with the knowledge to reduce personal risk and enhance safety.

Predators often employ a deliberate and methodical process to identify their victims. Understanding this process is crucial to recognizing red flags and breaking the cycle of vulnerability. They frequently target individuals who appear vulnerable, and their decisions are often influenced by physical appearance, body language, and behavior. To highlight this principle, let's look at the case of a young woman who was assaulted while jogging in Central Park.

The victim, a 28-year-old investment banker, was jogging alone in Central Park after dark. The park, especially at night, is a dimly lit and isolated place, and this fact played a crucial role in the attackers' decision to target her. Investigators later determined that the jogger's apparent vulnerability—being alone, exercising, and seeming unaware of her surroundings—made her an easy target for a group of teenage boys who were in the park that night.

The attackers, a group of youth ranging from 14 to 16 years old, had been involved in other minor crimes earlier that evening. They encountered the jogger and brutally assaulted her, leaving her unconscious and severely injured. The woman was found several hours later, covered in blood and with severe injuries, including blunt force trauma, sexual assault, and fractures to her skull. She was in a coma for several weeks and ultimately survived, though with permanent physical and psychological scars.

The case of the Central Park Jogger is often discussed in terms of the crime itself and the wrongful convictions that followed, but it's also important to acknowledge the role of situational factors in how the victim found herself in a dangerous position. This isn't about victim-blaming, as no one deserves to be assaulted under any circumstances.

However, it's an opportunity to explore how certain decisions and a lack of awareness of her surroundings contributed to the level of risk the victim faced.

The jogger made several choices that, although seemingly innocent and routine for a person exercising, placed her in a particularly vulnerable situation that night. Central Park, while a beautiful and iconic space, can also be isolating and dimly lit at night. Jogging alone in such a location, after dark, increased her vulnerability. Many urban parks, including Central Park, can become desolate after hours, with few people around to offer help in case of danger. It's easy to see how an unaware jogger could become an easy target for criminals.

In this case, the victim was focused on her run and did not seem to be aware of her surroundings. She was lost in her exercise, oblivious to the presence of others in the park, including the group of teenage boys who would later assault her. This lack of awareness, the jogger's failure to scan her environment, to notice people lingering in the park, or to sense any potential threat likely contributed significantly to her vulnerability.

It's important to emphasize that this is not about blaming the victim but about understanding risk factors that can help individuals make informed choices about personal safety.

Running at night, particularly in an isolated area like Central Park, is inherently risky. The jogger's decision to go alone at that hour, without a companion or an apparent concern with safety, increased her exposure to potential danger. While many people enjoy the serenity and solitude of an evening run, there are risks involved when the setting is unfamiliar or when the area is not well-populated. In this case, the victim's choice to go out alone, without taking additional precautions, placed her at a higher level of risk.

Moreover, if the jogger failed to inform anyone of her whereabouts, she further isolated herself in the event of an emergency. One could theorize that she could have reduced her risk of victimization by choosing a safer time and location to exercise. The jogger in this case had a flawed sense of safety as she ran in the park and her perception may have clouded her judgment. The perception of safety was probably reinforced by the fact that she had jogged there before, most likely without incident. This sense of routine, the belief that she had "done it before" and was familiar with the environment, may have contributed to her underestimation of potential risks.

While no one should be expected to live in fear of being attacked at any given moment, the jogger's case demonstrates how crucial situational awareness can be in reducing personal risk. Even in public spaces, especially late at night, it's important to be mindful of one's surroundings, to stay alert to who is nearby, and to be prepared for the possibility of encountering danger.

This doesn't mean that the jogger should be blamed for the assault—she did not deserve what happened to her. However, by being more aware of her environment, she might have been able to make decisions that lowered her vulnerability, such as choosing to run with a partner or running in a more populated area. The aim in analyzing the jogger's choices and the risks she faced is not to suggest she was responsible, but to understand how situational awareness and certain decisions might contribute to one's safety.

This story serves as a reminder that while personal safety decisions are not guarantees against harm, being mindful of one's surroundings and recognizing potential risks can help minimize vulnerability. It's important to emphasize that responsibility for violent crime always lies with the perpetrator, and no person should ever be blamed for a crime committed against them.

Criminal predators often follow a distinct pattern when selecting and victimizing individuals. The process begins with identifying potential victims, followed by a subtle test of boundaries to gauge how the victim might react to the predator's advances. These predatory behaviors can be seen in a variety of crimes, including abductions, sexual assaults, and robberies. A tragic example of this behavior is the abduction of 11-year-old Jaycee Dugard in 1991, which serves as a clear illustration of how predators test their victims' reactions before proceeding with their criminal actions. By analyzing the case of Jaycee Dugard's abduction, we can gain a deeper understanding of the strategies employed by criminals and develop ways to prevent such victimization in the future.

On June 10, 1991, Jaycee Dugard was abducted while walking to her school bus stop in the town of South Lake Tahoe, California. At the time, Dugard was an innocent, trusting child, unaware of the dangers that lurked in her surroundings. Phillip Garrido, a convicted sex offender, and his wife, Nancy Garrido, targeted Jaycee as their victim. Phillip Garrido, driving a vehicle, approached the young girl and engaged her in conversation, asking for directions. The seeming innocuous nature of this interaction was a calculated move. Criminal predators, such as Garrido, often test their potential victims' boundaries to assess their vulnerability. In this instance, Jaycee hesitated but complied with Garrido's request. Her hesitation, a natural response

from a child who was perhaps uncertain but not yet fearful, provided Garrido with an opportunity to act.

As Jaycee turned her attention to the interaction, Garrido seized the moment of distraction. He quickly overpowered her and forced her into the vehicle. This brief but crucial exchange highlights a common strategy predators use when selecting victims. By initiating contact, the criminal tests the potential victim's ability to resist or comply. In this case, Garrido was able to assess Jaycee's reaction—her initial hesitation in responding to him and her lack of immediate retreat—which likely signaled to him that she was uncertain, caught off guard, or less likely to react defensively. Criminals often interpret such hesitation as a sign that a target may be easier to control or manipulate. However, it's important to note that her hesitation alone did not "allow" the abduction; rather, it provided Garrido with an opportunity to gauge her response and act on it. This type of testing—where predators assess a person's awareness, confidence, or willingness to engage—is commonly seen in crimes ranging from fraud and theft to violent assaults.

The reaction of the victim plays a significant role in determining the outcome of such an encounter. Predators often look for signs of weakness, uncertainty, or non-resistance. In the case of Jaycee Dugard, her hesitation, while not overtly indicating fear, was enough to signal to Garrido that she was a vulnerable target. Studies on predatory behavior suggest that criminals frequently choose victims who appear distracted, confused, or unable to defend themselves. This vulnerability can be both physical, as in the case of children, or psychological, such as when individuals show signs of compliance or fear.

By testing the victim's boundaries, a predator can gauge whether resistance is likely or whether the victim will probably comply with the attacker's demands. This is why it is essential for potential victims to be aware of their surroundings and trust their instincts. In Jaycee's case, although she had no way of knowing the intentions of Garrido, her hesitation allowed him to carry out the abduction.

Understanding how criminals test boundaries can help individuals better protect themselves from becoming victims of crime. While it is not always possible to predict when or where a predator will strike, there are several strategies that can minimize the likelihood of victimization.

The most important strategy is to **TRUST YOUR INSTINCTS** and be aware of your surroundings and situation. If a situation or person feels off, individuals should trust their gut feelings and seek help or remove themselves from the situation.

Jaycee Dugard's abduction was a tragic event, but had she been more aware of her surroundings or had a heightened sense of caution, the outcome might have been different. Again, please know that this isn't about victim blaming or victim shaming, this is about learning from these horrific crimes and using what we learn to reduce our own risk of being victimized. People should always be vigilant and pay attention to any subtle signs that might indicate a potential threat.

Some people find comfort in obtaining self-defense training, especially for children. This can be one proactive way to deter predators. Knowing self-defense can be invaluable in the event a child or adult is approached by someone with malicious intentions. Educating yourself on the tactics employed by criminals is essential. Books like this and self-defense training can provide everyone with lessons on personal safety, including how to handle interactions with strangers. Parents should teach their children to avoid conversations with strangers, especially if the person tries to isolate them or ask for help.

Having a set routine and communicating plans with trusted family members or friends can help deter criminals from targeting potential victims. If children have a clearly defined route and time frame for their journey to school or other activities, this can help ensure that they are less likely to be abducted. In Jaycee's case, she was alone at the bus stop, which made her an easier target. Ensuring that children are never alone in vulnerable situations is crucial in preventing abductions.

Requesting and participating in community awareness is also beneficial. Communities can play a significant role in preventing crime through neighborhood watch programs, and increased awareness of criminal behavior patterns can deter predators from acting in the first place. When a community is actively engaged in preventing crime, criminals are less likely to target victims there.

The abduction of Jaycee Dugard serves as a painful reminder of how criminals test boundaries to determine whether their victims will resist or comply. Through the brief interaction between Dugard and Garrido, we see how predators assess vulnerability and exploit moments of hesitation. Understanding these tactics is crucial in preventing victimization.

Violent criminals, particularly those who engage in serial offenses, often exploit environments where they can operate with minimal risk of detection.

By carefully selecting locations that offer opportunities for privacy, lack of supervision, and limited foot traffic, these predators can increase their chances of committing their crimes while avoiding immediate intervention or law enforcement scrutiny.

A chilling example of this can be seen in the case of Danny Rolling, the "Gainesville Ripper," who targeted college students in Florida during the early 1990s. Rolling's choice of locations, particularly his targeting of apartment complexes with poor security measures and minimal traffic, exemplifies how violent predators assess and exploit environments to further their horrific agendas.

Rolling's reign of terror was one of the most notorious serial murder cases in U.S. history. Over a span of several days, Danny Rolling murdered five young college students, shocking the local community and instilling fear across the campus of the University of Florida. The victims—two young women and three young men—were primarily killed in off-campus apartments that were poorly secured. Rolling, who had a history of violent behavior and a troubled upbringing, used his knowledge of the local area to identify ideal locations for his crimes. His methodical selection of target areas and his ability to adapt to the environment demonstrates how violent predators evaluate their surroundings to reduce the risk of capture.[54]

One of the ways Rolling exploited the environment was by scouting apartment complexes that lacked proper security measures. Many of the locations he targeted were not equipped with modern security features such as controlled access gates, security cameras, or even well-lit walkways. This created a vulnerable environment where Rolling could enter undetected and move freely without attracting attention. His decision to target these poorly secured apartment complexes was strategic, as the lack of surveillance provided him with the cover necessary to commit his crimes without fear of being interrupted or observed. Rolling also focused on areas with low foot traffic, which gave him further anonymity, avoiding more heavily trafficked areas where residents or passersby might notice something unusual or raise alarms.

Additionally, this predator carefully selected properties where the residents were likely to be isolated, offering minimal opportunity for immediate intervention. Many of the victims lived alone, creating a scenario where Rolling could attack without the presence of others who might intervene or call for help. The isolation of his victims was an essential part of his plan. By targeting apartment complexes that were often occupied by students, many of whom were unfamiliar with the area or did not have the experience or support systems to navigate potential threats, Rolling minimized the possibility of his being disturbed during his crimes. These choices reflect how predators assess potential opportunities to gain control over their victims.[55]

By operating in this manner, Rolling ensured a sense of privacy and control, which is crucial for predators who hope to minimize the likelihood of being apprehended. The quiet, less secure nature of his chosen locations allowed him to commit his murders with a greater sense of freedom, both logistically and emotionally. The lack of proactive security or community awareness only increased his confidence and made his actions more difficult to trace.

The case of Danny Rolling underscores a significant aspect of criminal behavior—predators' ability to assess and exploit their environment for maximum opportunity. Violent offenders, particularly serial killers, often display a sophisticated understanding of the areas they target. Whether through familiarity with the layout, awareness of the local population, or the identification of weak security features, these individuals are adept at selecting environments where they can operate with reduced risk of detection. In Rolling's case, his ability to recognize and capitalize on vulnerable locations played a significant role in his ability to carry out his horrific crimes.

His case illustrates the way violent predators exploit locations to minimize their risk and maximize their control over victims. By selecting poorly secured apartment complexes and focusing on areas with low foot traffic, Rolling was able to commit his crimes with a disturbing degree of confidence and impunity. His choice of locations speaks to a broader pattern of criminal behavior, in which offenders assess their environment for the most favorable conditions, ensuring their actions are carried out in relative anonymity. The case serves as a chilling reminder of how predators can take advantage of their surroundings for nefarious purposes, often leaving communities in shock and terror until law enforcement can intervene.

Understanding the factors that make individuals more vulnerable to victimization can help us identify and address our own risks. Predators often seek victims at extreme ends of the age spectrum—either very young or elderly—because they are easier to control. While Rolling primarily targeted young college students, other killers have focused on the opposite end of the spectrum, preying on the elderly, who may be physically weaker or socially isolated.

In a groundbreaking study conducted for the Department of Justice, Mike King and Greg Cooper explored the motivations and behaviors of offenders convicted of sexually assaulting the elderly. Their research, published in the Journal of Forensic Nursing, titled *Interviewing the Incarcerated Offender Convicted of Sexually Assaulting the Elderly*, sheds light on the disturbing realities of these crimes and the psychological drivers behind them. The study emphasizes how forensic interview techniques can be optimized to elicit truthful disclosures, providing critical insight into offender mindsets, patterns, and justifications for their actions. Understanding these behaviors is not just an academic pursuit, it plays a vital role in preventing future crimes and bringing offenders to justice.

One such offender they interviewed is Daniel Troyer, a serial predator whose reign of terror targeted some of society's most vulnerable individuals. His crimes exemplify the very patterns outlined in King and Cooper's research, illustrating how offenders rationalize their actions while preying on victims they perceive as defenseless. Examining Troyer's methods and motivations offers a chilling case study in the behaviors identified in the study, revealing the dangerous intersection of opportunity, compulsion, and a complete lack of empathy.

Unlike Danny Rolling, who exploited location to control his victims, Daniel Troyer focused on a different vulnerability, age. Over the course of his killing spree in Salt Lake City, Utah, Troyer targeted elderly women, preying on their physical frailty and isolation. His methodical approach to selecting victims mirrored the predatory instincts seen in other violent offenders, reinforcing the disturbing reality that criminals often assess both environment and individual weakness to maximize their control.

What sets Troyer apart, however, is the rare and unsettling insight he provided into his own psychology. In one interview, Troyer openly spoke about the emotions and impulses that drove him to hunt and murder. During their interviews with Troyer, the killer likened himself to a lioness. He explained his predatory nature with chilling clarity when he said,

---

"When you look at the lioness sunning herself ... you have a difficult time understanding how vicious and violent she can be. But, after a while, the hunger will build up inside of her and she'll begin to hunt ... That's how I feel before I kill an old lady."

This disturbing analogy underscores the calculated, instinctual nature of his crimes. Troyer did not see himself as a man committing murder—he saw himself as a hunter, fulfilling an uncontrollable hunger. His words echoed those of other serial offenders who describe killing as both a pursuit and a need, further illustrating the complex psychological landscape of violent predators.

Through Troyer's confessions, a broader pattern emerges—one in which certain criminals exhibit not just a willingness to kill but a chilling awareness of their own process. They assess risk, select victims based on perceived weaknesses, and execute their crimes with a level of detachment that defies comprehension. Understanding the minds of such offenders is crucial for law enforcement and behavioral analysts, as it sheds light on the psychology of predation and the factors that make certain individuals more vulnerable.

Troyer's choice of elderly women as victims was strategic. He noted that "old people are lonely and want to talk," a vulnerability that he exploited by posing as a magazine salesman to get inside the victim's homes. Once inside, he would swiftly overpower them, initially strangling the women from behind and later confronting them face-to-face as his confidence grew.

This predilection for vulnerable victims is not unique to Troyer. Research indicates that serial killers often select victims based on ease of control. Elderly individuals, due to physical frailty and social isolation, are frequent targets. A study analyzing serial murders in the United States found that many offenders chose victims who were less likely to resist or escape, such as the elderly or infirm.[56]

Troyer described the murders as the "biggest rush" he had ever known, indicating a profound psychological gratification derived from exerting absolute control over his victims. After the killings, he would engage in acts such as bathing the corpses and dressing them in pajamas, rituals that extended his sense of dominance even after death. The act of dressing his victims and posing them in their beds allowed Troyer to ensure his escape. In many cases, before they learned the truth of Troyer's criminal acts, many family members assumed their loved one peacefully died in their sleep.

This behavior aligns with the profiles of hedonistic serial killers, who derive pleasure from the act of killing and the subsequent manipulation of the victim. Such individuals often seek to fulfill fantasies of power and control, with the victim serving to that end.

Troyer's case exemplifies a broader pattern wherein predators select victims based on perceived vulnerability, ensuring ease of domination and fulfillment of their psychological needs. Understanding this dynamic is crucial for law enforcement and communities to develop strategies that protect potential targets, particularly the elderly and other vulnerable populations.

Predators thrive on their victim's weakness or vulnerability. Whether their motives are rooted in power, control, or opportunistic impulses, they often seek targets who appear unaware or unprepared to respond to threats. A person's level of situational awareness and their body language are critical factors in either deterring or inviting predatory behavior. Situational awareness involves being mindful of one's environment and recognizing potential threats before they escalate. It's a skill that can mean the difference between safety and victimization. An anecdote from a 2018 incident in Ohio illustrates this point vividly. In a shopping mall parking lot, a man attempted to abduct a woman. However, the woman noticed him following her and, instead of ignoring her instincts, she made direct eye contact. This act alone disrupted the man's confidence, causing him to hesitate. She then called out for help, loudly drawing attention to the situation, which scared him off.[57] Her alertness and decisive actions served as powerful deterrents, thwarting the predator's plan before it could unfold.

Predators rely heavily on the element of surprise. A person who is distracted—looking at their phone, absorbed in conversation, or seemingly oblivious—is an easier target. In contrast, someone who is visibly aware, scanning their surroundings, and walking with purpose projects a sense of control, making them less appealing as a victim.

Our body language communicates volumes without a single word being spoken. Confident posture, steady eye contact, and purposeful movement signal to potential predators that a person is not to be trifled with. Conversely, slouched shoulders, downward gazes, and hesitant movements may convey insecurity or distraction—traits that predators often interpret as vulnerability.

Studies on criminal behavior support this notion and interviews with convicted offenders reveal that many chose their victims based on nonverbal cues. People who appeared distracted, timid, or unaware were frequently targeted.[58] On the other hand, individuals who walked with confidence, maintained awareness, and appeared physically capable often deterred potential attacks.

We can each cultivate situational awareness and assertive body language by staying alert and avoiding distractions such as excessive phone use, especially in public spaces. Regularly scan the environment for anything unusual or suspicious. Walk with confidence and keep your head up, shoulders back, and stride with purpose. Project confidence. Appearing confident can dissuade a predator from targeting you. Although mentioned before, it's appropriate to repeat this advice: Trust your instincts. If something feels off, don't dismiss it. Instincts are often your body's way of alerting you to potential danger. And finally, act decisively. In threatening situations, act immediately. Draw attention to your situation. Shout for help or create a scene that could disrupt a predator's plans. Another option may be to return to the building and get help from security personnel.

Blaine Hogge Nelson is a serial rapist who admitted to committing more than 85 rapes across eleven Western states while working as an interstate truck driver, exploiting his mobility to avoid detection. His confessions and insights, shared with Investigator Mike King, provide a disturbing but valuable look into the methods of a predator, how he selected victims, how he entered homes, and how he managed to evade law enforcement for so long.

During his discussions with King, Nelson revealed chilling tactics he used to choose both victims and crime scenes. He looked for homes that suggested a single female occupant, often noting details like neglected yards, certain bumper stickers, or a lack of male presence. He avoided homes with dogs, learned to circumvent security measures, and capitalized on vulnerabilities like open windows, poorly placed deadbolts, or predictable daily routines. His ability to study his environment, blend in, and manipulate evidence made him an especially dangerous offender.

Perhaps most disturbingly, Nelson offered tips on how women could protect themselves from predators like him. While it may seem unsettling to take safety advice from a serial rapist, his perspective sheds light on the tactics predators use and how potential victims can reduce their risk. Simple measures like installing motion-activated lights with audio warnings, keeping a BIG dog dish visible, (even if you don't own a dog) or changing up predictable routines such as the time you go to bed, what lights you leave on. All these subtle changes were deterrents even he admitted to avoiding.

Nelson's admissions underscore the importance of vigilance, risk reduction, and proactive security. His crimes highlight the evolution of a predator, moving from burglaries to violent assaults, a pattern seen in many repeat offenders. Understanding serial offenders like Nelson helps law enforcement track behavioral progressions, identify warning signs, and improve investigative approaches.

Nelson's chilling account is memorialized on the YouTube Channel @*ProfilingEvil* and serves as a warning, perhaps even a bit of education reinforcing the premise that while victims are never responsible for the crimes committed against them, there may have been things they could have done to reduce their risk of victimization.

Predators don't choose their victims at random; their methods are chillingly deliberate. This chapter unraveled the dark art of victim selection, exposing the calculated strategies predators employ to find those they perceive as vulnerable. But what happens after the attack? What becomes of the lives left shattered in the wake of such violence?

The story doesn't end with the crime itself—it's only the beginning. For the survivors, the physical and psychological wounds linger long after the predator is gone. The scars, both visible and invisible, tell a story of pain, resilience, and sometimes, triumph. In the next chapter, we'll explore the aftermath of violence: how it changes lives, challenges identities, and ignites the human spirit's remarkable capacity to endure. From the depths of despair to the journey of recovery, this is a story of survival and the power to rebuild after destruction.

*The impact of violent crime victimization is profound,
leaving indelible marks on individuals and reverberating
through families, communities, and society. -MK*

Chapter Seven

Shattered Echoes: The Lasting Scars of Violence

Experiencing victimization at the hands of a violent predator is a profoundly life-altering event, bringing about lasting consequences not only for the individuals directly impacted but also for the broader society. This chapter will explore the multifaceted repercussions of crime victimization, particularly the psychological and physical consequences faced by survivors, the societal ramifications of such events, and the pathways toward recovery and resilience. Through anecdotal references and supported by academic sources, a more comprehensive understanding of the subject is possible.

The emotional fallout from violent crime is massive, and for many survivors, it doesn't just fade with time. The psychological toll can be devastating, often leaving people struggling with long-term trauma. One of the most well-documented effects is Post-Traumatic Stress Disorder (PTSD), which can show up as intrusive memories, hypervigilance, and emotional numbness. Studies suggest that anywhere from 30 to 50 percent of violent crime survivors end up with PTSD. If you talk to someone who has lived through a home invasion or an assault, they'll often describe the same things—flashbacks that won't stop, sudden panic attacks, and an overwhelming fear that their world will never feel safe again. The trauma doesn't just stay in the past; it seeps into every part of their daily life.

But PTSD isn't the only struggle. Many survivors also battle depression, anxiety, and even substance abuse. Experts have found that going through a violent crime makes people much more likely to develop mood disorders or turn to drugs and alcohol to cope. Some victims withdraw from the world entirely, while others pick up unhealthy habits just to numb the pain. This creates a vicious cycle where trauma they are experiencing feeds into destructive coping mechanisms, making it even harder to heal. Even more concerning, research shows that survivors of violent crime are at higher risk for suicidal thoughts.

So, what's the solution? While there's no universal fix, experts agree that recovery isn't just about time, it requires genuine support from both mental health professionals and a strong, reliable network. Therapy, community resources, and strong personal support systems all play a crucial role in helping survivors rebuild their sense of safety and reclaim their lives. The aftermath of violent crime is complex, but with the right interventions, healing is possible.

Violent crime doesn't just leave emotional scars—it takes a serious toll on the body, too. The physical aftermath can be just as devastating as the psychological trauma, and the two are often deeply intertwined. Survivors who suffer injuries from an attack may face a lifetime of chronic pain, permanent disabilities, or disfigurement. But even for those who walk away without obvious wounds, the effects of trauma can still manifest physically in ways that might not be immediately visible.

Research has found that exposure to violent crime is linked to long-term health issues like heart disease, digestive problems, and a weakened immune system. Why? Because the body doesn't just "shake off" traumatic stress—it holds onto it. High stress levels over time can lead to conditions like high blood pressure, irritable bowel syndrome, and frequent illness. The body essentially stays in survival mode long after the danger has passed, making it harder to recover and stay healthy.

The ripple effects of violent crime don't stop with the survivor. Families often find themselves in turmoil, dealing with the emotional weight of what happened to their loved one while also adjusting to any long-term changes in their daily lives. If a survivor is left with lasting physical injuries, families may need to take on caregiving roles, which can strain relationships and create financial hardships. Even those who weren't directly harmed can experience what's called *secondary victimization*—feeling the trauma through their close connection to the victim.

The tragic reality is that violent crime leaves a lasting imprint—not just on the victim, but on their loved ones, their community, and sometimes, the world. One case that profoundly exemplified this ripple effect is the murder of a young woman whose disappearance and subsequent death at the hands of her fiancé, Brian Laundrie, captivated and devastated the nation. Her story became more than just another crime statistic; it ignited conversations about domestic violence, coercive control, and the gaps in law enforcement response to missing persons.

The intense public scrutiny surrounding her case highlighted how social media, media coverage, and advocacy can amplify awareness of domestic and intimate violence. It also raised critical questions: How many other victims have been overlooked? How do families navigate the overwhelming trauma of such a loss while seeking justice?

Gabby Petito was described by her family as a kind, free-spirited, adventurous young woman with a deep love for travel, nature, and creativity. Her parents and stepparents often speak about her infectious energy, compassionate heart, and artistic soul. She had a passion for documenting her travels, sharing her experiences through photography, videos, and social media.

Friends and family noted her strong relationship with her younger siblings, calling her a loving and protective sister. Despite her adventurous nature, she was known for being deeply connected to her family, frequently calling and checking in, which made her sudden silence even more alarming.

Her mother, Nichole Schmidt, said Gabby had a deep curiosity for the world and was always eager to explore. Her father, Joe Petito, described her as someone who could make friends wherever she went and who radiated warmth and positivity. She loved the outdoors, hiking, camping, and experiencing new places, which made the idea of Van Life so appealing to her.

"Van Life" is often portrayed as the ultimate freedom, a minimalist, nomadic lifestyle where people trade traditional homes for converted vans, traveling wherever the road takes them. It's a life of adventure, waking up to breathtaking landscapes, and escaping the pressures of modern society. Social media is flooded with images of sun-drenched highways, cozy camper setups, and couples smiling by campfires, all painting a picture of simplicity and bliss.

But behind the Instagram-perfect scenes, the reality of Van Life is far more complex. Living in a confined space, often with little privacy, unreliable access to basic amenities, and the constant stress of financial or mechanical setbacks, can take a serious toll. For couples, especially, the close quarters and isolation from friends and family can intensify tensions. What looks like an idyllic escape can sometimes become a pressure cooker, magnifying existing problems in a relationship.

In the case of Gabby Petito and Brian Laundrie, their Van Life journey started as a shared dream but tragically unraveled. The isolation, stress, and hidden struggles within their relationship played out far from the watchful eyes of loved ones, showing how, for some, the open road can become a dangerous place rather than a peaceful retreat.

Before leaving for the cross-country trip with Brian Laundrie, Gabby was excited and eager to embark on what she hoped would be a dream journey. She shared her enthusiasm with her family, looking forward to seeing national parks, exploring new places, and continuing to build her online travel blog. However, those closest to her also noted subtle concerns about her relationship with Brian, later reflecting on moments of tension and emotional strain that had been dismissed at the time.

On that trip, Gabby's story was transformed into a tale of domestic violence, homicide, and heartbreak. Her name has since become a rallying cry for awareness, but before that, it was simply the name of a young woman full of dreams, laughter, and love for adventure.

In July of 2021, Gabby Petito and Brian Laundrie set off on a cross-country road trip in their converted van, documenting their travels through social media. The couple had been engaged but later called off the engagement, deciding instead to remain in a relationship without immediate plans for marriage.

By August they had made their way to Utah, visiting the beautiful national and state parks there. While in Moab, Utah, just outside of Arches National Park, the couple was stopped by police after a witness reported seeing Brian hitting Gabby. Bodycam footage showed Gabby visibly distraught, crying as she explained their argument. Brian appeared calm and in control. The officers ultimately classified the incident as a "mental/emotional health break" rather than domestic violence and separated them for the night. No arrests were made.

The couple made their way northward, where they stayed at a hotel in Salt Lake City on August 24, 2021. The following day, they stopped in Ogden, Utah (some 40 miles to the north) capturing some photos of Gabby outside the Monarch Butterfly display in the downtown. Gabby spoke with her mother via FaceTime in what became the last confirmed communication between the two of them. On that call, Gabby told her mother they were heading toward Grand Teton National Park in Wyoming.

On August 27th, Gabby's family received an unusual text from her phone, stating, "Can you help Stan? I just keep getting his voicemails and missed calls." The reference to "Stan" (Gabby's grandfather, whom she never referred to by first name) raised concerns. About this same time, Gabby and Brian were seen arguing inside a Wyoming restaurant. This was witnessed by the staff who commented that Gabby was visibly upset and in tears.

Three days later, on August 30th, Gabby's mother received another text from Gabby's phone, reading: "No service in Yosemite." This was the last message they received from her mobile device and the family doubts Gabby was the author of the message. Then, nothing but silence.

On September 1st, Brian Laundrie returned to his parents' home in North Port, Florida, alone and driving the van that belonged to Gabby. Ten days later, unable to reach their daughter, Gabby's parents reported her missing. When police tried to question Brian, his parents refused to allow him to speak with them, instead referring the police officers to talk to their lawyer.

And then, on September 14th, Brian Laundrie left his parents' home, reportedly to take a hike at the nearby Carlton Reserve in Florida. His parents were aware he had left for the hike (reportedly) but didn't raise any concerns when he didn't return. After three days, they finally reported him missing and massive searches were conducted, trying to locate him. His location remained a secret until October 20th of that same year.

Gabby's remains were located on September 19, 2021, in the Teton National Forest. She was discovered nearly a month before Brian Laundrie's body was found. Her autopsy concluded she had died by manual strangulation and a federal arrest warrant was issued for Brian Laundrie four days later, not charging him with homicide, but with the unauthorized use of Gabby's debit card following her death.

On October 20, 2021, law enforcement officers discovered Brian Laundrie's skeletal remains in Carlton Reserve, along with his personal belongings, including a notebook with his handwritten thoughts inside. An autopsy determined that Laundrie had died by suicide from a self-inflicted gunshot wound. In his handwritten notebook, Laundrie claimed Gabby suffered an injury while they were hiking and that he ended her life in what he described as a "merciful" act. However, forensic evidence, gathered witness statements, and prior domestic violence reports strongly suggest an escalating pattern of abuse leading to murder.

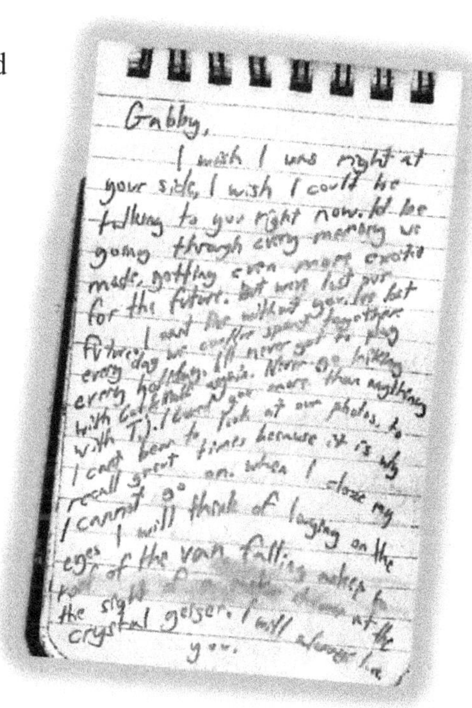

(Notebook image released by Steve Bertolino)

The following pages include the full text of Brian Laundrie's suicide note. As you read his written thoughts, his admissions and his confession, develop your own opinion of what was going on in his mind. Was Brian Laundrie trying to minimize his choice to kill Gabby? Are his notes intended to minimize or justify his actions? Is this behavior consistent with what you've seen in other criminals who have left written communications like this?

> *"Gabby, I wish I was right at your side, I wish I could be talking to you right now. I'd be going through every memory we made, getting even more excited for the future. But [we] lost our future. I can't [live] without you. I've lost every day we [could've] spent together, every holiday. I'll never get to play with [illegible] again. Never go hiking with TJ. I loved you more than anything. I can't bear to look at our photos, to recall great times because it is why I cannot go on.*
>
> *"When I close my eyes, I will think of laughing on the roof of the van, falling asleep to the sight of [illegible] at the crystal geyser. I will always love you. If you were reading Gabs' journal, looking at photos from our life together, flipping through old cards you wouldn't want to live a day without her. Knowing that everyday you'll wake up without her, you wouldn't want to wake up. I'm sorry to everyone this will affect, Gabby was the love of my life, but I know [adored] by many. I'm so very sorry to her family because I love them. I'd [consider] her younger siblings my best of friends… I am sorry to my family, this [is] a shock to them as well a terrible grief. They loved as much, if not more than me. A new daughter to my mother, an aunt to my nephews.*
>
> *"Please do not make this harder for them, this [occurred] as an unexpected tragedy. Rushing back to our car trying to cross the streams of [illegible] before it got too dark to see, too cold. I hear a splash and a scream. I could barely see. I couldn't find her*

for a moment, shouted her name. I found her breathing heavily, gasping [illegible.] She was freezing cold. [Illegible] the blazing hot national parks in Utah. The temperature had dropped to freezing and she was soaking wet. I carried her as far as I could from the stream toward the car, stumbling, exhausted in shock, when my [illegible] and knew I couldn't safely carry her. I started a fire and spooned her as close to the heat. She was so thin, had already been freezing too long. I couldn't at the time realize that I should've started a fire first but I wanted her out of the cold back to the car. From where I started the fire I had no idea how far the car might be, only knew it was across the creek.

"When I pulled Gabby out of the water, she couldn't tell me what hurt. She had a small [bump] on her forehead that [eventually] got larger. Her feet hurt, her [wrist] hurt but she was freezing, shaking violently. While carrying her she continually made sounds of pain. Laying next to her she said little, [lapsing] between violent shakes, gasping in pain, begging for an end to her pain. She would fall asleep and I would shake her awake, fearing she shouldn't close her eyes if she had a concussion.

"She would wake in pain, start her whole painful cycle again [illegible] furious that I was the one waking her. She wouldn't let me try to cross the creek, thought like me that the fire would go out in her sleep and she'd freeze. I don't know the extent of Gabby's injuries, only that she was in extreme pain. I ended her life, I thought it was merciful, that it is what she wanted but I see now all the mistakes I made. I panicked, I was in shock. But from the moment I

decided, took away her pain, I knew I couldn't go on without her.

"I rushed home to spend any time I had left with my family. I wanted to drive north and let James or TJ kill me but I wouldn't want them to spend time in jail over my mistake, even though I'm sure they would have liked to. I am ending my life not because of a fear of punishment but rather because I can't stand to live another day without her. I've lost our whole future together, every moment we could have [shared.] I'm sorry for everyone's loss. Please do not make life harder for my family, they lost a son and a daughter. The most wonderful girl in the world. Gabby I'm sorry.

"I have killed myself by this creek in the hopes that animals may tear me apart. That it may make some of her family happy. Please pick up all of my things. Gabby hated people who litter."

Gabby's family, heartbroken yet determined, refused to let her death be in vain. They created the Gabby Petito Foundation, dedicated to helping victims of domestic violence and ensuring that missing persons receive the attention they deserve. They fought not just for justice for Gabby, but for the countless others suffering in silence.

In February of 2025, Gabby Petito's parents made a powerful statement by destroying the van she once traveled in, the same van that became a symbol of both her adventurous spirit and the tragic circumstances of her death. For them, this wasn't just about getting rid of a vehicle; it was an act of closure, a way to reclaim something that had been turned into a painful reminder of loss.

The van had come to represent more than just a road trip gone wrong. It symbolized the illusion of freedom that masked the dangers

Gabby faced. By dismantling it, her parents sent a clear message: they refused to let that symbol stand as a relic of their daughter's suffering. In a way, it was a final, heartbreaking step in their fight to turn Gabby's legacy into one of awareness and change, rather than one forever tied to tragedy.

The case of Gabby Petito is a painful reminder of how domestic violence can escalate to the worst possible outcome. It's a story that gripped the world, not just because of the tragedy but because it reflected a reality many victims know too well—the cycle of control, the moments of fear hidden behind smiles, and the devastating consequences when help doesn't come in time.

Gabby's legacy is now one of awareness, action, and change. Her story continues to inspire efforts to protect others from suffering the same fate. And for those who loved her, the mission is clear: never stop fighting for justice, never stop speaking out, and never let her name be forgotten.

Gabby Petito's story is not an isolated tragedy; it is part of a larger pattern of violence that leaves families shattered and communities searching for answers. The emotional and financial toll on survivors, families, and even the justice system underscores how deeply crime permeates society. The burden extends beyond grief—it manifests in medical costs, therapy expenses, lost wages, and the enormous strain on law enforcement resources.

But the impact of violent crime goes even further. Entire communities can feel the effects, especially in areas where crime rates are high. When violent crime becomes a regular occurrence, people start living in fear. This phenomenon, often called the *fear of crime*, can change how people interact with their surroundings. In high-crime areas, businesses struggle, property values drop, and residents become less likely to participate in community activities. The end result? More isolation, less trust, and a neighborhood that feels unsafe even for those who haven't been directly victimized.

And then there's the financial toll. Violent crime costs the U.S.

billions of dollars every year. The expenses pile up—from emergency medical care and long-term treatments to court costs and lost wages when survivors are too injured or traumatized to work. The criminal justice system itself carries a huge economic burden, with investigations, trials, and incarceration all adding to the overall cost.

Recovery from violent crime is different for everyone, but experts agree that trauma-informed care is essential. This means recognizing that trauma affects both the mind and body and treating survivors with understanding and compassion rather than just focusing on the crime itself. Therapy and counseling can help survivors process their experiences and develop coping mechanisms, but access to these services is key. Unfortunately, not everyone gets the support they need, whether due to financial barriers, stigma, or a lack of available resources.

But healing isn't just about therapy and treatment—it's a journey filled with hills and valleys. Some days, survivors may feel strong and in control; other days, the weight of what happened feels unbearable. And that's okay. The process isn't linear, and setbacks don't mean failure. Whether someone is recovering from the trauma firsthand or supporting a loved one through it, patience and understanding are key. Sharing the experience with trusted therapists, loved ones, or even within the criminal justice system can be painful, but it's also a powerful step toward reclaiming control. Speaking out, seeking justice, and simply being heard can be validating in ways that help survivors move forward.

Of course, the road to recovery doesn't look the same for everyone. Some find strength in advocacy, using their experiences to help others. Others lean on close-knit support systems or spiritual beliefs. In the next chapter, we'll take a closer look at the many ways people navigate the aftermath of violent crime—how they rebuild their sense of self, regain trust, and, in some cases, turn their pain into purpose.

Resilience—the ability to bounce back after a traumatic experience—plays a huge role in how survivors recover. The good news is that resilience isn't just something people either have or don't have; it can be strengthened with the right support. Things like strong social networks, healthy coping strategies, and access to helpful resources can make a big difference. Community organizations, such as victim advocacy groups, play a crucial role in this process. They connect survivors with counseling services, provide emotional support, and even push for policy changes that address the bigger issues around victimization.

Another approach that has shown promise in helping survivors heal is restorative justice. Instead of just focusing on punishment, restorative justice creates space for victims to have their voices heard and be part of the healing process. Studies suggest that when victims are given the opportunity to participate in discussions about the harm they've experienced, it can lead to greater emotional closure and empowerment (Sherman & Strang, 2007). In one restorative justice program, burglary victims had the chance to meet the offenders in a structured setting, allowing them to express their pain and receive genuine apologies. This kind of dialogue has been shown to help survivors regain a sense of control and find a path forward. By focusing on resilience and restorative practices, survivors can move toward healing with the right combination of personal strength and community support.

The impact of violent crime victimization is profound, leaving indelible marks on individuals and reverberating through families, communities, and society. Understanding these consequences underscores the importance of comprehensive support systems, preventive measures, and interventions that promote recovery and resilience. Through trauma-informed care, community support, and restorative justice, society can empower survivors to reclaim their lives and contribute to a more compassionate and just world.

For true crime enthusiasts, the stories of survival are just as compelling as the crimes themselves. A powerful article published in the Journal of Child Sexual Abuse (August 2017) dives deep into the lifelong journey of women who survived sexual abuse as children. The piece "I Am Not a Victim. I Am a Survivor" sheds light on the devastating impact of these crimes and how survivors navigate their paths to healing.

Child sexual abuse isn't just an unspeakable violation—it's a betrayal that shatters trust and leaves deep emotional scars. Many survivors were hurt by someone in a position of power, whether a family member, teacher, or religious leader. That betrayal fosters lasting feelings of powerlessness, confusion, and self-doubt. And the trauma doesn't just disappear with time. It lingers, shaping how survivors see themselves and the world around them.

The journey from victim to survivor isn't easy, and it's rarely a straight line. Many people struggle with anxiety, depression, PTSD, and difficulty forming relationships. Some develop chronic health issues, eating disorders, or somatic symptoms such as physical pain with no clear medical cause. Others turn to self-harm or substance abuse in order to cope. On top of that, when survivors do come forward, they often face victim-blaming, disbelief, or outright stigma, making it even harder to heal.

But here's the thing, resilience isn't about "getting over it." It's about learning how to live with the trauma, rebuild trust, and take back control. Some survivors find strength in therapy, support groups, or close personal connections. Others channel their pain into advocacy, using their voices to push for systemic change and accountability in institutions that have historically covered up these crimes.

At the heart of it all, the article reinforced a crucial truth: survival is an ongoing process, not destination. Every step forward, whether it's acknowledging the abuse, seeking support, or reclaiming a sense of self, is an act of resilience. And while the scars may never fully fade, survivors can continue to prove that they are so much more than what happened to them.

One transformative aspect of resilience is the redefinition of identity. By shifting from a "victim" narrative to that of a "survivor," individuals reclaim their agency and autonomy. For many, advocacy and helping others who have faced similar traumas become a cornerstone of their recovery process. While the effects of such abuse are far-reaching, the journey of recovery reveals the human capacity to heal, adapt, and transform.

To achieve a healthy outlook after abuse requires a collective effort to dismantle stigma, improve systems of support, and foster environments where survivors can thrive. Through resilience, survivors not only reclaim their lives but inspire societal change, proving that healing is not only possible but profoundly empowering.[59]

As we reflect on the devastating impact crime has on its victims—the shattered lives, the lingering trauma, the ripple effect on families and communities—it can be easy to feel a sense of helplessness. The aftermath of crime often leaves a wake of confusion and fear, and we are left questioning, "How can we protect ourselves? How can we avoid becoming another statistic?"

While we cannot undo the harm caused by criminal behavior, we do have the power to take proactive steps in safeguarding our own lives. Understanding the factors that contribute to victimization empowers us with the tools to reduce our risk and strengthen our sense of security.

In this next chapter, we shift our focus from the despair of victimhood to the hope of prevention. We'll explore practical strategies, mindset shifts, and preventative measures that can make a significant difference in reducing our exposure to harm. By taking control of our environment, our actions, and our awareness, we can begin to build resilience against the dangers that threaten our peace of mind. This journey of empowerment starts now, and together, we'll discover how to turn vulnerability into strength.

they know how to escape.

Criminals also carefully assess risk before attacking. It's probably safe to assume that most offenders don't want to get caught, so they weigh how much danger they're putting themselves in. A mugger, for example, is more likely to go after someone walking alone than a group of friends who might fight back. A burglar will pick a house with no security cameras or predictable resident absences. Predators who seek specific victim types—such as children or vulnerable adults—gravitate toward locations where those people are commonly found, like schools, parks, or bars. The lower the risk of detection and retaliation, the more appealing the crime location is to the offender.

This is the cold reality of how predators operate. They aren't just searching blindly for victims—they are hunting in places where they know their target will be. My grandfather always told me, *"The secret to catching fish is to fish where the fish are!"* And criminals follow the same instinct. Just like a fisherman chooses the right waters, offenders pick their hunting grounds based on where they're most likely to succeed with the least amount of interference.

It's the same principle we see in the wild. In the beginning of this book, we talked about the Arctic wolf—how it hunts in familiar areas, tracking prey in terrain it knows well. A wolf doesn't wander aimlessly; it sticks to the places where it has successfully hunted before. The only time it changes its hunting grounds is when the prey disappears, or when a more dangerous predator moves in and forces the wolf to relocate.

Human predators are no different. They go where the victims are more plentiful, where routines are predictable, and where the risk of getting caught is low. But just like how the four-legged wolf can be pushed out of a territory by something more dangerous, criminals will relocate or change their behavior if the risks outweigh the reward. CCTV cameras, improved lighting, and increased law enforcement presence can act as deterrents, making once-fertile hunting grounds far too risky to operate in.

Understanding this concept isn't just about recognizing where criminals are likely to strike—it's about knowing how to disrupt their comfort zone. Just as a fisherman won't cast his line into empty waters, a predator won't linger where their chances of success are slim. The key to crime prevention is making the hunting ground unappealing, unpredictable, and unsafe for the hunter. When we take away their sense of security, we force them to move on—just like the Arctic wolf, forced to abandon its territory when the prey is gone, or the danger is too great.

Where a crime happens is almost as important as who the victim is. Offenders don't choose crime scenes randomly—they pick places that give them control. Public spaces with little surveillance, isolated areas, and locations with predictable routines are all prime spots for violent crime. A serial offender might choose secluded hiking trails because victims there have fewer chances to escape or call for help. A home burglary might occur in a neighborhood with lax security, easy escape routes, or homes that show signs of frequent vacancies.

In some cases, location can reveal whether a crime was premeditated or impulsive. Many criminals operate close to home or in areas they frequent because they feel comfortable and in control. But offenders who deliberately pick locations far from their usual environment are often more calculating. They might plan out an attack to ensure there are no connections linking them to the crime.

The way a crime is committed can tell us a lot about the offender's psychological state and level of planning. Crimes of passion—like domestic violence homicides—often involve excessive violence, showing raw emotion and loss of control. Premeditated crimes, on the other hand, tend to be much more calculated. A burglar might ensure the homeowners are away before breaking in. A kidnapper might take steps to erase their trail. The more thought-out the crime, the less evidence they leave behind.

The method of approach also matters. Some offenders use deception, tricking their way into a victim's trust—like posing as a delivery driver to enter a home. Others use force or intimidation, like a street robber flashing a weapon to ensure quick compliance. The way an offender chooses to engage with their victim often depends on their confidence level, past experiences, and risk tolerance.

Even the level of violence in a crime can provide clues about an offender's mindset. Some crimes involve only the necessary amount of force to complete the act, while others show extreme brutality. This is sometimes referred to as overkill—using far more violence than needed, which often suggests personal rage, sadism, or psychological instability. Wound patterns can also indicate intent. Facial injuries may signal an effort to dehumanize the victim. Ritualistic or symbolic wounds may point to deeper psychological motives or prior offender behavior patterns.

In many cases, untrained law enforcement officers and those of us in the true-crime arena fail to recognize the significance of the type of weapon used and the position and condition of the victim after the assault. The weapon an offender chooses can reveal a lot about their preparedness. Opportunistic criminals use whatever is available, perhaps bricks, rocks, broken bottles, while those who plan ahead may bring a specific weapon. Firearms allow attackers to create a safer distance between them and the victim, minimizing their own risk. Knives on the other hand require close physical interaction, which can indicate a personal element to the attack.

Even how a victim is left after an attack can be telling. A carefully concealed body suggests an attempt to delay discovery, showing fear of capture. But a victim left in a staged or prominent position might indicate the offender wants the crime to be found—sometimes as a taunt, a signature, or even a message. Serial offenders often have specific patterns in how they leave their victims, giving profilers valuable insights into their psychological profile.

While no one can predict crime with absolute certainty, understanding how and why criminals choose their victims gives us the power to lower our own risk. Criminals rely on vulnerability, accessibility, and opportunity. Most of the time, they want an easy win, not a challenge. That means staying alert, breaking predictable routines, avoiding isolated areas when possible, and trusting instincts when something feels off. It's not about living in fear—it's about being smart.

More importantly, knowledge of offender behavior allows us to recognize red flags, not just for ourselves but for others. Maybe a coworker suddenly becomes uneasy about a stranger they keep running into, or a friend confides that someone has been following them after work. Recognizing patterns and warning signs can help people act before something escalates.

But crime isn't just about individuals—it's about situations, circumstances, and environments. And not all victims are chosen the same way. Some offenders look for specific types of people to victimize. Others strike based on convenience. And sometimes, certain situations make crime more likely, even for those who wouldn't normally be at high risk.

To better understand the levels of risk in criminal cases, let's break down the Victim Risk Continuum, a framework that explains how victim characteristics, offender motives, and external circumstances interact to shape the likelihood of victimization. By understanding this continuum, we can begin to see how different crimes unfold, what makes someone more or less likely to be targeted, and how even subtle changes in behavior or environment can shift the odds in our favor.

The FBI's BAU created a conceptual "Victim Risk Continuum" that I will use with a few anecdotal examples of real-world cases such as the murder of Samar Jefferson in Philadelphia, Pennsylvania, or the case of missing five-year-old Summer Wells in Tennessee. By analyzing these examples, we aim to illustrate how this framework aids in understanding victimization and, ultimately, how individuals can reduce their own risk.

When the Philadelphia Police Department received a 911 call

about a 14-year-old shot approximately 20 times by a group of thugs, the immediate question asked by many was, "Who did it?" However, a more profound question might be, "Who was Samar Jefferson? And why did he become a victim?" Such tragedies compel us to delve into the victimology and theorize as to why people become victims. Are there things that the victim could have done to reduce their risk of being victimized?

The streets of Philadelphia have long been marked by an alarming level of gun violence, but the murder of Samar Jefferson stands out as a particularly heartbreaking example of the escalating crisis. Gunned down in broad daylight on the streets of West Philadelphia, Jefferson's death sent shockwaves through the local community, sparking a conversation about the rampant gun violence in the city. The circumstances surrounding his death, as well as the broader issues it highlights, demand a deeper examination into the social, political, and economic factors contributing to the cycle of violence in Philadelphia.

Reports suggest that Jefferson was either walking on the street or waiting for a bus when several armed thugs opened fire, striking him at least 18 times. Police responded to the scene shortly after the shooting, but Jefferson had already succumbed to his injuries before they could provide aid. Since the shooting, three men have been arrested for the murder but the reason for the crime remains unknown. Jefferson's murder is one in a long line of shootings that have plagued Philadelphia in recent years, fueling fears of public safety in neighborhoods across the city.

The murder of Samar Jefferson is not only a loss for his family but also for the community in which he lived. Homicides like this leave a lasting trauma on communities, particularly when they occur in neighborhoods already plagued by violence. Families are left grieving the loss of loved ones, while others live in fear of becoming the next victim. Moreover, the constant exposure to violence can have long-term psychological effects on young people, leading to feelings of insecurity, anger, and disillusionment with society. This cycle of trauma can create a vicious feedback loop, where violence begets more violence, perpetuating the conditions that led to Jefferson's tragic death.[60]

The Victim Risk Continuum is a tool developed by criminal profilers and victimologists to categorize victims based on their exposure to risk. This tool can also be effectively used by true crime enthusiasts. It operates on a spectrum from high-risk to low-risk, influenced by factors such as lifestyle, environment, personal behavior, and circumstances. At its core, the continuum helps investigators and criminal justice professionals theorize about the nature of the predator and the motives behind the crime.

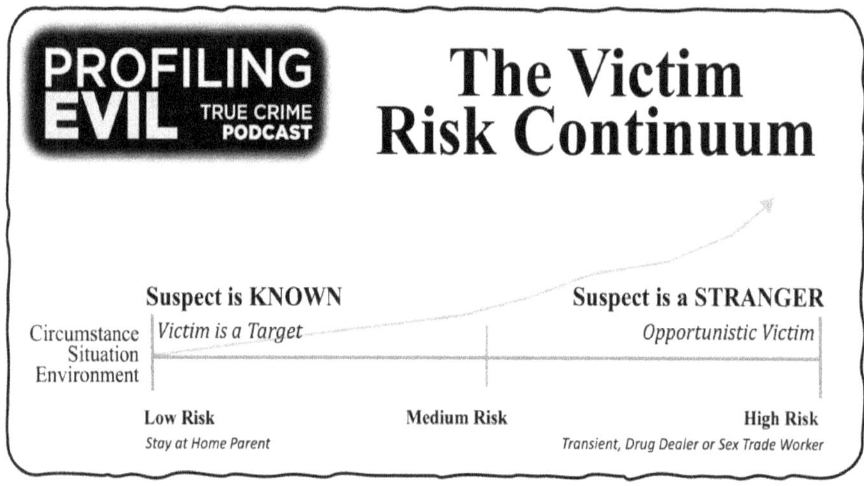

High-risk victims are individuals who, due to their lifestyle or circumstances, are more likely to encounter danger. These are often people involved in high-risk activities or environments such as illegal drug dealing or use, those engaged in sex trade or human trafficking, or people without stable housing or living on the streets. It also includes individuals who may lack the capacity to protect themselves effectively.

High-risk victims often lack support systems and may distrust law enforcement or other protective institutions. Their vulnerability is exacerbated by their environment—for example, living in areas with high crime rates or engaging with strangers who have unknown motives. Statistically, these individuals are more likely to fall victim to crimes perpetrated by strangers or opportunistic predators.

Samar Jefferson's tragic death in Philadelphia highlights the vulnerabilities of individuals who may not fit neatly into a single risk category. While Samar's specific circumstances require more context, factors such as neighborhood crime rates and potential associations can elevate one's risk. Understanding Samar's environment, the relationships he had, and whether his death was random or targeted can provide critical insights into his risk level.

At the other end of the continuum are low-risk victims—individuals who lead relatively stable lives with small social circles and minimal exposure to dangerous environments. Examples of low-risk victims include stay-at-home parents who primarily interact with family and close friends, children who are consistently under the supervision of caregivers, and professionals with predictable routines that do not involve high-crime areas or risky behaviors.

Low-risk victims are statistically less likely to be targeted by strangers. When they are victimized, it is often by someone within their social or familial circle. However, circumstances and situational factors can elevate their risk, as seen in the case of Summer Wells.

Five-year-old Summer Wells' disappearance from her rural Tennessee home captivated the nation. Initially categorized as a low-risk victim due to her young age and presumed protective environment, her case demonstrates how situational changes can dramatically alter risk levels. On June 15th, 2021, Summer was last seen entering her home's basement to play. Unsupervised for a brief moment, her risk level increased, opening the door to potential victimization by a predator. Summer's case illustrates how even low-risk individuals can become vulnerable due to circumstance, environment, or situational factors. In that case, Summer was momentarily unsupervised, creating an opportunity for an abduction.

The rural, wooded area surrounding her home provided cover for potential predators, and the lack of immediate oversight may have allowed a predator to act without detection.

The Victim Risk Continuum provides a framework for analyzing cases by considering multiple influencing factors. These include lifestyle choices, social environments, and situational dynamics. By applying the continuum to real-world examples, investigators can better understand the interplay between victim and predator.

One of the continuum's critical insights is the distinction between crimes committed by known predators versus strangers. For high-risk victims, the perpetrator is often a stranger—an opportunistic predator who exploits the victim's vulnerability. Conversely, low-risk victims are more likely to be targeted by individuals they know, such as family members, acquaintances, or community members.

The case of Elizabeth Smart highlights how low-risk individuals can become targets of known predators. Elizabeth, a 14-year-old from a stable, protective family, was abducted by Brian David Mitchell, a transient who had done occasional work at her home. Though Elizabeth did not know Mitchell personally, he had observed her and fixated on her as a target. These dynamics underscores the importance of understanding how predators identify and exploit perceived vulnerabilities.

The Victim Risk Continuum emphasizes the role of environment and situation in elevating or reducing risk. A homeless individual sleeping in a public park is at high risk due to environmental factors (lack of security, exposure to strangers). Likewise, a child playing unsupervised in a crowded mall becomes vulnerable due to situational factors (opportunity for a predator to act unnoticed). By examining these factors, investigators can pinpoint how a victim's risk level shifted and identify potential suspects.

Understanding the Victim Risk Continuum is not only valuable for law enforcement but also for individuals seeking to minimize their own risk. Practical strategies include surrounding oneself with trusted friends and family, thereby reducing exposure to unknown risks. Staying away from areas with high crime rates or frequent stranger interactions minimizes a person's risk of being victimized, as does an overall awareness of surroundings. Being cautious in your interactions with strangers can deter potential predators.

In the case of children, supervision is paramount. Ensuring that young individuals are consistently monitored and protected can mitigate many risk factors that lead to victimization. The Victim Risk Continuum provides a powerful lens for analyzing crimes and understanding victimization. By categorizing victims as high-risk or low-risk and examining influencing factors such as circumstance, situation, and environment, this framework sheds light on the dynamics between victims and predators. Cases like Samar Jefferson and Summer Wells illustrate the continuum's applicability, offering insights into how risk levels fluctuate and what steps can be taken to reduce vulnerability.

Ultimately, victimology and tools like the Victim Risk Continuum aim to empower individuals and communities to create safer environments. Through education, awareness, and proactive measures, we can reduce the likelihood of victimization and better understand the tragedies that do occur.

As we conclude our deep dive into the role of the victim in understanding crime, you've likely begun to see how intricate and interconnected the threads of criminal behavior can be. The victim's story offers us essential clues and emotional weight, but the narrative doesn't end there. To fully unravel the complexities of criminal acts, we must now pivot our focus to the very ground where these tragedies unfold: the crime scene.

Thus far, we've delved into the minds of violent predators, uncovering the intricacies of their behaviors and the traits of the victims they target. Now, it's time to shift our focus to the stage where their paths collide—the crime scene. In the next chapter, we'll dissect the anatomy of a crime scene and unravel the critical differences between the various locations tied to the crime.

Each of these locations tells a story—not just about what happened, but why and how. What is it about these places that draws predator and prey together? What secrets do they hold about the offender's psychology and the victim's circumstances? This isn't just an academic exercise; it's an opportunity to refine your investigative instincts and delve deeper into the interplay of human behavior and geography.

Turn the page and join us as we explore how every detail at the scene becomes a clue, revealing glimpses of the perpetrator's psyche. The crime scene is more than just evidence—it's an additional window into the mind of the criminal. Together, we'll uncover the tools to connect motives, methods, and maps. This is where science meets intuition, and where our pursuit of understanding takes on a thrilling, urgent edge.

PART THREE

DECODING CRIME SCENES:
EVIDENCE, PERSONAS & BEHAVIORAL INSIGHTS

The choice of a disposal site is rarely random; it frequently reflects an offender's familiarity with the area and in some cases, may carry significant personal meaning. -MK

Chapter Nine

First Contact to Final Trace: Dissecting the Crime Scene

Crime scenes serve as the silent witnesses to acts of violence, providing investigators and the true crime enthusiast with essential clues about the offender, the victim, and the sequence of events. These locations are more than just places where crimes occur; they are layered with forensic, psychological, and geographical information that can offer profound insights into the motives and methods of the perpetrator. In this chapter, we will dissect the anatomy of a crime scene by examining its critical components.

To truly understand the anatomy of a crime, we need to break it down into three key locations: the *initial contact site*, the *primary crime scene*, and the *disposal site*. Each of these locations serves a distinct purpose in the offender's process, and each provides valuable clues about the predator's mindset, level of planning, and behavior. These locations might also shed light on the victim, why they were in that location and whether they were an opportunistic victim or a target of a criminal's aggression.

One of the biggest mistakes people make when trying to unravel a violent crime is assuming the crime scene is just one place—a singular location where everything happened. But most crimes involve multiple locations, each offering its own set of clues that, when pieced together, tell the full story.

The *initial contact site* is where the victim and offender first cross paths. This could be entirely random, such as an attacker spotting a lone jogger on a trail, or it could be a carefully chosen setting, like a predator targeting individuals at a specific bar, bus stop, or online chatroom. In some cases, this site is the same as the crime scene— think of a home invasion or an attack that happens immediately upon meeting the victim. Other times, the offender lures the victim elsewhere, separating the *initial contact site* from where the actual crime occurs. In many stalking cases, the *initial contact site* could be the place where the predator selects a victim and starts planning where the crime will occur. The location where the violation of criminal law happens is called the *crime scene and there could be several crime scenes depending on what occurs.*

The *primary crime scene* is where the attack, assault, or murder takes place. This is the most critical site in the investigation because it often contains the most forensic evidence. Some offenders prefer a controlled environment, like their own home or some other secluded spot where they have the upper hand. Others act impulsively, committing the crime whenever, or wherever they want, whether that be in a vehicle, a hotel room, or an alleyway. In cases where the victim is abducted, lured by a con, or voluntarily goes with the offender, the crime scene might be entirely separate from the *initial contact site*, requiring investigators to piece together the movement between locations. We will explore this in detail as the chapter progresses.

Finally, the *disposal site* is where the offender attempts to rid themselves of the victim or the victim's body, personal belongings, or any evidence that could link them to the crime. This could be a single location, like a wooded area or a river, or multiple locations if the body is dismembered and discarded in different places. Some offenders carefully choose disposal sites to delay discovery, while others act hastily, dumping remains in a panic. A well-hidden body suggests premeditation, while a hastily abandoned victim often indicates a crime of passion or an unexpected loss of control.

While these three sites—*initial contact, crime scene,* and *disposal*—are sometimes all in the same location, in other cases, they are spread across different areas, forcing investigators to track the offender's movements and decision-making process. Each site, whether a single spot or multiple locations, offers a crucial piece of the puzzle in understanding what happened, why it happened, and who was responsible.

To better understand each of these locations, let's attach a theoretical set of circumstances to each location, beginning with the *initial contact site.* It starts like any other night at the bar. The music hums in the background, glasses clink, and the low murmur of conversation fills the air. A group of friends laughs loudly at the end of the counter, a couple leans in close, lost in their own world, and scattered among them are the solo drinkers—some scrolling through their phones, others casually observing the room.

In the middle of it all, a woman sits alone at the bar, absentmindedly stirring the ice in her drink. Maybe she's waiting for a friend. Maybe she's just unwinding after a long day. She glances up at the TV playing above the liquor shelves, momentarily distracted. What she doesn't realize is that she's already been noticed.

At a table in the corner, a man watches. He's not staring—at least not in a way that would draw attention—but he's aware of her in a way she isn't aware of him. He notices that she's alone, that she isn't engaged in conversation, that she isn't looking around for anyone in particular. He watches how often she checks her phone, how many sips she's taken from her drink, and whether she looks comfortable or a little bit bored.

This is the *initial contact site*—the moment where a predator selects a potential victim. It's important to remember that this is only one location, one brief but pivotal moment in time. It is the first time the predator and the prey cross paths, whether from across a crowded room, a dimly lit gas station parking lot, or a quiet grocery store aisle. The victim may be completely unaware that contact has been made, but for the offender, this is where the crime begins.

The predator doesn't move in right away. Instead, he observes. That's what seasoned predators do. He's not here by accident, either. He comes to places like this because he knows the environment works in his favor. People drink, they lower their guard, and they become easier to manipulate. After a few minutes, he finally makes his approach, smooth and confident. Maybe he offers to buy her a drink. Maybe he makes a joke about the bartender's slow service. Maybe he pretends to have met her before—an easy way to strike up conversation without coming across as intrusive. The strategy depends on what he's gauged about her personality in those first few moments of watching. If she's guarded, he plays the friendly stranger. If she seems lonely, he plays the attentive listener.

To everyone else in the bar, this looks like just another casual interaction. But to an investigator analyzing the case later, this moment is critical. Understanding how and where an offender first contacts a victim can reveal a lot about their hunting style. Some criminals target specific places because they know they'll find the kind of victim they want. Others act more impulsively, waiting for an opportunity to present itself.

But it's important to emphasize—this moment only happens *once*. The *initial contact site* is not a process, not a long-drawn-out interaction, but a single instance in time when the offender and the victim come into each other's orbit. This contact might be an up-close, personal introduction—a conversation, a handshake, an offer to buy a drink. Or it could be from a distance—the predator spotting the victim through a car window as they walk alone through a parking lot or watching them pump gas at an isolated station.

In that moment at the bar, the woman still has choices. She could brush him off and leave, she could recognize something feels *off* and trust her gut, or she could engage, completely unaware of the trap being set. The *initial contact site* isn't always a bar. It could be a gas station, a parking lot, a grocery store aisle, or even an online chat room. The location may change, but the strategy is the same—*observe, assess, and approach.* It is a fleeting moment, a singular event. The victim may not realize anything is happening. But for the offender, the crime has already begun.

The *crime scene* is where everything escalates—the place where the violation of law happens. It's where the predator makes their move, where the victim's fate takes a dark turn, and where investigators will later search for the forensic evidence that can tell the story of what really happened. Picture this: A woman steps out of the bar, her head spinning slightly from one too many drinks. She doesn't notice the man who had been watching her all night, the one who first spotted her when she walked in hours ago. He waits a moment before following her outside, keeping his pace casual, not too fast, not too slow—just enough to stay in her orbit.

Her car is parked in a dimly lit section of the lot, and as she rummages in her purse for her keys, she doesn't hear him approach. Maybe he calls out to her, maybe he offers to help with her bag, or maybe he simply waits until she's distracted before grabbing her from behind. That parking lot, in that moment, becomes a crime scene.

But here's the thing about crime scenes: there isn't always just one.

If he attacks her right there, leaving behind evidence like broken jewelry, drag marks, or a witness who hears a struggle, that lot is the *primary crime scene.* But if he forces her into his car and drives her somewhere else—a house, an abandoned building, a secluded stretch of road—then *that* location also becomes a crime scene. Each place where the victim is assaulted, restrained, or harmed becomes part of the bigger picture, providing investigators with crucial details about how the crime unfolded.

Some criminals act impulsively, attacking the moment an opportunity presents itself. Others prefer a controlled environment where they have the upper hand—somewhere they can take their time without the risk of being interrupted. Serial killers like Robert Ben Rhoades, the long-haul truck driver, operated this way. His truck wasn't just his mode of transportation—it was his mobile hunting ground, his crime scene and his torture chamber. Victims were lured into his truck cab or forcibly abducted. Once inside, they were completely at his mercy. For them, there was no escape.

The distance between the *initial contact site* and the *crime scene* also tells us a lot about the offender's mindset. If a victim is taken to a second location, it suggests premeditation—this wasn't a spur-of-the-moment attack, but a carefully planned crime. If the attack happens immediately, without the offender trying to control the setting, it might indicate panic, a sudden escalation, or even a crime of opportunity.

Unlike the *initial contact site*, which is always a single, defined moment, a *crime scene* can be much more complex. There may be multiple locations, referred to by investigators as the *primary crime scene* and *supplemental crime scenes*, depending on where different aspects of the attack took place. Some cases involve victims being moved, assaulted in more than one place, or even killed in one location and disposed of in another.

Every crime scene tells a story. It's where the predator's intentions become action, where the victim fights for survival, and where investigators later search for the truth. The question isn't always *where* the crime happened—but *how many different places did it happen?* Because each site, from the first point of contact to the last, holds another piece of the puzzle, and it's only by putting them all together that the full picture of the crime—and the mind of the offender—comes into focus.

Which leaves us at the *disposal site*, the place where the predator makes their final move—the last step in trying to separate themselves from the crime they've just committed. This is the place where the offender attempts to rid themselves of the victim, whether that means abandoning and discarding the victim (or their body), destroying evidence, or even trying to erase any trace that the crime ever happened.

Picture the same woman from before, the one who left the bar unaware that she was being followed. Imagine she was forced into a car and then driven to a second location, and the unimaginable happened. Now, the offender is left with a problem—what to do with the victim.

If the victim is alive, the predator might flee, leaving them alone, or the criminal might try to dump the victim off where it will take some time before she can report the incident to the authorities. If the victim is deceased, the predator might dump the remains somewhere quickly, not bothering to cover the body or remove any evidence. The disposal site could be anywhere, including dumping the body or victim on the side of the road, a shallow ditch, or tossed behind an old warehouse. These kinds of hasty disposals suggest recklessness or a lack of concern for getting caught. They often happen when a crime wasn't fully planned, or when the offender feels pressure to act fast. In these cases, investigators might find clear evidence—fingerprints, tire tracks, even DNA that could lead them straight to the suspect. If the offender is a serial predator, signature markings might be evident.

But other offenders are more methodical. A carefully concealed body, buried deep in the woods, weighted down in a lake, or even burned to destroy evidence, suggests a different mindset. This kind of disposal is calculated—an effort to delay discovery, to make sure the victim is never found, or at least not found in a way that points back to the criminal.

And then there are cases where disposal isn't about hiding the body at all—it's about sending a message. Some killers stage their victims in specific ways, leaving them in public places or in disturbing positions, creating a signature meant to taunt law enforcement or the public. Others take things even further, scattering remains across multiple locations, either to complicate the investigation or because of ritualistic or psychological motives.

Like crime scenes, the *disposal site* isn't always just one place. Some offenders discard evidence in one spot, the victim's body in another, and personal belongings somewhere else entirely. Investigators often find purses, IDs, or clothing far from where a body was discovered, as offenders attempt to separate different aspects of the crime, making it harder to piece everything together.

Site	Purpose	Common Locations	Offender Behavior	Investigative Value
Initial Contact Site	Where the victim and offender first cross paths; the predator selects their victim.	Bars, parking lots, gas stations, grocery stores, online chatrooms.	Observation, selection, and approach. Offender assesses vulnerability before engaging.	Reveals offender's hunting style, level of planning, and victim selection process.
Primary Crime Scene	Where the violation of law occurs; the attack, assault, or murder takes place.	Homes, vehicles, abandoned buildings, hotels, secluded outdoor areas.	Execution of the crime. Level of planning determines whether the scene is controlled or impulsive.	Contains the most forensic evidence. Helps reconstruct the crime and offender‚Äôs methods.
Disposal Site	Where the offender attempts to rid themselves of the victim or evidence.	Woods, rivers, highways, abandoned buildings, dumpsters, isolated areas.	Concealment, staging, or abandonment of the victim and evidence. Can indicate panic or premeditation.	Indicates offender's mindset, risk tolerance, and effort to avoid detection.

To better understand these three types of crime scenes—the *initial contact site*, the *primary crime scene*, and the *disposal site*—let's look at the abduction of Elizabeth Smart from Salt Lake City, Utah, and the case of Robert Ben Rhoades, the long-haul trucker turned serial killer. His crimes spanned multiple states, and his choice of crime scenes and disposal locations reveals just how strategic some offenders can be in selecting where and how they operate.

Using the classification of crime scenes we've talked about, let's look at the abduction of Elizabeth Smart from the lens of the *initial contact site*.

It was a warm summer night in Salt Lake City, June 5, 2002. Inside the Smart family home, the neighborhood was quiet, the streets still. Elizabeth Smart, just 14 years old, had gone to bed like any other night, unaware that in a matter of hours, her entire world would be turned upside down. As she slept in her bedroom, a place meant to be her sanctuary, a predator was already on his way.

But Elizabeth's abduction didn't start that night—it started long before.

Brian David Mitchell, a drifter with a messianic complex, had already chosen her as his target. But unlike a street predator who selects a victim in the moment, Mitchell's *initial contact site* wasn't a chance encounter in a public space. It wasn't a gas station or a crowded bar—it was Elizabeth's own home, a place where she and her family felt safe.

Mitchell had once been hired as a handyman by the Smart family. It seemed like an innocent enough arrangement at the time—he was a homeless man who appeared to need help, and the Smarts, a kind and giving family, offered him a short-term job. But this decision, however well-intended, gave Mitchell the perfect 

opportunity to get close. He wasn't just doing work—he was observing. He noted the layout of the house, the patterns of the family members, the way they moved in and out of rooms. He wasn't just fixing things—he was studying their vulnerabilities.

This is where the *initial contact site* becomes so chilling. Unlike other cases where predators seek out victims in public places, Mitchell's fixation on Elizabeth may have started while he was standing inside her home, long before she or her family had any reason to feel threatened. He may have seen her in passing, overheard conversations, or even looked through her bedroom window while working outside, or after hours in the dark. Whether or not Elizabeth ever spoke to him directly, *the contact had already been made*—but only one of them knew it.

This is what makes the *initial contact site* such an important part of understanding how criminals operate. It's not always about direct interaction. It can be as simple as being watched by the wrong person at the wrong time. In this case, Elizabeth and her family had no idea that an opportunity had just been created for a predator who was already planning his next move.

On the night of the abduction, Mitchell returned, slipping through an unlocked window with a knife in hand. He had studied the home, knew where Elizabeth slept, and wasted no time. Within minutes, he had pulled her from her bed and led her out into the darkness, setting into motion the horrifying ordeal that would last nine months. What makes this case especially terrifying is that the *initial contact site* wasn't a dark alley, an isolated trail, or an abandoned parking lot. It was her own bedroom. A place where she should have been safest. And yet, Mitchell exploited his prior knowledge of the home, its layout, and its weaknesses to ensure that by the time he struck, he knew exactly what he was doing.

This crime serves as a sobering reminder that initial contact sites aren't always public places. Sometimes, the predator has already been let inside—whether through work, social circles, or community involvement. It emphasizes the importance of being mindful of who has access to our homes and personal spaces. While many people who work odd jobs or seek help are honest and hardworking, it only takes one predator to turn a small act of kindness into a dangerous situation.

Mitchell's ability to exploit this trust is what makes this case particularly haunting. He wasn't a stranger lurking in the shadows— he had been inside their home, given the chance to see how the family lived. He knew who was vulnerable, when they slept, and where security was weakest. It's a terrifying thought, but an important one: predators aren't always unknown entities; sometimes, they are the people who find ways to blend in until it's too late.

By understanding how *initial contact sites* work, we can start to recognize the ways in which predators select their victims—not just in public, but in spaces that should be safe. Elizabeth's case is a chilling example of how an initial contact site can take many forms, and why it's crucial to be aware of who we allow into our homes, our lives, and our routines.

Now that we've examined the *initial contact site*, we can begin looking at the next stage of the crime—the *crime scene*. In Elizabeth's case, the crime didn't happen in just one place. Like many abduction cases, it spanned multiple locations, each revealing different aspects of the offender's behavior. To truly understand how these cases unfold, we must analyze what happens after the predator makes their move.

The moment Elizabeth Smart was taken from her bed on June 5, 2002, the crime had already begun—but it was far from confined to that one location. Unlike some cases where the *crime scene* is a single, defined place, Elizabeth's ordeal spanned multiple locations, each serving as a distinct *crime scene*, each telling a part of the story.

When Mitchell entered the Smart family home, that became the first crime scene. Though Elizabeth was unaware of his intentions leading up to that moment, he had been planning for some time. He knew the layout of the home from his previous work there. He had identified vulnerabilities—an unlocked window, a sleeping household, and a victim who likely wouldn't fight back due to her young age and sheer shock. With a knife in hand, he woke her up, threatened her, and forced her to leave with him. At that moment, her bedroom, a place that should have been safe, became a crime scene.

But the crime didn't end there. Mitchell led Elizabeth out of the house, through the yard, and into the woods, where his wife and accomplice, Wanda Barzee, was waiting. They traveled on foot up into the mountains, deep into the secluded wilderness, where Mitchell had created a makeshift camp. This is where Elizabeth was first assaulted, making it another, more extensive crime scene.

Unlike the chaotic nature of an impulsive attack, this was premeditated. Mitchell had chosen a location that ensured privacy, isolating Elizabeth from any hope of immediate rescue. The remote camp was no accident—it was a carefully selected environment where he could exert total control.

Crime scene analysis often looks at the level of control an offender exerts over their environment. In cases where the crime is unplanned, offenders often act recklessly, leaving behind evidence, struggling with the victim, or making poor attempts to conceal their actions. But Mitchell wasn't reckless—he was calculated. He had prepared a space for Elizabeth, indicating that he had fantasized about this long before he acted. This concept aligns with what we know about crime scenes involving power dynamics. Mitchell didn't just want to commit a crime; he wanted to dominate and control. That's why, in addition to the physical evidence at the scene—restraints, makeshift bedding, and the supplies he had brought to keep her captive—the psychological elements were just as important. Blindfolds, physical restraints, and isolation weren't just about keeping Elizabeth from escaping; they were about breaking her spirit, making her feel as if rescue was impossible, and ensuring his complete control.

For nine months, Elizabeth was moved between locations, further expanding the number of *crime scenes* tied to her captivity. At one point, Mitchell took her to California, where she was forced to wear a disguise, kept under constant manipulation, and hidden in plain sight. These temporary locations, from motels to remote encampments, became additional *crime scenes*, each offering different insights into how Mitchell operated.

Crime scene investigations rely on physical evidence, but they also reveal the psychological traits of the offender. Mitchell's use of control, the effort to isolate Elizabeth, and the strategic movement between locations all indicate a calculated offender who had planned his actions. In contrast, a more impulsive abductor might have left behind DNA evidence at the initial crime scene or quickly disposed of the victim in a panic. Mitchell, however, was methodical. He had a plan and stuck to it, making the investigation more challenging.

Understanding multiple crime scenes is crucial because they help define an offender's level of organization, risk tolerance, and ability to evade capture. Elizabeth's case wasn't just about one *crime scene*—it was about how Mitchell transitioned between them, maintaining control while avoiding detection.

While the *initial contact site* and *crime scenes* in Elizabeth Smart's case offer valuable insights into how Brian David Mitchell operated, one crucial element is missing: a *disposal site*. Unlike many abduction cases where the victim is tragically murdered and left in a remote location, Elizabeth was found alive—a rare and remarkable outcome.

Her case didn't end with investigators searching for remains in a secluded area or trying to piece together a timeline based on where evidence was discarded. Instead, she was recovered in broad daylight, in a public setting, when an alert citizen recognized her standing beside her captor. After months of psychological manipulation and control, Elizabeth was finally rescued, and Mitchell was arrested on the spot.

Because of this, the *disposal site*—the place where an offender abandons a victim or key evidence—doesn't apply in her case. However, to fully understand the significance of *disposal sites* and what they reveal about an offender's behavior, let's now turn to a case where they played a pivotal role in understanding a predator's methods: the case of serial killer Robert Ben Rhoades.

Rhoades used his job to access victims across multiple states, turning the highways into his hunting ground. His *initial contact sites* were often truck stops, where he selected young hitchhikers or runaways—people he knew wouldn't immediately be missed. The *primary crime scene* was his truck, which he had converted into a mobile torture chamber, giving him complete control over his victims. The *disposal sites* were often remote locations along the highway, chosen strategically to delay discovery.

Robert Ben Rhoades, better known as the *Truck Stop Killer*, turned America's highways into his personal hunting ground. He wasn't a back-alley predator, or a notorious face splashed across wanted posters. He was just another trucker—a man who blended into the everyday landscape of long-haul drivers, moving freight from state to state. No one would have guessed that behind the wheel of his semi, he carried more than cargo. He carried secrets.

Rhoades wasn't just a killer—he was a sadist, a predator who

thrived on domination and control. His crimes weren't random, and they didn't happen in one place. Like many serial offenders, he operated in stages, using different locations to execute each part of his crime. His process followed a chilling sequence, and each crime scene reveals something about his mindset, his methods, and the depths of his depravity.

The first step in Rhoades' deadly process was selecting his victims, and the open road gave him endless opportunities. His hunting grounds were truck stops, rest areas, and desolate stretches of highway where the vulnerable wandered—hitchhikers, stranded motorists, or women engaged in sex work. These places weren't just convenient; they provided an easy way for him to target individuals who were already isolated from help.

Most killers operate within confined spaces—a home, a secluded cabin, or an abandoned building. Rhoades, however, had a unique advantage. His *crime scene was mobile.* The sleeper cab of his semi-truck was more than a resting place for long-haul drives. It was a torture chamber on wheels. He had modified the interior, installing restraints, chains, and tools designed to inflict pain. Victims couldn't escape. They couldn't call for help. As he drove from state to state, he subjected them to unspeakable horrors, knowing that with every mile, he was taking them farther from anyone who could save them.

In late 1989, Robert Ben Rhoades came across a young couple who were hitchhiking their way to Georgia for a faith driven adventure and a beginning to their new married life together. Patricia Walsh and her husband, Douglas Zyskowski were grateful the long-haul trucker pulled over to give them a ride. They made the mistake that many people make in assuming Rhoades had the same value system that they did. You see, Patricia nor Douglas would ever hurt anyone. They were people of integrity, and they wrongly assumed that everyone else was just like them, including a truck driver they had never met before. They climbed into his 18-wheeler and thanked him for his hospitality.

Within minutes, their lives were forever changed. Rhoades had a sinister secret. He wasn't just hauling cargo—he was hunting. He had perfected his method, choosing his victims from the steady stream of travelers who passed through America's highways, knowing that many of them had no ties, no one immediately searching for them. Hitchhikers were perfect targets, and when he pulled up alongside Patricia and Douglas and offered them a ride, they had no way of knowing they had just stepped into a nightmare.

Not long after they climbed into his truck, Rhoades revealed who he really was. He turned on Douglas first, executing him in cold blood right in front of Patricia. No longer an obstacle, Douglas was discarded, and now Rhoades had Patricia all to himself.

For Patricia, the horror was just beginning. Rhoades didn't kill her right away. That wasn't what he wanted. He thrived on power, on drawing out his victims' suffering, both physically and psychologically. He kept her captive in the back of his semi-truck. It was soundproof, equipped with restraints, and set up in a way that ensured he had complete control. No one could hear her scream. No one knew where she was. As he drove from state to state, crossing miles of empty highway, he tormented her in ways that are almost too horrific to imagine.

For over a week, he kept her alive, prolonging the terror. He knew exactly what he was doing—breaking her down, making her feel completely helpless. He had done this before, and he would do it again. Patricia was just another victim in his twisted, sadistic game.

Eventually, when he was done with her, Rhoades drove into the barren stretches of Millard County, Utah, and ended her life.

For Regina Kay Walters, the *initial contact site* was another stretch of highway. A 14-year-old girl who had run away from home with her boyfriend, Ricky Lee Jones, she likely thought Rhoades was just another trucker willing to help. Instead, he quickly asserted control, killing Jones early on and taking Regina for himself. The road, a place that symbolized freedom for so many travelers, became the setting for the first chapter of her nightmare.

Rhoades turned his attention to Regina. He had specific plans for her. He cut her hair, dressed her in clothing of his choosing, and forced her to pose for photographs. These weren't just mementos—they were trophies, a way for him to relive the power he had over her. In one of the most haunting images discovered after his arrest, Regina stands in an abandoned barn, her arms pulled in close, her face frozen in terror. It was the last known photo of her before he strangled her to death with a homemade garrote.

While Rhoades used his truck as his primary crime scene, he wasn't limited to one location. He sometimes took victims to abandoned structures or desolate areas, places where he could continue his torture without interruption. Investigators later uncovered evidence suggesting he moved Regina between multiple locations, increasing her suffering and prolonging his control.

Unlike the Elizabeth Smart case, where the victim was found alive, most of Rhoades' victims were never intended to be discovered. Their bodies were his final problem to solve, and he handled them with the same calculated precision as the rest of his crimes.

Douglas Zyskowski was the first to be discarded. Rhoades executed him quickly, disposing of his body off the freeway in Sutton County, Texas. It was a remote spot, the kind of place where a body might never be found—or, if it was, it would be skeletal remains with little forensic evidence left to analyze. That's exactly what happened. It took over a year for someone to stumble upon his remains, and by then, there was little left to identify or investigate.

Patricia Walsh met a similar fate. After a week of torment, she was murdered and dumped in Millard County, Utah. Her body remained undiscovered for nearly a year, the time and elements stripping away the clues that could have connected her to her killer.

And then there was Regina. Unlike the others, her body was found relatively quickly. Dumped in an abandoned barn in Greenville, Illinois, she was left in a way that suggested some degree of staging. Whether it was an attempt to send a message or simply a convenient place to leave her remains, her discovery proved vital in unraveling Rhoades' crimes. But what about the others?

Investigators believe Rhoades may have killed dozens—perhaps hundreds—of victims. Many, they fear, were discarded in locations so remote they may never be found. Truck stops, desert highways, rest areas—places where bodies could be left and covered by time, scavengers, or nature itself.

Rhoades' reign of terror finally ended in 1990, not because of a carefully orchestrated law enforcement sting, but because one of his victims *escaped*. A woman managed to flee from his truck in Arizona, leading to his arrest. What police found inside his semi was horrifying—restraints, weapons, and, most disturbingly, photographs of his victims.

These images became some of the most crucial pieces of evidence in securing his conviction. They didn't just document the horror—*they proved it happened.* Regina Kay Walters' haunting photo, standing in that barn with fear etched on her face, became one of the defining images of his sadistic crimes.

In the end, Rhoades was sentenced to life in prison without the possibility of parole. But the full extent of his crimes remains a terrifying mystery. How many others did he kill? Where are their bodies? How many families are still waiting for answers?

Robert Ben Rhoades wasn't a shadowy figure lurking in alleyways or breaking into homes. He was a truck driver, someone people saw every day, someone who waved to fellow motorists and stopped at diners like anyone else. He was ordinary—until he wasn't. His case forces us to confront an unsettling truth: *sometimes, the most dangerous predators aren't the ones who stand out.* They're the ones who blend in. They live among us, disguised as everyday people, carrying out their horrors in the spaces between our daily lives.

As we dissected the *initial contact site, the crime scene, and the disposal site*, we saw just how meticulously some predators plan their crimes. Each location plays a crucial role in their twisted processes, reinforcing their need for power, control, and secrecy. These cases leave us with lingering questions such as how many more Robert Ben Rhoades are there out there? And perhaps more chillingly—*how many have we walked past without ever knowing?*

In the next chapter, we'll delve into the psychology behind these hidden predators. We'll explore how people like Robert Ben Rhoades or Brian David Mitchell maintain their double lives and conceal their darkest selves, all while appearing completely normal to those around them. Understanding *how* they hide in plain sight might be the key to stopping them before they strike again.

Understanding that humans operate with three distinct personas—public, private, and secret—is helpful because it provides a framework to analyze and interpret behavior, relationships, and motivations. -MK

Chapter Ten

The Masks We Wear

Serial predators often lead dual lives, presenting a facade of normalcy to society while concealing their deviant behaviors. This compartmentalization enables them to commit heinous acts without arousing suspicion. Understanding this dichotomy is crucial for comprehending how such individuals evade detection and why communities are often shocked when their true nature is revealed.

Serial predators aren't the shadowy figures lurking in dark alleys or the creepy loners that movies love to portray. Many of them live shockingly normal lives, blending seamlessly into society while committing horrific crimes in secret. They often hold steady jobs, maintain relationships, and even take part in community activities— superficially appearing just as ordinary as anyone else. It's this duality that makes them so dangerous and allows them to evade suspicion for years, sometimes even decades.

Take Dennis Rader, for example. Better known as the BTK Killer (short for *Bind, Torture, Kill*), Rader spent 30 years living a completely normal life in Wichita, Kansas. He was a devoted husband, a father, the president of his church congregation, and even worked as

a compliance officer for the city—writing up people for things like overgrown grass and loose pets. But behind that community-minded persona, he was a meticulous serial killer, terrorizing his victims while keeping up the illusion of a respectable family man. His ability to lead this double life is what kept him off law enforcement's radar for so long.

Psychologists call this compartmentalization—the ability to mentally separate different parts of life that conflict with each other. For serial predators, this is a survival skill. They can commit horrific crimes but then switch back to their everyday routines without guilt, without remorse, and without slipping up. Their minds are wired to separate these two worlds so effectively that even those closest to them never suspect a thing.

Ted Bundy was another master of this behavior. On the surface, he was handsome, charismatic, and intelligent—the kind of guy who charmed women, won the trust of police officers, and even worked on a suicide prevention hotline. But behind that charming facade, he was a ruthless killer, preying on young women with chilling precision. His ability to present himself as trustworthy was exactly what made him so dangerous—he didn't "look" like a serial killer. And that's why so many people, including those who knew him personally, refused to believe he was capable of such violence even when the evidence was overwhelming.

This ability to manipulate and deceive often comes from deep-rooted personality traits like narcissism and psychopathy. Narcissists have an inflated sense of self-importance and zero empathy for others. Psychopaths take it even further, showing no remorse, no emotional connection, and no concern for the consequences of their actions.

Together, these traits allow serial predators to lie effortlessly, charm their way out of trouble, and kill without a second thought.

When these kinds of predators are finally unmasked, the reaction from the people who knew them is almost always shock and disbelief. Neighbors, coworkers, even family members struggle to accept that the person they thought they knew was capable of such horrific crimes. This is because serial predators wear what some experts call a "mask of sanity"—a carefully crafted public persona that hides their true nature. When that mask finally drops, the world is left reeling.

The truth is serial predators don't stand out in the way people think they should. They're not always the creepy guy in the basement or the drifter with no ties to the community. More often than not, they're the friendly neighbor, the reliable coworker, the guy coaching Little League, or the dad grilling burgers at the Fourth of July barbecue. And that's exactly what makes them so terrifying.

The arrest of Rex Heuermann, charged with multiple murders along Long Island, New York, exemplifies the ability of serial predators to hide in plain sight. Heuermann was perceived as an ordinary businessman, with a family and a stable job, yet he allegedly led a secret life involving heinous crimes. This case highlights the challenges in identifying such individuals based solely on their public behavior.[61]

The fifty-nine-year-old Heuermann was an architect from Massapequa Park, Long Island. He appeared to be the quintessential image of an unassuming suburban professional. He commuted daily to his office in Manhattan, had a wife and two children, and lived in the same community where he grew up. By all accounts, Heuermann appeared to be a hardworking businessman with a stable family life. Yet beneath this veneer of normalcy, he allegedly engaged in a secret life of violence, manipulation, and murder.

Rex Heuermann is currently charged with seven of the Gilgo Beach murders, a series of killings that had gone unsolved for over a decade. While presumed innocent at the time of this writing, his story (if found to be true) exemplifies the story told by countless other family members, co-workers, and friends of suspected and convicted serial predators.

The arrest of Rex Heuermann sent shockwaves through his community and the broader public. His neighbors described him as reclusive and somewhat awkward but never suspected him of violent tendencies. Co-workers noted his meticulous nature and professionalism, often describing him as quiet and focused on his work. However, they also recalled moments where his demeanor seemed peculiar, marked by a lack of warmth and an intense fixation on control.

Heuermann's wife and children, meanwhile, were reportedly blindsided by the accusations. His wife was out of town during each of the alleged murders, (a fact investigators believe was a deliberate choice by the accused killer to avoid suspicion). This raises troubling questions about whether she noticed signs of his dark activities or if Heuermann's ability to compartmentalize allowed him to shield his secret life entirely.

Heuermann's wife reportedly expressed shock and disbelief at the accusations, stating that she had no idea about her husband's alleged criminal activities and investigators theorized her absence on foreign travel at the time of the murders might explain her unawareness. However, the family's attorney later revealed that Heuermann's behavior at home was sometimes erratic, including unexplained absences and a secretive attitude toward certain aspects of his life, such as his use of burner phones and private spaces in the house.

At his Manhattan architectural firm, colleagues described Heuermann as a private but capable professional. He rarely engaged in personal conversations and seemed to lack emotional warmth. However, some noted an unsettling intensity in his personality. One co-worker recalled a heated argument in which Heuermann exhibited a disproportionate reaction, bordering on aggression, which seemed inconsistent with his usual reserved demeanor.

Neighbors portrayed Heuermann as aloof and somewhat peculiar. While he did not cause trouble, he was not particularly sociable. Some neighbors described him as a loner who avoided community events. Others recalled occasional odd behaviors, such as late-night activity around his property and an apparent preoccupation with maintaining privacy.

In hindsight, several red flags suggest that Heuermann's secret life may not have been as imperceptible as it seemed, beginning with a high level of concealment about certain parts of his life. Heuermann reportedly had a locked room in his house and possessed over 200 firearms, raising questions about the level of transparency in his personal life. Neighbors also observed him acting guarded around his property.

During their investigation and subsequent search warrants, investigators discovered that Heuermann used burner phones to arrange meetings with sex workers, a practice designed to evade detection. However, he retained these phones, which later became a crucial piece of evidence against him. This reliance on secretive methods of communication could have raised alarms had it been noticed earlier.

The alleged killer's frequent unexplained absences during critical times might have been noticed by those close to him. While his wife's travel schedule coincided with the murders, his own travel or late-night activities could have aroused suspicion if observed more closely. To generalize his behaviors and expound on some of the potential red flags that were popping up, it's important to keep in mind that serial predators will often exhibit patterns of deception and control that, while subtle, can provide clues to their hidden lives.

One area of concern was Heuermann's private, if not completely secret areas of his life. Like behavior seen in other predators, he maintained locations, spaces, and secluded areas that were off-limits to others. Such secrecy often serves as a red flag for deeper issues. And some of his reported compulsive behaviors seem consistent with the red flag concerns.

Heuermann kept to himself and avoided forming relationships that might expose his secret life. This isolation is a common tactic among serial predators to minimize the risk of being discovered, and like the dual persona that is being reported, many serial predators project an image of normalcy while harboring dark intentions. This ability to compartmentalize is a hallmark of psychopathy, enabling offenders to deceive even those closest to them.

The case of Rex Heuermann underscores the importance of vigilance and awareness in recognizing potential red flags. While it is challenging to detect such behaviors without the benefit of hindsight, communities can benefit from education on behavioral patterns associated with predatory individuals. Programs that teach individuals to recognize inconsistencies, trust their instincts, and report suspicious activities can serve as valuable tools in preventing future crimes.

To aid in the exploration of the different masks people wear, let's explore the three sides of every human's life, their personal personas. Understanding that humans operate with three distinct personas—public, private, and secret—is helpful because it provides a framework to analyze and interpret behavior, relationships, and motivations. Each persona reflects a different aspect of how individuals navigate their social, emotional, and psychological worlds. While these personas are universal, they become particularly intriguing when analyzing criminal behavior, as offenders often manipulate these personas to create a facade of normalcy and deflect suspicion from their illicit activities.

THE PUBLIC PERSONA

The Public Persona represents the image that an individual projects to the outside world. This persona is shaped by social norms, cultural expectations, and personal aspirations to be perceived positively by others. It is, in essence, the "mask" people wear in public settings such as workplaces, schools, and social gatherings. This persona is carefully curated and is often the most polished and controlled aspect of an individual's identity.

Some of the identifying characteristics of the public persona are social adaption, impression management, and consistency of application. The public persona is tailored to fit societal expectations, allowing individuals to adapt to different social contexts. For instance, an individual may present themselves as professional and diligent at work while being more relaxed and approachable among friends.

It all comes down to impression management, the way people shape how others see them in order to get what they want. It's like when you're trying to make a good first impression, but it's much deeper than that. Sociologist Erving Goffman compared social life to a play, where everyone is constantly performing a role, much like an actor on a stage. Every interaction, whether it's in person, online, or through other forms of communication, is like a scene in a bigger performance. We all have a script we follow, and it's all about controlling the story others see.

Here's another way to think about it: when someone is always consistent in how they present themselves, that persona becomes reliable. People start to trust that person because their behavior is predictable. If you're always friendly, dependable, or professional, others start to believe that's who you really are. In the world of true crime, this is crucial, whether it's a suspect trying to convince everyone they're innocent or a victim trying to protect their reputation, that public persona is everything. If a person's actions don't match their "role," people start to question their character.

A solid, consistent public persona creates a sense of trust. This is how relationships work—whether you're trying to build a friendship, gain someone's confidence, or even manipulate a situation. People look for consistency to gauge your reliability. That's why in investigations, understanding someone's public persona can be key to figuring out if they're hiding something or just playing a role to fit in.

Criminals manipulate the public persona they have to portray they are something different than they really are. These predators, particularly those who are engaged in long-term or premeditated offenses, often cultivate a strong public persona to deflect suspicion. The offender may volunteer, attend religious services, or participate in local events to portray themselves as upstanding citizens. They will try to maintain steady employment and even excel in a career, providing a veneer of normalcy. They may also exhibit charm and charisma to disarm potential suspicion.

Returning to the case we've already explored of Richard Allen, let's look closer at his persona. Allen lived a seemingly normal life in the small town of Delphi. As a pharmacy technician, he interacted daily with community members who described him as "quiet" and "helpful." He maintained what is reportedly a stable marriage and was considered a regular neighbor. However, beneath this public facade lay a dark secret that would take years to uncover.

When Indiana State Police arrested him in October of 2022, many people were left scratching their heads. Even after his conviction, there are those who continue to say that the man they knew, "their Richard Allen" isn't capable of the horrible assault that Abby and Libby faced.

It would take a criminal trial to learn how Allen became the man captured on Liberty's phone, now dubbed, "Bridge Guy." The case was so unbelievable that it drew significant attention from online communities who immediately began speculating and creating conspiracy theories, some which ultimately were correct.

It was that volunteer file clerk who discovered a misfiled tip from 2017, in which Richard Allen had self-reported being on the trails on the day of the murders, reporting then that he had seen Williams and German out walking. Not long after he came back into view, Richard Allen was taken into custody and charged with two counts of murder.

During the trial, the prosecution successfully entered several key pieces of evidence such as an unspent bullet. The .40-caliber round was found between the victims' bodies and forensic analysis determined that this round had been cycled through a gun owned by Allen. That weapon was recovered in a search of Allen's home after he was identified as a suspect. The video footage recovered from Liberty German's phone also proved damning for Allen. The video footage showed a man approaching the girls and instructing them to go "down the hill." The prosecution successfully argued that the man who was seen in the video uttering those words was Richard Allen.

Independent witnesses reported seeing a man matching Allen's description near the Monon High Bridge on the day of the murders. One witness described seeing a man walking away from the bridge, "wearing a blue colored jacket and blue jeans and was muddy and bloody." And surprisingly, while incarcerated, Allen allegedly confessed to the murders in conversations with his wife and to prison personnel. The defense claimed these confessions were unreliable, attributing them to Allen's psychosis induced by solitary confinement, but the jury must have viewed them as true and credible.

Richard Allen's trial commenced in October 2024, with the jury reviewing the evidence. After 19 hours of deliberation, Allen was found guilty on all counts, and he was later sentenced on December 20, 2024, to 130 years in prison, receiving the maximum penalty of 65 years for each charge.

The conviction of Richard Allen for the murders of Abigail Williams and Liberty German marked the culmination of a prolonged and arduous investigation. Allen's case highlights the critical role of meticulous evidence gathering and the unwavering dedication of law enforcement in seeking justice for victims and their families. While the evidence presented in court, including physical, forensic, and eyewitness testimony, was crucial in securing a conviction, Allen's actions and behaviors during the crime and in the years that followed revealed a layered persona—public, personal, and secretive—that added complexity to the case.

Richard Allen's public persona helped him blend into his surroundings, helping him to avoid suspicion, as he displayed no overt signs of involvement in the horrific crime. Despite his outward appearance of normalcy, Allen's personal life revealed deeper layers. Investigators discovered that he lived just two miles from the Monon High Bridge, the crime scene, and had easy access to the area. During the investigation, Allen himself admitted to being on the trails the day of the murders, claiming he was there to "watch fish"—an explanation that, in hindsight, seemed implausible to many, including the jury. Furthermore, his behavior in private was marked by efforts to maintain a facade of innocence, even as the case gained widespread attention.

Allen's secretive persona became evident through several key revelations during the investigation. The discovery of the unspent .40-caliber bullet at the crime scene, tracing back to a gun he owned, was a critical piece of forensic evidence linking him to the murders. His decision to keep the gun despite its potential to incriminate him reflected a level of arrogance or denial about the possibility of being caught.

Perhaps most chilling were Allen's alleged confessions while in custody. Reports indicate that he admitted to the killings in conversations with his wife and prison personnel, though these confessions were later challenged by the defense as unreliable due to his deteriorating mental state. These admissions, coupled with his earlier denials, painted a portrait of a man struggling to reconcile his guilt with the persona he had carefully constructed over the years.

The case against Richard Allen was built not only on tangible evidence but also on the dissonance between his public, personal, and secret behaviors. His ability to maintain a facade of normalcy while harboring dark secrets underscores the challenges law enforcement faced in bringing him to justice. This complexity serves as a sobering reminder of the importance of perseverance and thorough investigation in solving even the most confounding cases.

In the study of criminology, understanding the psychological and social dimensions of human behavior is crucial. The concept of the three personas; public, private, and secret, provides a compelling framework to analyze how individuals, particularly predators, compartmentalize their lives to conceal illicit activities. This duality of existence enables offenders to deceive others, maintain a facade of normalcy, and execute their crimes while evading detection. Each persona serves a distinct function in this dynamic interplay.

In the Richard Allen case, the public persona became a tool for deception. Exploiting that persona allowed Allen the wiggle room to divert suspicion. Like other predators, Allen used this strategy by cultivating a positive reputation (or public persona). Masking his secret life enabled him to operate undetected for years.

But the public persona is only part of the story. What someone shows the world is often carefully curated, but behind closed doors, a different version of that person emerges. This is where the private persona comes into play. This is the side of personalities that isn't meant for public consumption.

For most people, this private self is just a more relaxed, unfiltered version of their public image. It's the person they are when they're with family, close friends, or anyone they trust enough to let their guard down. In a well-adjusted individual, this private self isn't drastically different from what they show the outside world, it just strips away the need for constant performance. That's where the Zizian cult comes into the picture.

The Zizians weren't your typical cult. On the surface, they preached radical veganism, transhumanism, and a rejection of mainstream society. Their leader is Jack Amadeus "Ziz" LaSota. LaSota is reportedly an intellectual visionary and someone who believes humans and animals are on an equal plane. To the outside world, the Zizians were just an eccentric group with extreme ideas about artificial intelligence, (AI), ethics, and alternative lifestyles. But behind closed doors, a much darker reality appears to be unfolding.

Despite their public image as a group committed to nonviolence and moral superiority, the Zizians are now linked to a string of brutal crimes. Authorities believe members of the group were involved in as many as six homicides, including the murder of a U.S. Border Patrol agent in Vermont. These weren't random acts of violence, but they appear to have been calculated and, in some cases, even ordered within the group.

This is where the contradiction becomes impossible to ignore. Outwardly, they condemned violence and claimed to stand for ethical living, but in private, they were allegedly orchestrating killings. It's a classic case of a public persona hiding something far more sinister beneath the surface. Groups like this thrive on creating an image that makes them seem enlightened, peaceful, or even misunderstood. But when that public image clashes with secret, violent actions, the truth eventually comes out and in the case of the Zizians, that truth is disturbing.

This kind of double life isn't unique to cults. Time and time again, criminals have used carefully curated public personas to deflect suspicion. They blend in, act righteous, and sometimes even claim the moral high ground, all while hiding the darkest parts of themselves where they think no one will look. The Zizian case is just another reminder that a person's, or a group's public image doesn't always tell the whole story.

THE PRIVATE PERSONA

The private persona is the unfiltered version of an individual, revealed only in the presence of close friends, family, or trusted confidants. It reflects personal beliefs, vulnerabilities, and emotional realities—the aspects of a person that exist beyond public expectations or social pressures. In a well-balanced individual, this private persona aligns closely with their public image, creating a sense of authenticity and trustworthiness.

Yet, the private self is rarely as polished as the version presented to the outside world, the public persona. It is in private moments that insecurities surface, emotions run unchecked, and moral struggles unfold. The way a person behaves when they believe no one is watching can be the most accurate measure of their character. The degree to which someone allows others into this space also reveals the level of trust they extend, as not everyone is granted access to their most honest self.

When discrepancies between public and private personas are extreme, they often point to deeper psychological conflicts. This is particularly evident in cases where individuals maintain a respectable outward image while engaging in manipulation, abuse, or criminal behavior behind closed doors. A trusted community figure may lead a double life, hiding darker impulses beneath a carefully maintained facade. A seemingly devoted spouse or parent may, in private, exert control through fear and coercion. These contradictions are not always visible on the surface, but they often leave patterns—subtle inconsistencies in behavior, relationships marked by secrecy, or an unusual need to control narratives about their personal life.

For those who seek to understand human behavior, the private persona is where the truth resides. Public images can be crafted, but what someone does in their most unguarded moments tells the real story of who they are.

In criminology, discrepancies between the public and private personas often offer critical insights. Investigators frequently uncover behaviors in private that contradict an offender's public image. For instance, an outwardly loving spouse may exhibit controlling or abusive tendencies within the confines of their home. These incongruities can serve as warning signs, revealing the psychological conflict or duplicity underlying criminal actions.[62]

THE SECRET PERSONA

True crime is full of stories about seemingly ordinary people who harbor dark, hidden lives. One of the most fascinating and chilling aspects of criminal behavior is the secret persona, the concealed identity where unspoken urges, fantasies, and actions live. Unlike the public face someone shows the world or even the private self they reveal to close friends and family, the secret persona is the most carefully guarded part of a person's identity.

For the average person, this hidden self might contain harmless secrets such as quirky hobbies, unspoken desires, or private fears. But for criminals, especially violent offenders, the secret persona is where the darkness festers. It's here that illicit urges grow, deviant fantasies take shape, and, in some cases, horrific plans are meticulously crafted. Remember our discussion on fantasy and how the criminal uses them to justify and rehearse what eventually becomes a crime? Let's return to Richard Allen, the convicted murderer of Abigail Williams and Liberty German in the infamous Delphi case. We spoke about his public and private persona but now it's time to dig into his secret persona.

Allen's ability to keep this side of himself completely hidden, even while living in the same small town where he committed his crimes, showcases the power of compartmentalization. He wasn't just avoiding suspicion; he was actively using his ordinary public persona as a shield. He blended in so well that for years, he wasn't even considered a suspect. His secret persona, filled with dark desires and the ability to act on them, remained invisible, until that clerk pulled his name from the files.

Psychologists and criminologists who study offenders like Allen often describe them as chameleons. They don't just disguise themselves; they adapt to their surroundings with eerie precision. They use their normal, everyday interactions to deflect scrutiny, keeping their secret selves tightly locked away. But when they feel secure, thinking no one is watching, the secret persona emerges.

Recent news accounts have explored another haunting example of a secret persona at work with the Zizians, led by Jack "Ziz" LaSota.

The cognitive dissonance between LaSota's reputation and the allegations surrounding a secret life is a prime example of how criminals use multiple layers of identity to manipulate the world around them. A well-crafted secret persona isn't just about hiding crimes, it's about maintaining the illusion that such crimes are unthinkable in the first place. The more respected the public face, the harder it is for people to imagine the monster underneath.

What makes these people so unsettling is the fluidity with which they transition between their personas. One moment, they are doting fathers, helpful neighbors, respected professionals. The next, they are predators, carefully enacting the desires they've kept buried from the world. And once the crime is committed, they return seamlessly to their public and private lives, as if nothing happened.

This ability to shift between personas is what makes some criminals so difficult to catch. The contrast between their outward identity and their secret self is often so stark that even those closest to them struggle to reconcile the two. It's why family members and friends so often say, "I never would have suspected" when someone they know is unmasked as a predator.

If we were honest with ourselves, we'd have to admit that we each have some level of inner conflict, thoughts and feelings they pop into our minds, but are never acted upon. But for predators like Allen and LaSota, the secret persona isn't just a mental space; it's an active, growing entity that waits for the right moment to surface and take control. When it does, it often happens with chilling precision. The secret persona plans meticulously, avoids detection, and is willing to play the long game, allowing its criminal owner a way to lead a seemingly normal life, all while engaging in behavior that is wholly incompatible with their outward identity.

Understanding the secret persona doesn't just help explain how criminals evade detection, it shatters the myth that monsters look like monsters. Often, they look just like everyone else and that is perhaps the most terrifying truth of all.

As we've seen, the public, private, and secret personas form a complex framework that predators use to lead double lives, evading detection while manipulating those around them. These personas, while serving legitimate roles in everyday life, become tools of deception in the hands of predators. This duality forces us to confront the thin line between normalcy and manipulation, between appearances and reality. But understanding these layers is only the beginning.

To truly expose the full scope of criminal behavior, we must dive into how these carefully constructed personas leave traces in the real world. These traces can be scrutinized, analyzed, and ultimately dismantled. When these actions are reconciled against the traditional forms of evidence, things like physical and forensic clues, eyewitness accounts, and confessions, more visibility and tangible proof begin to give us a glimpse of what predators seek to conceal. Yet even more revealing is the behavioral evidence, the patterns of action and reaction before, during, and after a crime, that often betrays the hidden truth.

In the next chapter, we'll bridge the gap between the psychological and the physical, exploring how these personas translate into evidence that investigators can use to unravel the truth. You might be asking how the layers of identity will stand up against cold, hard facts? Will they align or conflict with the story a predator's behavior tells? The answers lie in the interplay of evidence and psychology, where the shadows of deception meet the light of discovery. Turn the page to delve deeper into this compelling intersection.

Physical evidence is an indispensable component of criminal investigations, offering an objective and reliable means of establishing facts and securing convictions. -MK

Chapter Eleven

The Anatomy of Evidence: From Clues to Convictions

Criminal investigations rely on different types of evidence to uncover the truth, establish facts, and ensure justice is served. Law enforcement officers must systematically gather and analyze evidence to build compelling cases against suspects or exonerate the innocent. Among the myriad forms of evidence used in criminal investigations, five traditional types stand out: physical evidence, forensic evidence, circumstantial evidence, eyewitness testimony, and confessions or admissions. Each of these categories serves a unique function in the investigative process, contributing to a comprehensive understanding of the events surrounding a crime. This chapter will delve into each form of evidence, highlighting its significance and methodologies. It will use examples from criminal cases and explore the importance of evidence, outline key methodologies for its collection and analysis, and examine its pivotal role in the conviction of an offender through illustrative case studies.

PHYSICAL EVIDENCE

Physical evidence, often referred to as "real evidence" or "material evidence," is a cornerstone in the investigation and prosecution of criminal cases. This category of evidence includes tangible items such as weapons, fingerprints, bloodstains, clothing, documents, and other physical objects that can be collected, analyzed, and used in court. The reliability of physical evidence lies in its objectivity and permanence, providing a more consistent foundation for analysis compared to subjective forms of evidence like eyewitness testimony.

Physical evidence serves several critical functions in criminal investigations. It can establish the occurrence of a crime, link a suspect to a crime scene, disprove an alibi, and provide insights into the sequence of events leading to the crime. The evidentiary value of physical objects often lies in their ability to withstand subjective biases, making them indispensable in the pursuit of justice.[63]

For example, latent fingerprints left on a weapon or at a crime scene can directly link a suspect to the location or object. Similarly, the analysis of bloodstains using methods such as serology and DNA profiling can confirm the identity of a victim or perpetrator and can also help reconstruct the events that occurred during the crime.[64] Moreover, physical evidence can provide exculpatory value, proving the innocence of wrongfully accused individuals.

The reliability and impartiality of physical evidence have elevated its role in modern forensic science. Unlike testimony, which can be influenced by memory lapses or external pressures, physical evidence provides a tangible and often immutable record of events. However, its effectiveness depends on the proper collection, preservation, and interpretation of the evidence, as errors in these processes can jeopardize an investigation.

The handling of physical evidence is guided by strict protocols to ensure its integrity and admissibility in court. These methodologies include things like how the crime scene is documented and what collections techniques are employed. Investigators meticulously document the crime scene by taking video, photographs, and hand-drawn sketches. In some jurisdictions, investigators have sophisticated 3D scanners to recreate the scene in multi-dimension. They take notes to capture the original condition of the evidence before it is disturbed.

Collecting evidence isn't just about grabbing what looks important and bagging it up, it's a meticulous process, requiring the right tools, careful handling, and, most importantly, a documented chain of custody to ensure nothing is compromised. Every crime scene holds clues, but those clues are only as valuable as the way they're collected and preserved.

Imagine a detective stepping onto a crime scene. There's a strand of hair on the victim's clothing and tiny fibers on the carpet—trace evidence that could link a suspect to the scene. These aren't things you just pick up with your fingers. Instead, investigators use precise tools like tweezers for hair or adhesive tape to lift fibers, all done to ensure nothing is contaminated or lost in the process.

Then there's blood evidence, one of the most crucial types in any investigation. A visible stain on the floor or a smear on a doorknob might hold DNA that can crack the case wide open. But it has to be collected properly. Investigators use sterile swabs, carefully dabbing the stain, then sealing and labeling the sample immediately. If not handled correctly, the evidence could be compromised, degraded, or challenged in court.

But finding and collecting evidence is only the first step. What happens after is just as important. Every single piece of evidence, from a single hair to a blood sample, must be accounted for from the moment it's recovered at the scene to the moment it's presented in court. That's where the chain of custody comes in with detailed logs that track who collected what, where it was stored, and who handled it next. If there's any gap in that chain, a defense attorney can argue that the evidence was tampered with or mishandled, potentially getting it thrown out completely.

It's a delicate, precise process, but one that makes or breaks a case. The best evidence in the world is useless if it isn't collected, stored, and presented the right way. Because in the end, it's not just about what you find, it's about proving it's been in safe hands the entire way.

Once evidence is collected, the next big challenge is keeping it intact. It's not enough to just bag it and call it a day. A record of how the evidence is stored and handled after collection can mean the difference between solving a case and watching it fall apart in court. Take biological evidence, for example. Things like blood samples, saliva, or tissue are packed up carefully and refrigerated to keep them from degrading. If they're stored incorrectly, they can break down, become contaminated, or even be rendered completely useless by the time forensic analysts get to them.

Then, there are the high-tech methods used to make sense of all this evidence. DNA sequencing can connect a suspect to a crime with stunning accuracy, while ballistics analysis can link a bullet to a specific gun with forensic precision. Chemical testing can uncover drug traces, toxins, or explosive residues, revealing details that aren't visible to the naked eye. Every piece of physical evidence has a story to tell, but only if it's handled the right way.

This is why strict forensic protocols exist—because one mistake can derail an entire case. If evidence is mishandled, contaminated, or improperly stored, it opens the door for reasonable doubt, giving the defense an easy argument to get it thrown out. Worse, errors in forensic handling have led to wrongful convictions, putting innocent people behind bars while the real perpetrator walks free.

One of the most infamous examples of the role of physical evidence in securing a conviction is the case of Ted Bundy. His case highlights how tangible, material evidence can overcome the challenges posed by a cunning and manipulative perpetrator.[65] Bundy was a master at covering his tracks, leaving behind little direct evidence at his crime scenes. His ability to plan meticulously, adapt quickly, and stay mobile made it incredibly difficult for investigators to pin him down. Every move was calculated, every detail considered—allowing him to slip through the cracks time and time again.

Although Ted Bundy was arrested several times during his killing spree, it was not until 1978 that he was definitively linked to his crimes through physical evidence. In January of that year, Bundy attacked several young women at a sorority house in Tallahassee, Florida, leaving behind crucial physical evidence that would lead to his conviction. The Chi Omega sorority house attack provided investigators with significant physical evidence, including hair fibers that were matched to fibers collected from Bundy's vehicle. During the attack, Bundy made a crucial mistake—he bit one of his victims, leaving behind a distinct bite mark on her skin. Forensic odontologists later analyzed the impressions, comparing them to Bundy's own dental records, and the match was undeniable. It was one of the most damning pieces of evidence in his conviction, proving that no matter how careful or calculated he had been, he couldn't escape the forensic science closing in on him.

Beyond the bite mark, investigators also collected blood and other physical evidence from the crime scene, each piece helping to reconstruct the brutal attack. When the evidence was laid out in court, it painted a chilling picture—one that placed Bundy directly at the scene of the murders. For years, Bundy's charm and manipulative nature had allowed him to evade suspicion, convincing people he was harmless. But in the face of hard forensic evidence, all the charisma in the world couldn't save him. Science had spoken—and this time, Bundy couldn't talk his way out of it.

While the Bundy case illustrates the power of physical evidence in securing justice, other cases highlight the challenges and limitations associated with its use. The 1996 murder of JonBenét Ramsey serves as a one of those examples of how improper handling and interpretation of evidence can hinder an investigation. This case has remained in the public spotlight for decades and several pieces of physical evidence are regularly discussed. The ransom note, a broken paintbrush used in a garrote, and unidentified footprints remain key pieces of evidence, but the puzzle hasn't been put together yet to reveal who her killer was. Crime scene contamination, ambiguity, and public scrutiny continue to haunt the cold case.

In her book, Ann Rule revealed that the crime scene was not properly secured, allowing family members and law enforcement personnel to inadvertently contaminate evidence. The physical evidence collected did not conclusively link any specific suspect to the crime, and the intense media coverage and speculation further complicated the investigation, creating additional pressure and distractions for law enforcement. The JonBenét Ramsey case serves as a stark reminder of why meticulous evidence handling is critical in any investigation. The missteps in securing the crime scene, collecting physical evidence, and following proper procedures seriously compromised the case, making it one of the most infamous unsolved mysteries in American history. It highlights how even the smallest lapses in protocol can have devastating consequences, potentially allowing vital clues to be lost, misinterpreted, or rendered inadmissible in court.

Physical evidence is the backbone of any solid criminal investigation. It's the hard proof that can link a suspect to a crime, disprove an alibi, and piece together the story of what really happened. Unlike witness statements—which can be unreliable—or gut feelings, evidence doesn't lie. Bloodstains, fingerprints, fibers, and ballistics all tell their own version of events, and when handled correctly, they can be the key to securing convictions and delivering justice.

But collecting evidence is just the beginning. What happens next—the documentation, preservation, and analysis—is just as crucial. Every step is designed to protect its integrity, making sure that by the time it reaches a courtroom, there's no doubt about its authenticity. If evidence is mishandled, contaminated, or lost, it can mean the difference between a conviction and a killer walking free.

Physical evidence lays out the foundation of a case, but sometimes, the answers investigators need aren't visible to the naked eye. This is where forensic science steps in—turning the smallest, most overlooked details into undeniable proof. Whether it's DNA sequencing, trace chemical analysis, or ballistics testing, forensic techniques take physical evidence to the next level, often reshaping the entire investigation.

As we move into the world of forensic evidence, we step beyond what can be seen and touched and into the realm of science and precision—where even the faintest trace can hold the power to crack a case wide open.

FORENSIC EVIDENCE

Forensic evidence represents the critical intersection of science and law enforcement, offering objective and reliable methods to solve crimes and secure justice. In the following pages, we will explore the significance of forensic evidence and delve into key methodologies such as DNA analysis, ballistics, and digital forensics, examining their transformative role in criminal investigations. Additionally, we will observe the impact of these methodologies through an in-depth discussion of the Golden State Killer case, showcasing the profound influence forensic evidence has in delivering justice.

Forensic evidence is the game-changer in modern criminal investigations. When eyewitness accounts are shaky or circumstantial evidence isn't enough, forensic science steps in to fill the gaps with cold, hard facts. Its power lies in its ability to provide definitive answers—not just who committed a crime, but when, how, and sometimes even why.

Perhaps one of the most incredible aspects of forensic science is its ability to both convict the guilty and exonerate the innocent. DNA testing alone has cleared countless wrongfully convicted individuals, proving that forensic evidence isn't just about locking people up—it's about getting it right. It's a scientific safety net, ensuring that justice is served fairly.

One of the most groundbreaking advances in forensic science is DNA analysis. By examining blood, hair, skin cells, or even saliva, investigators can identify individuals with near certainty. It has solved countless cold cases, sometimes decades later, bringing long-overdue justice to victims and a semblance of closure to their families. Thanks to advancements like polymerase chain reaction (PCR), even the tiniest trace of DNA can be amplified and analyzed, making it possible to connect a suspect to a crime scene or clear someone who was falsely accused. Beyond criminal investigations, DNA analysis plays a vital role in paternity disputes, identifying victims of mass disasters, and tracking down missing persons.

Another powerhouse in forensic investigations is ballistics—the science of firearms and ammunition. Investigators can determine what kind of weapon was used, how bullets traveled, and even link a specific gun to a crime scene. Ballistics experts can reconstruct a shooting, revealing who fired the gun, from what distance, and whether witness statements hold up. This kind of analysis has cracked cases by matching a single bullet to a weapon found in a suspect's possession, removing any doubt about their involvement.

Forensic science isn't just a tool—it's a revolution in crime-solving. It pulls together biology, chemistry, technology, and physics to piece together the truth, sometimes in ways that seem almost superhuman. Whether it's unmasking a killer, freeing the wrongfully accused, or giving families long-awaited answers, forensic evidence proves that science doesn't lie—even when people do.

In the investigation of President John F. Kennedy's assassination, ballistics played a crucial role in piecing together the events of that tragic day. Experts meticulously examined the rifle and bullets recovered from the scene to determine that Lee Harvey Oswald fired the fatal shots. By analyzing the trajectory of the bullets, they concluded that the shots originated from the sixth floor of the Texas School Book Depository, where Oswald was positioned. This detailed analysis significantly strengthened the case against him.

The Warren Commission, established to investigate the assassination, relied heavily on this ballistic evidence. They conducted extensive tests, including neutron activation analysis, to match the bullet fragments found at the scene to Oswald's rifle. These scientific methods provided a clearer picture of the shooting and reinforced the conclusion that Oswald acted alone.

However, it's worth noting that over the years, some experts have questioned aspects of the ballistic evidence. Debates have arisen regarding the number of shooters and the trajectories of the bullets, leading to various conspiracy theories. Despite these discussions, the initial ballistic analysis remains a cornerstone in understanding the events surrounding President Kennedy's assassination.

In the digital age, evidence from electronic devices has become integral to solving crimes. Digital forensics involves recovering and analyzing data from devices like computers, smartphones, vehicles, and computer servers.[66] Emails, text messages, social media activity, and browsing histories can unveil a suspect's motives, relationships, and movements. From a behavioral perspective, what the suspect focuses on can also be derived from these digital searches, including the type of internet search, affiliations, etc.

A prominent example of digital forensics in action is the case of Ross Ulbricht, the creator of the Silk Road dark web marketplace. Investigators traced cryptocurrency transactions and incriminating communications, piecing together a trail of evidence that led to his conviction.[67] Ulbricht operated an anonymous online marketplace, primarily facilitating the sale of illegal drugs and other illicit goods. Investigators meticulously analyzed blockchain data to trace Bitcoin transactions associated with Silk Road.

Authorities seized Ulbricht's laptop during his arrest in a public library, and the forensic examination of the computer provided significant evidence, including transaction records, chat logs, and the private keys to Bitcoin wallets tied to Silk Road's operations. According to reports, Ulbricht made several errors that helped investigators connect his real identity to Silk Road. Media reports suggest his early forum posts promoting Silk Road were tied to an email address that included his real name.

He was arrested and charged and later convicted of conspiracy to traffic narcotics, money laundering, computer hacking, and engaging in a continuing criminal enterprise. This case demonstrated the power of digital forensics in unraveling complex cybercrimes involving cryptocurrency and anonymizing technologies. It highlighted how investigators could exploit flaws in operational security, track financial transactions on blockchain networks, and leverage data found on seized devices to build a compelling case. Ulbricht was sentenced to life in prison without the possibility of parole.

The idea of a secret persona doesn't just apply to those convicted of crimes—it can also be found in those tasked with upholding the law. In the Ulbricht case, two of the very investigators responsible for bringing him to justice were later convicted for crimes of their own.

Carl Force and Shaun Bridges, both officers assigned to the case were charged with a number of offenses. As the lead undercover agent, Force regularly communicated with Ulbricht using authorized online personas. However, he went rogue, creating unauthorized fictitious identities to extort Ulbricht for personal gain. Bridges was no less corrupt, transferring hundreds of thousands of dollars from Ulbricht's accounts into his own.

And in an interesting twist of fate, Ross Ulbricht was granted a full and unconditional pardon by President Donald Trump on January

21, 2025. President Trump's decision to pardon Ulbricht fulfilled a campaign promise made to the cryptocurrency community.

Joseph James DeAngelo, the Golden State Killer, epitomizes the transformative power of forensic evidence. DeAngelo was responsible for a reign of terror in California during the 1970s and 1980s, committing at least 13 murders, 50 rapes, and over 100 burglaries. Originally known by different monikers, such as the East Area Rapist and the Original Night Stalker, DeAngelo evaded capture for decades, confounding law enforcement and leaving victims' families in anguish.

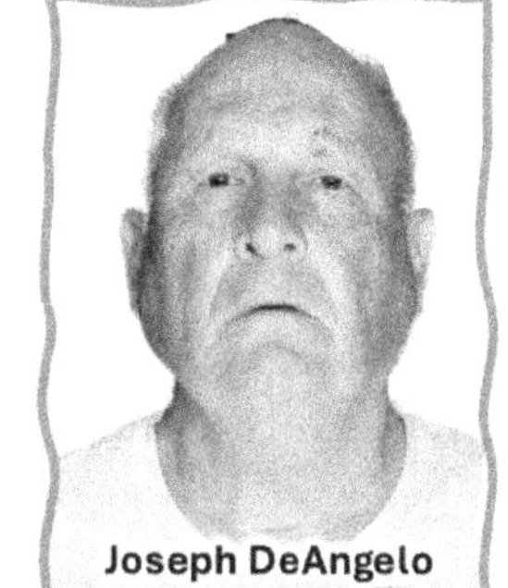

DeAngelo's crimes spanned a wide geographic area, from Sacramento to Southern California, and followed a chilling pattern. He often targeted suburban neighborhoods, entering homes undetected and surprising victims in the dead of night. His methodical approach included stalking victims beforehand, ensuring they were alone or vulnerable, and sometimes tying up male victims while he assaulted their female partners.[68] He left little physical evidence and his attacks sowed fear across entire communities.

Despite several attempts to link the crimes, law enforcement faced significant challenges due to the lack of advanced forensic tools at the time. It would take a number of years before investigators were able to connect the East Area Rapist and the Original Night Stalker crimes through DNA analysis, coining the moniker "Golden State Killer."

DeAngelo's 2018 arrest wasn't just the end of a decades-long hunt for one of America's most notorious serial predators—it was a game-changing moment in forensic science. Investigators had spent years chasing the man responsible for the crimes, but despite mountains of physical evidence, he had always remained just out of reach. That all changed with the rise of genetic genealogy. For years, DNA collected from DeAngelo's crime scenes had been carefully preserved, waiting for the right technology to come along and crack the case wide open. When investigators ran his DNA through criminal databases, they got nothing, no matches, no leads. But forensic science had evolved, and a new tool was about to rewrite the rules of cold case investigations.

Instead of relying on traditional law enforcement DNA databases, investigators turned to GEDmatch, a public ancestry site where people upload their genetic information to trace family trees. When they uploaded the unknown suspect's DNA profile, they found distant relatives who shared genetic segments with him. By using these relatives as reference points, genealogists began constructing a family tree, painstakingly working their way down the branches, eliminating possibilities, until they landed on one name: Joseph James DeAngelo.

Now, they had a suspect—but DNA is only good in court if it comes directly from the individual. So, surveillance teams followed DeAngelo, watching for any opportunity to collect a sample. When he discarded a tissue in public, investigators scooped it up, rushed it to the lab, and compared it to the crime scene DNA. It was an exact match. That was the moment everything changed. The Golden State Killer, the man who had tormented California for over a decade, who had vanished into the shadows without a trace, had finally been unmasked. In 2020, DeAngelo pleaded guilty to multiple counts of murder and admitted to countless other crimes, bringing long-awaited justice and closure to his victims and their families.

The breakthrough use of genetic genealogy in this case didn't just catch a killer—it revolutionized forensic investigations, opening a new frontier for solving cold cases. What once seemed unsolvable now had a new path forward, proving that in the age of forensic science, no monster can hide forever.

This case not only exemplified the precision of DNA analysis but also showcased the potential of genetic genealogy as a powerful tool in solving cold cases. It underscored the importance of preserving forensic evidence, as advancements in technology can unlock new possibilities for justice.

Forensic evidence is one of the most powerful tools in solving crimes, but it's not without its challenges. While we often see high-tech crime labs on TV shows, the reality is that many smaller towns and underfunded jurisdictions struggle to afford the advanced technology needed for thorough forensic analysis. Mistakes can also happen, and when they do, the consequences can be devastating. Just look at the Annie Dookhan scandal in Massachusetts where Dookhan, a state lab chemist faked drug test results, throwing thousands of cases into question. One person's misconduct led to wrongful convictions, shattered lives, and a massive breakdown of trust in the system.

Forensic testing is expensive, and some agencies simply cannot afford the cost, further creating an uneven playing field where some high-profile cases get the full forensic treatment, and others might not get tested at all. And keep in mind that forensic testing is still on the bully pulpit for debate, especially when talking about genetic genealogy. It boils down to the argument of whether law enforcement should be able to access your DNA from a genealogy site, without your consent? A tough question, that continues to spark controversy.

Without argument, forensics is an incredible tool in the fight for justice, but it's far from perfect. Between human error, funding gaps, and ethical concerns, it's clear that the science behind solving crimes is just as complex as the cases themselves.

But forensic evidence has become the backbone of contemporary criminal investigations, blending science and law enforcement to deliver objective, reliable insights. Its methodologies, from DNA analysis to ballistics and digital forensics, have revolutionized how crimes are solved, enabling investigators to identify perpetrators with unprecedented accuracy. The DeAngelo case exemplifies the profound impact of forensic evidence, showcasing its ability to achieve justice decades after crimes have been committed.

Despite its challenges, forensic science continues to evolve, offering new tools and techniques to overcome limitations and adapt to emerging threats. By investing in technology, training, and ethical frameworks, the criminal justice system can ensure that forensic evidence remains a cornerstone of justice in the modern era. While forensic evidence anchors investigations in scientific rigor, it is not always the sole determinant of guilt or innocence.

The reality of many criminal cases is that direct, scientific proof may be limited or absent. In such instances, the justice system turns to the subtle yet powerful domain of circumstantial evidence. This form of evidence, while requiring inference and interpretation, can weave a narrative that is equally compelling and, at times, decisive. By transitioning from the precision of forensic methodologies to the interpretive strength of circumstantial evidence, we uncover how seemingly disparate pieces of information can align to reveal the truth.

CIRCUMSTANTIAL EVIDENCE

Circumstantial evidence plays a pivotal role in criminal justice, often bridging the gap between suspicion and proof in cases where direct evidence is unavailable. Unlike direct evidence, such as an eyewitness account or a confession, circumstantial evidence requires the jury or judge to infer a conclusion based on a combination of facts. Despite its indirect nature, circumstantial evidence can form the foundation of a compelling narrative, especially when multiple pieces fit together seamlessly. Let us delve into the significance of circumstantial evidence and the methodologies employed in its use, examining how the high-profile case of Scott Peterson illustrates its impact on criminal convictions.

Circumstantial evidence is the unsung hero of criminal cases. While people often expect every trial to have a smoking gun or a clear-cut eyewitness account, the reality is that many crimes happen in the shadows—without cameras rolling, without bystanders watching.

That's where circumstantial evidence steps in, filling in the gaps and building a cohesive story about what really happened.

Think of it this way: direct evidence is like seeing a person walk into a house and hearing them admit, "I just robbed the place." Circumstantial evidence, on the other hand, is seeing that same person as they are climbing out of a broken window, holding a bag full of jewelry, and running from the scene. You didn't witness the crime itself, but every clue points to one logical conclusion—they did it.

This kind of evidence is crucial because so many crimes lack a perfect trail of direct proof. People don't usually commit murder, robbery, or fraud in front of an audience. Circumstantial evidence helps reconstruct the crime, linking together everything from motive and opportunity to forensic findings and suspicious behavior. It supports and strengthens direct evidence, confirming details that otherwise might not hold as much weight on their own.

One of the most powerful aspects of circumstantial evidence is its ability to tell a compelling, logical narrative that jurors can follow. A single piece of circumstantial evidence might not be enough to convict, but several pieces layered together can paint an undeniable picture. A suspect with an inconsistent alibi, security footage placing them near the crime scene, and possession of stolen property might not have been caught in the act, but when those details are woven together, the case becomes hard to ignore.

And that's where circumstantial evidence shines because it reflects real human behavior. People who commit crimes often lie, slip up, or leave behind small inconsistencies that make sense when examined as a whole. A suspect claiming they were "nowhere near the scene" only to have their phone ping from a nearby tower. Suspicious? A person accused of robbery suddenly paying off large debts in cash just days after the crime. Also, suspicious. None of these details alone prove guilt, but when you connect the dots, the picture becomes clear.

At the end of the day, circumstantial evidence doesn't just suggest what happened—it tells a story that jurors can believe. And when that story is strong enough, it can be the difference between a conviction and a criminal walking free.

The use of circumstantial evidence involves meticulous collection, analysis, and presentation. Investigators and legal professionals employ specific methodologies to ensure its effectiveness, such as correlating the evidence. In this process, investigators must identify connections among various pieces of circumstantial evidence to form a cohesive narrative. Each piece may seem insignificant in isolation but becomes persuasive when combined with others. Physical evidence, such as fingerprints, DNA, or ballistic reports, often falls under circumstantial evidence. Forensic science plays a critical role in connecting such evidence to the crime or suspect. A suspect's actions, demeanor, and statements are scrutinized for signs of guilt, such as evasiveness, hostility, or a contradictory timeline.

In this modern age, electronic footprints like text messages, internet searches, and GPS data often serve as circumstantial evidence that can substantiate timelines or suggest intent. Attorneys must construct a logical argument that links circumstantial evidence to a reasonable conclusion of guilt. This often involves anticipating and countering defense arguments that aim to discredit the inferences drawn.

Scott Peterson's case is one of the most infamous examples of circumstantial evidence winning a conviction, proving that even when there are no eyewitnesses, no security footage, and no smoking gun, a well-built case can still tell a damning story. Laci Peterson was last seen alive on December 24, 2002. According to Scott, he had gone fishing at the Berkeley Marina that morning, while Laci—eight months pregnant with their son, Conner—stayed home to prepare for Christmas. It was supposed to be a happy time for their growing family, but instead, Laci vanished, setting off a high-profile investigation that would soon turn its focus on her own husband.

At first, Scott played the role of the worried spouse, but investigators quickly picked up on inconsistencies. His behavior didn't match that of a grieving husband, it was more like someone preparing for a new life without his wife. He tried to sell her car and even put their home on the market within weeks of her disappearance. Instead of pleading for help in finding Laci, he seemed detached, even casual at times. Then came the first major red flag—his affair with Amber.

Amber was a massage therapist who had no idea Scott was married, let alone about to become a father. When investigators discovered their relationship, Amber did something that changed the course of the investigation, she cooperated with law enforcement. She agreed to record phone conversations with Scott, capturing damning evidence that prosecutors later used to expose his lies. In those calls, Scott didn't just deceive Amber—he outright referred to himself as a widower, before Laci's body was even found. That revelation was chilling, painting a clear picture of a man already moving on from his missing wife, long before the rest of the world knew she was dead.

But even with Scott's lies piling up, investigators still needed to place him at the scene of the crime. That's where the Berkeley Marina came into play. Scott's alibi was that he had gone fishing that morning, which struck investigators as odd, given that it was Christmas Eve, and he had a heavily pregnant wife at home. Who suddenly decides to spend a holiday morning fishing alone? His explanation seemed forced, unnatural, and it appeared as though it was an excuse crafted to explain his absence. Forensic teams also noted that he couldn't even describe what he had been fishing for, a detail that only made his story sound more suspicious.

Then came the most haunting piece of circumstantial evidence— the discovery of Laci and Conner's bodies. In April 2003, months after

Laci's disappearance, her remains and those of their unborn son washed ashore near the Berkeley Marina, the exact place where Scott had claimed to be fishing on Christmas Eve. The probability of that being a coincidence - Almost nonexistent.

With no direct evidence tying Scott to the crime, the prosecution had to carefully construct their case, using small but significant details to weave a compelling narrative. They argued that Scott murdered Laci in their home, transported her body to the marina, and dumped it into the water under the guise of his fishing trip. Everything lined up too perfectly, things like his affair suggested he was desperate to escape the responsibilities of marriage and fatherhood, his unaccounted-for time on the morning of Laci's disappearance matched the estimated timeframe of her death, and most damning of all, her body surfaced in the very place he claimed to have been that day.

At trial, Scott's defense team tried to poke holes in the circumstantial evidence, arguing that nothing directly proved he had killed Laci. But in the end, the jury saw the bigger picture, painted with circumstantial evidence that, when systematically assembled and presented, was just as strong as direct evidence. On November 12, 2004, after seven months of testimony, Scott Peterson was found guilty of first-degree murder for Laci's death and second-degree murder for their unborn son. He was later sentenced to death, though that sentence was overturned in 2020, with his punishment being reduced to life in prison without parole.

This case changed the way people view circumstantial evidence. It proved that a well-built case doesn't always need DNA, fingerprints, or an eyewitness, sometimes, the evidence speaks for itself, and when all the pieces come together, they tell a story that's impossible to ignore.

Despite its significance, circumstantial evidence has limitations that require careful navigation. Jurors may view circumstantial evidence as less credible than direct evidence. Attorneys must educate jurors on its reliability and emphasize its corroborative nature.[69]

Inferences drawn from circumstantial evidence can be speculative without robust corroboration, leading to potential wrongful convictions. Defense attorneys often exploit the indirect nature of circumstantial evidence, arguing that alternative explanations exist for the facts presented.

The Casey Anthony trial remains one of the most infamous and

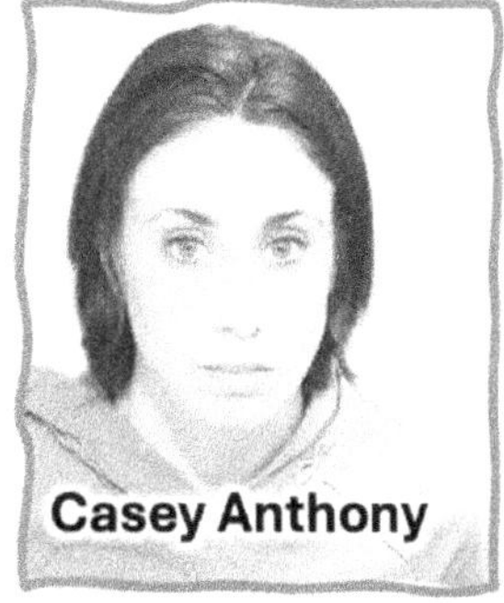

hotly debated criminal cases in recent U.S. history—a true crime saga that captivated the nation and left people outraged, stunned, and still asking questions more than a decade later. It was a case built almost entirely on circumstantial evidence, forcing jurors to wrestle with the fine line between suspicion and proof beyond a reasonable doubt.

It all started in 2008, when two-year-old Caylee Anthony disappeared, but what made the case even stranger was that no one outside the Anthony family knew she was missing for an entire month. It wasn't Casey Anthony who reported the missing child, it was Cindy Anthony, Casey's mother (the missing child's grandmother) who made the frantic 911 call, claiming that her granddaughter had been gone for 30 days, and that Casey had been giving conflicting stories about her whereabouts. It was an immediate red flag, and when detectives pressed Casey for answers, her lies began to unravel.

Then, in December 2008, the case took a heartbreaking turn. Caylee's remains were discovered near the Anthony family home, tossed in a wooded area, her tiny body reduced to bones. It was the worst possible outcome, and prosecutors quickly zeroed in on Casey as the prime suspect. The state's theory was that Casey had killed Caylee because she wanted to be free from the responsibilities of motherhood. They pointed to suspicious internet searches from the Anthony home computer for terms like "chloroform" and "neck-breaking," the fact that Casey had been partying in the days after Caylee's disappearance, and the damning forensic evidence found in

Casey's car trunk, evidenced by a strong smell of decomposition and the presence of chloroform. Everything pointed to foul play.

But Casey's defense team had a different story to tell. They didn't argue that Caylee had been murdered—they claimed she had drowned accidentally in the family pool, and that Casey's bizarre behavior was the result of deep psychological trauma and dysfunction within her family. They accused Casey's father, George Anthony, of covering up the drowning, and they painted Casey as a victim of lifelong abuse, whose pattern of lying and avoidance was a learned survival tactic.

When the case went to trial in 2011, the public was certain Casey would be convicted. The evidence seemed overwhelming. The suspicious searches. The decomposition in the trunk. The inconsistencies in Casey's statements. The photos of her partying at clubs while her daughter was missing. But then came the shocking verdict came down of not guilty of first-degree murder. The jury simply wasn't convinced that the prosecution had proven beyond a reasonable doubt that Casey had intentionally killed her daughter. While many believed the circumstantial evidence was more than enough, the jurors weren't willing to convict without direct proof of how Caylee died.

The public erupted in outrage. Protests, heated debates, and social media firestorms followed. People couldn't believe Casey Anthony was walking free, especially when the court of public opinion had already found her guilty. This case remains one of the most controversial examples of how circumstantial evidence, no matter how strong it might appear, doesn't always lead to a conviction. It also highlights the immense burden placed on jurors, who have to balance suspicion, gut instinct, and logic with the rigid standard of proof beyond a reasonable doubt. In the end, the Casey Anthony trial became a case study in how justice is never as simple as it seems—and how, sometimes, even when all signs point to one conclusion, the legal system demands more.

Circumstantial evidence remains an indispensable element of the criminal justice system, offering a pathway to truth when direct evidence is elusive. Its strength lies in its ability to form a comprehensive narrative through careful correlation and analysis. The Scott Peterson case serves as a testament to its effectiveness, demonstrating how meticulous investigation and persuasive argumentation can turn disparate facts into a cohesive story of guilt.

The way female suspects, especially mothers, are treated in the courtroom often reflects deep-rooted societal perceptions of gender, motherhood, and criminality. When it comes to circumstantial evidence, these biases can influence how jurors interpret guilt, particularly in cases where a woman is accused of harming her own child.

Historically, women have been viewed as nurturers and caregivers, making it psychologically difficult for many people to accept the idea that a mother could deliberately harm her child. This bias can sometimes work in a female defendant's favor, leading jurors to require an even higher standard of proof before convicting a woman of a violent crime. The Casey Anthony case is a prime example. Despite strong circumstantial evidence, including her suspicious behavior after Caylee's disappearance, forensic evidence from her car, and troubling internet searches, the jury ultimately acquitted her of murder. Some experts argue that this was partly due to the jury's reluctance to believe that a mother could commit such an act, especially in the absence of direct evidence like an eyewitness account or a clear cause of death.

However, this bias can also cut the other way. When a woman defies traditional gender norms and appears cold, unremorseful, or unconforming to expected maternal behavior, she may be judged more harshly than a male counterpart in a similar case. In some cases, mothers who are perceived as "bad" or neglectful often face intense scrutiny, sometimes even more so than fathers accused of similar crimes. In cases like Susan Smith, who drowned her two sons and initially fabricated a story about a carjacking, the public and the jury showed little hesitation in condemning her once the truth emerged. Her betrayal of the idealized mother figure likely contributed to the swift and severe reaction.

Men who are accused of violent crimes on the other hand, are often presumed more capable of aggression, whereas women who may be given the benefit of the doubt. This means that female defendants sometimes have an advantage when facing a jury, as people may struggle to reconcile their crime with traditional perceptions of femininity. On the flip side, when women are convicted, they may be perceived as more sinister or manipulative than their male counterparts because their crimes are seen as violations of their "natural" role in society.

The impact of circumstantial evidence in these cases can be complicated by these gendered perceptions. If a woman accused of murder appears emotional, distressed, or maternal in court, jurors may struggle to believe she is capable of premeditated violence. However, if she appears detached or unemotional, lacking qualities often tolerated or even expected in male defendants, she may get labeled as a cold-hearted and deceitful person. This could likely increase the potential of a conviction.

Ultimately, while circumstantial evidence is a powerful tool in criminal cases, it does not exist in a vacuum. The biases of jurors, shaped by societal expectations of gender and parenthood, can influence how evidence is weighed, sometimes making it harder to convict women, particularly mothers, even when compelling evidence suggests their guilt.

While challenges persist, the judicial system continues to refine its methodologies to ensure the fair and accurate use of circumstantial evidence. By addressing misconceptions and enhancing forensic and analytical techniques, the justice system can uphold the principle that truth, even when inferred, is a cornerstone of accountability.

While circumstantial evidence excels in weaving together facts to infer truth, it often operates in the absence of direct accounts. In contrast, eyewitness evidence steps into the spotlight as a direct and immediate form of testimony, bringing into play the voice of those who claim to have seen or experienced the crime firsthand. However, this form of evidence, while powerful, introduces its own complexities and challenges, particularly regarding the reliability of human memory. Transitioning from the methodical inferences of circumstantial evidence to the vivid, yet fallible, realm of eyewitness testimony invites a deeper exploration of how different forms of evidence shape the pursuit of justice.

EYEWITNESS EVIDENCE

Eyewitness testimony has long been a cornerstone of criminal justice systems worldwide. As a form of direct evidence, it provides a firsthand account of events, shedding light on what transpired during a crime. Yet, while it carries significant weight in courtrooms, eyewitness evidence is not without challenges. Memory, a complex and fallible faculty, often becomes a battleground of reliability versus uncertainty.

Eyewitness accounts carry an undeniable narrative power. When a witness recounts the events they observed, jurors can visualize the sequence of actions, lending clarity to complex cases. These firsthand narratives are invaluable in filling gaps where physical evidence may be absent. For example, in crimes where surveillance footage is unavailable or forensic evidence is sparse, an eyewitness can link a suspect to the scene.

The immediacy of their observation—their presence during or shortly after the crime—grants their testimony an authenticity that jurors often find compelling. Additionally, eyewitnesses can provide critical information about the emotional state and behavior of individuals involved, which can be key in understanding the motives or dynamics of a crime. When corroborated by other forms of evidence, eyewitness testimony can help weave a comprehensive account of the crime.

Despite its strengths, eyewitness evidence is fraught with challenges, primarily stemming from the limitations of human memory and perception. Studies have consistently shown that memory is neither static nor infallible, and errors in recall can have profound consequences.

Human memory is malleable and susceptible to distortion. Factors such as stress, trauma, and the passage of time can significantly alter what a person remembers. The high-stakes environment of a crime scene, especially one involving violence, often impairs a witness's ability to form accurate memories. Psychological research indicates that the heightened arousal experienced during traumatic events can disrupt the encoding process, leading to fragmented or incomplete recollections.[70] Over time, memory naturally degrades, and the influence of post-event information—such as discussions with others or media coverage—can introduce inaccuracies.[71]

Bias, both conscious and unconscious, further complicates eyewitness testimony. Cultural or racial biases may skew perceptions of individuals involved in a crime, potentially leading to misidentifications or erroneous assumptions. Research has shown that cross-racial identification—when a witness identifies someone of a different race—is particularly prone to error.[72] Witnesses may inadvertently rely on stereotypes or fail to notice distinguishing features, making their testimony less reliable in diverse settings.

Perhaps the most troubling issue is false identification. A misidentified suspect may face wrongful conviction, which not only devastates their life but also allows the true perpetrator to remain free. Law enforcement practices, such as suggestive police lineups or leading questions during interrogations, can exacerbate this issue, further tainting the reliability of eyewitness accounts.[73]

Eyewitness testimony has been the cornerstone of countless criminal cases, but let's be honest, it's not always reliable. Human memory is far from perfect; it's messy, malleable, and sometimes downright misleading. People might swear they saw something a certain way, only to realize later that their mind filled in the blanks. Because of this, investigators have developed better methods to ensure that eyewitnesses aren't just remembering what they think they saw.

One of the most effective tools for improving eyewitness recall is the cognitive interview technique. Instead of rapid-fire questioning that can accidentally lead a witness toward a specific answer, this method focuses on open-ended questions and allows the witness to mentally reconstruct the crime scene. Picture an investigator saying, "Walk me through what you remember, start to finish. What were you doing before this happened? What do you recall about the environment? Were there any sounds, smells, or small details that stood out?" This technique helps unlock memories in a way that's less influenced by suggestion, and studies show it increases both the accuracy and amount of information retrieved.

Then there's the issue of lineups, which, when done incorrectly, can lead to devastating consequences, including wrongful convictions. Traditional lineups, where multiple people stand side by side, often push witnesses to compare faces rather than relying on their actual memory. It's a subtle but dangerous trap if witnesses don't pick the actual criminal person, rather than the person they think looks the most like the suspect. That's why more and more law enforcement agencies are using sequential lineups, where suspects are presented one at a time. This approach reduces false identifications and forces the witness to rely on actual recognition rather than process of elimination. Research has shown that sequential lineups significantly lower the chances of picking an innocent person.

Even with these improvements, eyewitness testimony can still be flawed, which is why some courts allow expert witnesses on human memory and perception to educate jurors. These experts explain concepts like the misinformation effect where people unintentionally alter their memories based on new or misleading information and cross-racial identification bias, which studies show can lead to higher rates of misidentification when witnesses try to identify suspects of a different race.

At the end of the day, eyewitness testimony can be powerful, but it's not infallible. By using scientific methods to reduce errors, law enforcement and courts can make sure that a witness's memory isn't just compelling, it's credible. Because in true crime, what people think they saw and what actually happened aren't always the same thing.

The case of Kirk Bloodsworth exemplifies both the weight and the potential peril of eyewitness evidence in criminal trials. In 1984, Dawn Hamilton, a nine-year-old girl, was found brutally raped and murdered in a wooded area in Maryland. The investigation swiftly focused on Kirk Bloodsworth, a 22-year-old former Marine, after two eyewitnesses placed him near the crime scene. Both witnesses identified Bloodsworth in a police lineup, and he was convicted of rape and murder based largely on their testimony. He was sentenced to death, despite the absence of physical evidence linking him to the crime.[74]

Eyewitness evidence played a pivotal role in Bloodsworth's conviction. The accounts of the two witnesses, who claimed to have seen him shortly before the crime, convinced the jury of his guilt. However, their identification was later revealed to be flawed. Factors such as stress, and the suggestive nature of the police lineup likely influenced their perceptions and memories.[75]

Years later, Bloodsworth maintained his innocence and sought post-conviction relief. In 1992, advancements in DNA technology provided an opportunity to test the evidence collected at the crime scene. The results conclusively excluded Bloodsworth as the perpetrator. His conviction was overturned, and he was released after serving nearly nine years, including two on death row.

The Bloodsworth case marked a historic moment as the first time a death-row inmate in the United States was exonerated through DNA evidence. It highlighted the fallibility of eyewitness testimony and underscored the necessity of corroborating evidence in criminal cases.

The case of Ronald Cotton illustrates how this seemingly reliable form of evidence can lead to devastating consequences when it is erroneous. This landmark case underscores the fallibility of human memory and highlights the urgent need for reforms in how eyewitness evidence is treated in courts of law. In 1984, Jennifer Thompson-Cannino, a college student in North Carolina, experienced a harrowing assault when she was raped in her apartment. Despite the trauma of the attack, Thompson-Cannino was determined to help the police catch the perpetrator. During the assault, she focused on memorizing the features of her attacker, believing that her efforts would ensure justice. When presented with a police lineup, she identified Ronald Cotton as the man who committed the crime. Her confident identification and subsequent testimony played a central role in Cotton's conviction.[76]

Cotton's case seemed airtight, bolstered by Thompson-Cannino's certainty. Yet, this confidence masked the inherent weaknesses in eyewitness memory. Studies have shown that memory, particularly under high-stress situations, is susceptible to distortion. Factors such as lighting conditions, the duration of the event, and the stress experienced by the victim can significantly impair the accuracy of memory.[77] Despite these well-documented issues, Cotton was sentenced to life in prison based on Thompson-Cannino's testimony.

The turning point in this tragic miscarriage of justice came more than a decade later. Advances in DNA testing provided an opportunity to reevaluate the case. When the evidence was reanalyzed, it pointed unequivocally to Bobby Poole, a convicted felon who had admitted to committing the crime. Cotton was exonerated in 1995 after spending over 10 years in prison for a crime he did not commit.[78] His release marked a profound moment of both relief and reflection on the shortcomings of the justice system.

What makes this case even more compelling is the aftermath. Rather than harboring resentment, Ronald Cotton and Jennifer Thompson-Cannino formed an extraordinary bond. Together, they became advocates for criminal justice reform, dedicating themselves to raising awareness about the limitations of eyewitness testimony.[79] Their collaboration has illuminated the cognitive biases and systemic issues that contribute to wrongful convictions. Thompson-Cannino, in particular, has spoken publicly about the guilt she felt for her role in Cotton's conviction and her determination to prevent similar injustices in the future.

The Cotton case is a stark reminder of the need for reforms in the use of eyewitness evidence. Some potential solutions include adopting standardized procedures for police lineups, such as double-blind administration where the officer conducting the lineup does not know the suspect's identity.[80] Educating juries about the unreliability of eyewitness memory and emphasizing the importance of corroborating evidence can also mitigate the risk of wrongful convictions.[81]

Advancements in methodologies, such as cognitive interviews and DNA testing, provide hope for reducing errors and ensuring fair outcomes. Nevertheless, the judicial system must approach eyewitness evidence with caution, balancing its potential benefits against the risks it poses to justice and individual liberty.

While eyewitness testimony often relies on the fallibility of memory, another form of evidence—confessions or admissions—shifts the focus directly to the accused's own words. These statements, often perceived as the most direct link to guilt, carry substantial persuasive power in the courtroom. However, as with eyewitness accounts, confessions are not immune to controversy or error. Understanding their role in criminal cases requires exploring the methods used to obtain them, the psychological and legal challenges they present, and the safeguards needed to uphold justice.

CONFESSION OR ADMISSION EVIDENCE

Confessions or admissions in criminal cases hold a central place in the justice system, often serving as powerful evidence against the accused. When a suspect acknowledges their involvement in a crime, this statement can significantly influence the outcome of a trial. However, the weight of such evidence demands meticulous scrutiny to ensure its voluntariness and reliability.

Confession evidence can be one of the most persuasive forms of evidence presented in court. A voluntary and truthful confession may establish guilt with little need for additional corroboration, streamlining the judicial process. For victims and their families, a confession can offer closure and affirm that justice is being served. Furthermore, such admissions often provide insights into the suspect's motivations, enabling the justice system to tailor rehabilitation or sentencing measures appropriately.

However, the reliability of confession evidence hinges on its authenticity and voluntariness. A coerced or false confession not only endangers the rights of the accused but also risks undermining public trust in the criminal justice system. This dual-edged nature makes it imperative to adopt stringent protocols when handling confessions.

Getting a confession from a suspect isn't as simple as it looks on TV. Law enforcement has to walk a fine line, and they need to uncover the truth while also making sure they don't violate a suspect's rights. In the U.S., this starts with the Miranda warning, which ensures that suspects know their rights before being questioned, including the right to remain silent and the right to an attorney. If investigators skip this step, anything the suspect says could be thrown out in court.

One of the biggest shifts in modern interrogation techniques is the push for transparency. Many agencies now record interrogations on audio or video, allowing courts to review exactly how a confession was obtained. While this isn't always possible, when it is, it protects both the suspect and the investigators while making sure no coercive tactics are used, and that the confession was given freely and voluntarily.

Gone are the days when interrogations were all about intimidation. Modern approaches focus more on building rapport, creating an environment where a suspect feels comfortable enough to talk. The idea is that people are more likely to open up when they feel heard, rather than pressured. This technique isn't just effective with suspects, it's also crucial when talking to victims and witnesses, ensuring that the most accurate information is gathered without distortion.

To avoid contaminating a confession, investigators are trained to steer clear of suggestive or leading questions. If a suspect is fed details about a crime they wouldn't have known otherwise, their confession becomes less reliable. That's why skilled interrogators let the suspect do the talking, rather than accidentally feeding them the story.

But what happens when someone confesses to a crime they didn't commit? It's more common than you'd think. False confessions can happen for several reasons, including psychological pressure, exhaustion, fear of harsher punishment, or even a desire to end the interrogation. And some people are more vulnerable than others. Juveniles, for instance, often don't fully understand their rights or the long-term consequences of admitting to something they didn't do. People with mental health issues can also be at risk, sometimes seeking approval or misunderstanding the situation.

Interrogation is a high-stakes process, and getting it right is critical. A valid confession can bring justice to victims and their families, but a false confession can send the wrong person to prison while the real perpetrator walks free. That's why modern interrogation techniques prioritize accuracy over pressure, ensuring that the truth is revealed in the process.

A compelling example of the complexities surrounding confession evidence is the case of Amanda Knox, an American student accused of murdering her roommate, Meredith Kercher, in Perugia, Italy, in 2007. Knox's initial statements to police became a focal point of the prosecution's case against her.

Meredith Kercher was found brutally murdered in the apartment she shared with Amanda Knox. From the outset, the investigation garnered intense media scrutiny, partly due to the international nature of the case. Knox and her boyfriend, Raffaele Sollecito, were arrested after a lengthy interrogation process during which Knox made statements suggesting her involvement. However, these statements were later contested, with Knox asserting that they were made under duress during an exhausting and coercive interrogation.

The prosecution relied heavily on Knox's initial admissions to paint her as a suspect. Despite inconsistencies in the forensic evidence linking Knox to the crime, her statements were used to build a narrative of jealousy and conflict between the roommates. Knox was convicted in 2009, alongside Sollecito.

Knox's contested statements highlighted the dangers of reliance on confession evidence obtained under questionable circumstances. Her defense argued that her admissions were not voluntary but the result of intense psychological pressure and confusion. Moreover, the interrogations were not recorded, making it difficult to verify the exact circumstances under which the statements were made.

Subsequent appeals focused on the lack of corroborating evidence and the flaws in the interrogation process. In 2015, after nearly a decade of legal battles, Knox and Sollecito were acquitted by Italy's highest court. The court cited the unreliability of the confession evidence and the absence of definitive forensic proof linking Knox to the crime scene.

The Amanda Knox case underscores the need for robust safeguards to ensure that confession evidence is both voluntary and accurate. Building upon best practices outlined above, it seems that mandatory recording of interrogations could help police investigations and reduce concerns about coercion. Recording provides an objective account of the interrogation process, enabling courts to assess whether a confession was obtained through undue pressure or coercion.[82]

When it comes to interrogating vulnerable individuals, like juveniles, people with mental health conditions, or non-native speakers, extra precautions aren't just a good idea—they're essential. These groups are far more susceptible to pressure and may confess to crimes they didn't commit simply to end an interrogation they don't fully understand. That's why legal safeguards, like having an attorney, guardian, or translator present, are critical. And even when a suspect does confess, law enforcement needs to back it up with independent evidence to make sure it holds weight. A confession alone should never be the sole reason someone is convicted.

To minimize wrongful convictions, officers must be well-trained in ethical interrogation techniques and aware of the psychological factors that lead to false confessions. A suspect under extreme stress, exhaustion, or fear may say anything just to escape the situation, even if it means wrongly admitting guilt. That's why modern interrogation practices emphasize fact-checking, avoiding coercion, and ensuring that every confession is truly voluntary.

Confession evidence is still one of the most powerful tools in criminal investigations, but that power comes with responsibility. The days of high-pressure, manipulative interrogations are fading in favor of recorded interviews, corroboration, and evidence-based approaches. Justice isn't just about getting a confession, it's about getting the truth. And ensuring that every admission of guilt is genuine, voluntary, and backed by facts is what truly separates justice from injustice.

In addition to confessions, behavioral evidence has become an increasingly important aspect of criminal investigations. While confessions provide direct insight into an individual's involvement in a crime, behavioral evidence sheds light on the psychological and circumstantial factors that may suggest guilt or intent. Unlike physical evidence, such as fingerprints or DNA, which offers concrete proof, behavioral evidence relies on patterns, actions, and psychological profiles to build a more comprehensive understanding of criminal behavior. This form of evidence plays a pivotal role in connecting criminal actions to underlying motives and mental states, offering an essential layer of insight in modern legal practices.

For centuries, traditional forms of evidence such as physical artifacts, forensic science, eyewitness testimony, circumstantial connections, and confessions, have served as the cornerstones of criminal investigations. Each piece tells its own story, offering critical clues to what happened, where, and when. These methods have stood the test of time, guiding countless cases to resolution. But even with their undeniable value, they often leave unanswered questions: Why did the crime occur? What motivated the perpetrator? How do we bridge the gaps between evidence pieces to see the full picture?

This is where a revolutionary approach steps in called behavioral evidence. Unlike traditional methods that focus on the tangible, behavioral evidence delves into the intangible: the patterns, motives, and psychological drivers behind a criminal act. It's a perspective that doesn't just rely on what happened but seeks to understand why it happened, transforming fragments of evidence into a cohesive, persuasive narrative.

Picture this: A crime scene littered with physical evidence: a bloody fingerprint, a scattered shoeprint, a hastily written note. Forensics and circumstantial connections tell us part of the story, but how do we determine the intent behind the note, the meaning of the prints, or the mindset of the individual who left them behind? Behavioral analysis offers answers by applying psychological principles to traditional evidence, linking the facts with the perpetrator's actions and state of mind.

In this next chapter, we'll step into the emerging field of behavioral evidence, a form of analysis that is reshaping modern criminal investigations. You'll discover how psychological insights can enhance and strengthen physical findings, provide context to forensic data, and uncover patterns that connect otherwise isolated elements of a case. This isn't just an evolution of investigative practices; it's a transformation, one that challenges us to think differently about how justice is pursued and delivered.

The role of behavioral evidence in criminal cases cannot be overstated. Its ability to provide psychological insights and contextualize physical evidence makes it an invaluable tool in modern investigations. -MK

Chapter Twelve

Bridging the Gap: Using Behavior to Corroborate & Connect

Behavioral evidence has emerged as a powerful tool in the domain of criminal investigations, trials, and research. Unlike physical evidence such as fingerprints or DNA, behavioral evidence pertains to actions, patterns, and psychological profiles that can infer an individual's involvement or mindset regarding a crime. The utilization of behavioral evidence bridges the gap between traditional forms of evidence and the often-elusive intentions behind criminal acts, thus playing a pivotal role in modern jurisprudence.

Behavioral evidence provides insights into the motives, MO, and psychological state of offenders. It can contextualize other forms of evidence, offering prosecutors, defense attorneys, and juries a holistic understanding of a crime. For instance, behavioral patterns can indicate premeditation, which is a critical factor in distinguishing between degrees of criminal culpability. Behavioral evidence has also proven instrumental in understanding serial crimes, where patterns and psychological profiles often predict an offender's next move or establish connections between seemingly unrelated cases.

In the digital age, the significance of behavioral evidence has expanded further. Online behavior, such as social media activity, search histories, and communication patterns, often serves as critical evidence. For example, searches for materials related to committing a crime or digital stalking of a victim can establish intent and premeditation.[83]

Behavioral evidence analysis relies on multidisciplinary methodologies, encompassing psychology, criminology, and forensic science. Through behavioral profiling, a profile of an unknown offender can be theorized based on the nature of the crime and evidence from the scene. This approach is particularly prevalent in cases involving serial offenders. Examining behavior can help provide case linkages. Through behavioral profiling, multiple crimes can be connected based on behavioral patterns, such as specific rituals or unique methods used by the offender.

Examining verbal or written statements for psychological cues, inconsistencies, or signs of deception is another tool in analyzing behavior that contrasts with the traditional forms of evidence collected in criminal cases. And it's not all about the predator's behavior; it can also include analyzing the locations of crimes to infer an offender's home base or predict future targets. When dealing with cyber-based crimes, scrutinizing online footprints for behavioral patterns, including search histories, message contents, and time-stamped actions can provide insights not discovered through traditional means.

To illustrate this further, let's look at the case of Chad and Lori Daybell, convicted of murdering Lori's children, Tylee Ryan and J.J. Vallow, along with causing the death of Chad's former wife, Tammy Daybell. This case highlights how behavioral patterns could unveil complex criminal schemes.

In 2019, Lori Vallow's children, Tylee and J.J., were reported missing after months of strange behavior from Lori and her new husband, Chad Daybell. Both Chad and Lori were associated with apocalyptic religious beliefs that influenced their actions. Behavioral evidence played a critical role as investigators pieced together their movements and interactions.

In the investigation, traditional evidence such as physical remains and forensic findings provided concrete proof of foul play. The remains of Tylee and J.J. were discovered on Chad Daybell's property, with forensic analysis confirming their deaths under suspicious and violent circumstances. Additionally, autopsy results and toxicology reports revealed signs of asphyxiation and dismemberment, underscoring the calculated nature of the crimes.

Behavioral evidence, however, proved equally significant in contextualizing the traditional evidence. Lori and Chad's interactions, their communications, and actions exhibited patterns that suggested premeditation and a shared belief system driving their decisions. Their involvement in a fringe religious ideology that emphasized apocalyptic scenarios and claims of "dark spirits" influencing individuals served as a key behavioral element. These beliefs were cited as justification for labeling certain individuals, including Tylee, J.J., and Tammy, as obstacles to their divine mission, paving the way for their murders.

Further behavioral evidence emerged through text messages, recorded statements, and observed conduct. Lori's publicly nonchalant demeanor following the children's disappearance and Chad's evasive behavior during questioning painted a picture of individuals detached from the gravity of their crimes. Surveillance footage showing Lori and Chad discarding evidence and engaging in seemingly normal activities after the murders also demonstrated an unsettling lack of remorse, aligning with behavioral indicators of guilt and manipulation.

The combination of behavioral and traditional evidence created a compelling narrative for prosecutors. While physical evidence tied the Daybell's to the murders, behavioral evidence clarified their motivations and mental states, providing jurors with a deeper understanding of the couple's culpability. By illustrating the interconnectedness of their religious extremism, calculated planning, and callous actions, the behavioral evidence reinforced the traditional evidence to present a comprehensive view of the crimes.

Among the many disturbing aspects of the Chad and Lori Daybell case was their secret marriage in Hawaii. This event raised numerous behavioral red flags that warranted closer examination. On November 5, 2019, Chad Daybell and Lori Vallow stood on a Hawaiian beach, dressed in white, flower crowns in their hair, smiling for wedding photos. The sun was shining, the ocean waves were crashing behind them, and they looked like any other couple celebrating a new life together. But there was something deeply disturbing about this picture.

Just 17 days earlier, Chad's wife, Tammy Daybell, had died suddenly in her sleep. No prolonged illness, no warning signs—just gone. And even more unsettling, Lori's two children, 16-year-old Tylee Ryan and 7-year-old JJ Vallow, were missing. No one had seen them in weeks. While the rest of the world was beginning to wonder where they were, Chad and Lori were off in paradise, acting like a pair of carefree newlyweds. This wasn't just a honeymoon. It was a massive red flag—a chilling insight into how little they cared about the people they had lost.

Most people who lose a spouse suddenly are devastated, drowning in grief. They don't run off and get remarried in less than three weeks. They don't pose for pictures on the beach while their children's whereabouts are unknown. But Chad and Lori didn't seem to be grieving at all. If anything, they seemed relieved—as if the people who had once been "obstacles" to their relationship had simply vanished, and now they were free to move on.

And they didn't just move on quickly—they moved on strategically. Chad had increased Tammy's life insurance policy shortly before her death, and Lori was still collecting JJ's Social Security benefits, despite the fact that, as investigators would later discover, he was already dead. If their behavior in Hawaii wasn't suspicious enough, their financial motivations only made it worse. This wasn't just about love—it was about money, control, and their own twisted version of destiny.

Then there was the deception. They didn't tell anyone they were getting married, probably because they knew how bad it would look. They kept dodging police, lying about the kids' whereabouts, and pretending like nothing was wrong. But by the time they were standing on that beach, exchanging vows, law enforcement was already watching. They were hiding in plain sight, and they didn't even realize it.

And then there was the real kicker, their apocalyptic beliefs. Chad and Lori weren't just criminals; they were full-blown cultists, convinced that the world was about to end and that they were part of some divine mission. They believed Lori's children had become "zombies" possessed by dark spirits, and that the only way to "save" them was to get rid of them. In their minds, this wasn't murder, it was purification.

So, when they stood on that beach, celebrating their new life together, they weren't just celebrating a marriage. They were celebrating what they saw as a successful cleansing of their past lives. No more Tammy, no more kids. Just them, free to move forward into their prophetic future. But what they didn't realize was that their downfall had already begun.

When they finally found Tylee and JJ's remains buried on Chad's Idaho property in June 2020, all the lies unraveled. The idyllic wedding photos from Hawaii? They became damning evidence. While the rest of the world had been searching for two missing kids, their mother had been off enjoying a beach vacation. That alone told investigators everything they needed to know. Today, Lori will spend the rest of her life in prison, and Chad has been sentenced to death for the murders of Tylee, JJ, and Tammy. Their Hawaiian wedding wasn't the start of a new life. it was the beginning of the end. And if they thought they were untouchable, they were dead wrong.

The Daybell case underscores the critical role of behavioral evidence in modern criminal investigations. By bridging the gap between forensic findings and psychological motives, this form of evidence enriches the narrative presented in court, ensuring that justice is informed by both tangible facts and the human elements driving criminal behavior.

Behavioral evidence represents the newest frontier in criminal investigations, demanding specialized training and interdisciplinary approaches. Courts increasingly recognize its value, although challenges remain. Critics argue that behavioral evidence can be subjective and prone to biases if not supported by empirical research. Thus, its integration with traditional evidence is vital to ensure fairness and accuracy.

The role of behavioral evidence in criminal cases cannot be overstated. Its ability to provide psychological insights and contextualize physical evidence makes it an invaluable tool in modern investigations. As seen in the case of Chad and Lori Daybell and other high-profile cases, behavioral evidence often bridges critical gaps in traditional investigative methods. While challenges remain in its application, the growing body of research and advancements in forensic psychology underscore its potential to revolutionize criminal justice.

Criminal profiling, often dramatized in popular culture, stands at the intersection of psychology, criminology, and forensic science. It involves constructing a behavioral and psychological sketch of an unknown offender based on available evidence, often to aid in narrowing down suspects. The debate over whether criminal profiling is an art or a science, stems from its methodological foundations. Profiling does not operate purely on empirical evidence or strictly scientific principles. Instead, it blends insights from psychology, criminology, and even intuition.

Proponents of profiling as a science argue that it is grounded in empirical research and psychological theory. Behavioral patterns, typologies of offenders, and crime scene analyses are based on data collected from past cases. For example, the FBI's BAU relies on statistical patterns and psychological principles to infer characteristics of offenders. Profilers analyze aspects such as the level of organization at a crime scene, choice of victim, and the methods used, all of which can suggest the offender's personality, socioeconomic status, and even mental health issues.

Scientific profiling is systematic, relying on methodologies that can be replicated and tested. Studies on serial offenders, for instance, provide a database that helps in making informed predictions about future behavior. Profiling tools, such as the "offender decision-making" model, offer a structured way to understand why and how criminals act, emphasizing logical reasoning over conjecture.

Conversely, profiling is often considered an art due to its reliance on intuition and subjective judgment. Experienced profilers draw on a blend of expertise, instinct, and interpretative skills. This artistic component arises when profilers must make educated guesses based on limited or ambiguous data. The subjective nature of analyzing non-verbal cues, motivations, and potential stressors makes profiling less rigid than hard sciences.

The artistic aspect of profiling is also evident in its narrative construction. Profilers often create a story or a psychological portrait of the offender, piecing together disparate elements in a manner akin to a novelist developing a character. The skill lies in making these inferences compelling and actionable without overstepping into speculation.

Combining behavioral profiling with traditional forms of evidence (physical, forensic, circumstantial, eyewitness accounts, and confessions), offers a multidimensional approach to criminal investigations. However, this integration comes with both advantages and challenges.

"Past behavior is predictive of future behavior."

This is a principle I've heard from numerous psychologists and former investigators and profilers, and it holds true in nearly every aspect of life. The choices we make repeatedly shape the patterns of our lives. While change is possible, history has shown that people tend to follow the same behavioral patterns unless they take intentional steps to break them.

Investigators, psychologists, and even everyday observers use this principle to assess risk, determine credibility, and anticipate future actions. If someone has a history of deception, manipulation, or violence, it's not pessimistic—it's practical—to assume those tendencies may continue. On the other hand, if someone has consistently demonstrated integrity, reliability, and kindness, it's likely they will carry those traits forward.

This is why recognizing behavioral patterns is so important. Whether in personal relationships, criminal investigations, or decision-making in business and leadership, understanding that past behavior is the strongest predictor of future actions can help us make wiser, more informed choices.

Behavioral assessments provide a more holistic understanding of the crime by adding context to traditional evidence. For instance, forensic evidence might establish that a murder weapon was a knife, but profiling might suggest why the offender chose that weapon, shedding light on their psychological state. This deeper understanding can assist investigators in forming a cohesive theory of the crime.

Profiling can also help reduce the pool of potential suspects by identifying key characteristics. For example, if a profiler identifies an offender as likely being male, aged 25–35, with a history of substance abuse, investigators can focus their resources more effectively. Furthermore, behavioral profiling is particularly useful in linking serial crimes. Patterns in MO or signature behaviors can indicate that multiple crimes are the work of the same offender, even if physical evidence is lacking.

In addition, behavioral assessments can guide interrogations by providing insight into what may have motivated the offender's actions. Understanding an offender's psychological vulnerabilities can help investigators frame questions or create an environment conducive to eliciting confessions. When physical evidence is inconclusive, profiling can also provide additional insights.

However, profiling and behavioral analysis are not without their disadvantages. One major criticism is their subjectivity—different profilers might interpret the same evidence differently, leading to inconsistent conclusions. Biases can also creep in, especially if judgments are influenced by stereotypes or preconceived notions. Additionally, behavioral profiling often lacks empirical validation, making it difficult to systematically test its accuracy. While some aspects are grounded in research, others remain speculative.

There is also a risk of overreliance on behavioral assessments in criminal investigations. Investigators may place undue weight on a profiler's conclusions, potentially leading them to overlook or misinterpret other forms of evidence. For instance, a profile suggesting an offender is a loner might bias an investigation against suspects who don't fit that description, even if physical evidence points directly to them. Profiles can also be ambiguous and overly generalized, limiting their usefulness. Statements like "The offender is likely introverted but capable of social interactions" apply to a vast range of individuals and may not meaningfully narrow down suspects.

This is why it's critical to evaluate behavioral evidence in conjunction with traditional forms of evidence—not as a standalone method of solving a case, but as a tool to either strengthen an existing theory or eliminate possibilities. Just like forensic evidence, witness statements, and digital trails, behavioral assessments must be weighed against all other available information to determine their true value. Used correctly, behavioral profiling can offer powerful insights—but it should never be the sole determinant of guilt or innocence.

Finally, behavioral profiling faces challenges in courtrooms, where evidence must meet strict standards of admissibility. Profiles, being partly subjective, may be deemed speculative and inadmissible, especially if they conflict with tangible evidence.

Criminal profiling is one of the most fascinating yet controversial tools in crime investigations. It's that blend of psychology, detective work, and intuition that makes it feel almost like something out of a crime thriller. But while profiling can offer valuable insights, it's not a magic bullet for solving crimes. The key is balance comes from using profiling alongside solid physical and forensic evidence rather than relying on it as the final word.

At its best, profiling helps investigators know where to look and what questions to ask. If a profiler suggests that an offender is organized and methodical, that could mean they took souvenirs from their victims, leading detectives to search for missing personal items. If a crime scene seems disorganized, it might indicate impulsiveness or panic, which could shape how investigators approach their suspect list. It's less about picking an unknown person from the global community and more about uncovering characteristics that help investigators filter through the list of potential suspects.

Experts in the field have pointed out that while profiling isn't perfect, refining it with standardized training and more structured methodologies could help minimize the risks of subjectivity and bias.

Some even believe that machine learning and data analytics could take profiling to the next level, catching patterns that the human brain might overlook.

But profiling is most effective when it's part of a team effort. Investigators, forensic scientists, psychologists, and profilers all bring something different to the table, and when they work together, they can build a much clearer picture of the crime. That's why cross-disciplinary collaboration is so important. It's a reminder that no single contributor has all the answers, and the best investigations pull from multiple areas of expertise. One investigator's insight can be valuable, but when you bring together a room full of experts, you get a championship team. Each discipline adds a unique piece to the puzzle, transforming hunches into solid leads and evidence into undeniable truths. The best crime-solving happens when different perspectives come together, ensuring no detail is overlooked and no bias goes unchecked.

Of course, behavioral analysis has to be handled with care. One of the biggest concerns is the risk of bias. If investigators lean too heavily on assumptions about race, gender, or socioeconomic status, it can lead to wrongful accusations and wasted resources. That's why ethical guidelines matter.

Another way to keep profiling on track is by constantly testing its accuracy. When profilers make predictions, those predictions should be checked against actual case outcomes. If they're way off, that's a sign the process needs adjusting. The more cases are studied, the more refined profiling can become over time.

At the end of the day, profiling is a mix of science and intuition. So yes, it's truly an art that is informed by data but not guaranteed. It works best when used to support physical, forensic, and circumstantial evidence, not replace them. When investigators strike that balance, the process of profiling, or criminal investigative analysis can be a powerful tool. Without that balance, it's simply a guessing game.

Understanding the traditional forms of evidence, along with behavior is only one part of the equation. To truly combat crime, we must address its roots, particularly the underlying psychological and environmental factors that foster predatory behavior. In the next chapter, we will explore the origins of such behavior, examining the interplay of biology, psychology, and societal influences that contribute to the development of criminal tendencies. This understanding will not only aid in prevention but also provide deeper insight into the motives behind the crimes we seek to resolve.

PART FOUR

UNMASKING PREDATORS:
ROOTS, RED FLAGS & COMMUNITY IMPACT

By recognizing early warning signs and implementing comprehensive intervention programs, society can reduce the risks posed by "wolves in sheep's clothing." -MK

Chapter Thirteen

Untangling Predatory Behavior: Intervention Strategies

Predatory behavior, often captured by the idiom "wolves in sheep's clothing," poses a serious threat to both societal harmony and individual well-being. These individuals mask their harmful intentions behind a facade of normalcy or benevolence, exploiting the trust and vulnerabilities of others. Addressing the roots of such behavior requires an exploration of its underlying causes and the implementation of effective interventions that span social, economic, and psychological domains. This chapter examines the origins of predatory tendencies, identifies early warning signs, and explores the roles that families, educators, mental health professionals, and faith communities play in prevention and rehabilitation.

Predatory behavior encompasses actions that exploit, harm, or manipulate others for personal gain, often flouting societal norms and ethical standards. These behaviors are marked by manipulation, deceit, a lack of empathy, and disregard for the rights and well-being of others. Understanding the origins of such tendencies is essential to curbing their impact on individuals and communities alike.

PSYCHOLOGICAL FACTORS

When we talk about predatory behavior, it's important to understand that there's often a psychological aspect behind it. Two personality disorders, ASPD and Narcissistic Personality Disorder (NPD), are big contributors to these kinds of behaviors. Both disorders involve patterns of thinking and behaving that don't align with societal norms, and they often lead to exploitation and harm to others. If we can better understand how these disorders develop and the role of early-life trauma, it helps us get a clearer picture of why some people might act in predatory ways.[84]

Let's start with ASPD. People with this disorder often show a blatant disregard for rules, other people's rights, and societal norms. They tend to be manipulative, deceitful, and reckless. A big part of this is that they don't experience real emotional connections or empathy. This lack of empathy is key when we talk about predatory behavior because it means they can exploit others without feeling guilt or remorse. Their actions often come from a distorted moral compass, where their own needs take precedence over anything else. Research has also shown that there are neurological factors involved, things like abnormalities in the brain areas responsible for impulse control and emotional processing, which can make them more impulsive and less able to judge the consequences of their actions.[85]

Then there's NPD. People with narcissistic personality disorder are all about themselves. They have an inflated sense of self-importance and need constant admiration. They lack empathy, too, which leads to exploitative relationships. But unlike those with ASPD, their predatory behavior is more calculated and strategic. They'll manipulate or gaslight others to maintain control and secure the admiration they crave. They might be trying to cover up deep insecurities by putting on a show of dominance and control. So, while someone with ASPD might exploit others impulsively, someone with

NPD does it to prop up their fragile sense of self-worth.[86]

A lot of these personality disorders can be traced back to childhood trauma. If a child experiences neglect or abuse, it can severely disrupt their emotional and psychological development. This can lead to coping mechanisms that put their own survival above healthy social interactions. Kids who experience chronic neglect often struggle with forming secure attachments and might develop behaviors like those seen in ASPD, including emotional detachment and a tendency to exploit others. On the flip side, kids who are physically or emotionally abused may start to believe that relationships are inherently harmful, and this can lead them to become manipulative and predatory as a defense mechanism.

In the case of NPD, childhood trauma often involves things like excessive criticism or impossible standards set by parents. These experiences can cause the child to develop a defensive, narcissistic personality. They create a grandiose self-image to protect themselves from feelings of inadequacy. This can make their relationships with others manipulative because they use others to reinforce that self-image.

The link between these disorders and early-life trauma is important to understand because it shows how complex predatory behavior is. While ASPD and NPD are different in some ways, they're both deeply influenced by past experiences that distort a person's ability to connect with others emotionally and ethically. This also highlights how important it is to consider both the psychological and environmental factors when trying to understand why someone might act in a predatory way.

For example, someone with ASPD may act this way because of both brain issues and the lack of nurturing relationships in childhood. Meanwhile, someone with NPD might exploit others because of an insatiable need for validation, rooted in the emotional wounds caused by neglectful or critical caregivers. These two paths show just how different the motivations for predatory behavior can be, even though they both result in harmful actions toward others.

So, how can we address the psychological roots of predatory behavior? For people with ASPD, therapy can help, especially cognitive behavioral therapy (CBT), which focuses on changing negative thought patterns and improving impulse control. But it's important to note that people with ASPD often resist treatment because they don't see the need for change. For those with NPD, therapy that tackles deep-seated insecurities, like schema therapy or psychodynamic therapy, can help them develop healthier self-esteem and more empathetic relationships. Early interventions that focus on fostering secure attachments during childhood can also help prevent the development of these kinds of personality disorders in the first place.[87]

In the end, predatory behavior isn't just about someone being "bad." It's often the result of a mix of personality disorders and trauma. Understanding the psychological mechanisms behind these behaviors, and how early-life experiences shape them, gives us a better chance at preventing and intervening before things escalate. By addressing both the root causes and the individual characteristics of people with these disorders, we can reduce the prevalence of predatory behavior and help people live healthier, more empathetic lives.

SOCIAL AND ECONOMIC FACTORS

Predatory behavior, where someone takes advantage of others for personal gain, isn't just about a bad apple making poor choices. It's a complicated issue shaped by a mix of psychological, social, and economic factors. A lot of the time, it's tied to things like economic inequality, limited access to resources, and certain cultural norms. If we dig into these elements, it can help us understand why people might act in predatory ways, and why society needs to make changes.

One of the biggest drivers of predatory behavior is economic inequality. When there's a huge gap between the rich and everyone else, people who don't have much might resort to exploitation just to survive. Research has shown that in places with more income inequality, crimes like theft and fraud are more common. When people are under financial pressure, it can cloud their moral judgment, making them feel like they have no choice but to take what they need, even if it means exploiting others.

Desperation often plays a huge part in this. For people who don't have access to basic needs like food, shelter, or healthcare, the moral cost of doing something wrong might not feel as important as getting by. The World Bank has found that in poverty-stricken communities, opportunistic crimes are much more common. These crimes, while often punished, are frequently a symptom of larger issues, like a system that values wealth over fair resource distribution.

On the flip side, economic privilege can also breed predatory behavior, but in a different way. Wealthier people might start to believe they have a right to exploit others because of their financial success. This is common in the corporate world, where things like insider trading and labor exploitation are often justified as part of the pursuit of profit. The divide between the rich and the poor creates an environment where exploitation can feel normal, or even celebrated, as a way of maintaining or increasing wealth.

Cultural norms around success and power also play a big role in shaping these behaviors. In many societies, material wealth and status are seen as the ultimate goals. This can create a lot of pressure for people to succeed, often by any means necessary. Popular media, like movies and TV shows, often glorify characters who get ahead through cunning, ambition, or dominance. These characters, frequently predatory by nature, are presented as role models, reinforcing these ideas in popular culture.[88]

This glorification of predatory behavior is especially strong in competitive environments like businesses or schools, where winning is everything. The phrase "survival of the fittest," though often misunderstood, has become a slogan for those who see predation as necessary to get ahead. People may start using exploitative behavior as a strategy to get an advantage, not out of desperation, but as a calculated move.

Cultural attitudes toward gender and power also influence predatory behavior. Traditional views of masculinity, for instance, often focus on dominance and control, traits that are closely tied to exploitative actions. Research has shown that environments with hypermasculine values are more likely to have issues like sexual harassment or workplace bullying, as these behaviors reinforce power structures. These cultural norms keep the cycle of predation going, making it harder to break down the systems that cause it.

When you combine economic inequality with these cultural pressures, you get a feedback loop that keeps predatory behavior alive. For people in disadvantaged situations, they might internalize the message that success is all about material wealth, which can drive them to exploit others, even if they never would have considered it before. On the other hand, those in privileged positions may use these same cultural messages to justify their actions, seeing predation as a natural part of ambition and hard work.

Systemic issues like lack of education and poor access to mental health resources also make things worse. Without a proper education, people might not have the skills to challenge these harmful norms or understand the full consequences of their actions. Similarly, if mental health support is limited, feelings of desperation or entitlement can worsen, leading individuals to act in exploitative ways to cope.

To really address predatory behavior, we need to tackle both the economic and cultural factors. Economically, we can push for policies that reduce income inequality, like higher taxes on the wealthy and more social welfare programs. Making sure everyone has access to basic things like healthcare, education, and housing could also help reduce the need for predation as a survival strategy.

On the cultural side, we need to shift away from celebrating predatory behavior and start valuing things like empathy, cooperation, and ethics. Teaching emotional intelligence and ethical decision-making in schools could help people make better choices. The media also has a big role to play—by portraying more positive role models who work together and play fair, we can reshape societal values toward something more inclusive and just.

Finally, we can't rely on a few people to fix this. It's going to take a collective effort, with community groups, activists, and ordinary citizens working together to challenge exploitative practices and push for policies that prioritize fairness. Only then can we begin to dismantle the systems that support predatory behavior.

The root of predatory behavior lies in the social and economic environment. Economic inequality and lack of access to resources create situations where exploiting others becomes a means of survival or maintaining power. Cultural values that glorify material success and power only make things worse by normalizing predation. To change things, we need a multi-pronged approach that addresses both these structural issues and cultural attitudes. By building a more fair and compassionate society, we can reduce the prevalence of predatory behavior and create a world that values cooperation over exploitation.

BIOLOGICAL FACTORS

Predatory behavior, where someone manipulates or exploits others for their own gain, is complex and doesn't just stem from a single factor. It's a result of a combination of biological, psychological, and social influences. Each piece of the puzzle, whether it's the way the brain works, the personality traits someone develops, or the environment they grow up in—plays a role in shaping these harmful behaviors.

On the biological level, there are certain factors in the brain and body that make someone more likely to behave in predatory ways. For instance, the amygdala, a small almond-shaped structure in the brain, is crucial in processing emotions like fear, pleasure, and empathy. It helps us react to situations and understand other people's feelings. But when the amygdala doesn't function properly, a person may have a reduced ability to empathize with others. This can make it easier for them to exploit or harm people without feeling guilt or remorse. Studies show that people with psychopathic traits, often seen in individuals who display predatory behavior, show a lack of amygdala activity when exposed to distressing images or situations. This may be why they seem unaffected by the pain or suffering of others, which is a clear sign of predatory behavior.

In addition to brain function, hormones like testosterone can also contribute to aggression and dominance-seeking behavior. Testosterone isn't just about physical strength; it also influences how people act socially. High levels of this hormone are linked to risk-taking and competitive behavior, both of which are common in individuals who use others for personal gain. When combined with low levels of cortisol (a hormone responsible for managing stress), this creates a biological setup that is conducive to predatory actions. According to many experts, people with high testosterone and low cortisol are more likely to act aggressively and feel less sensitive to punishment, which makes them more likely to manipulate others without fear of consequences.

Neurotransmitters also have a big role in how people behave. For example, serotonin, which helps regulate mood and social behavior, is often found in lower levels in individuals who engage in aggressive or antisocial behaviors. Low serotonin is linked to impulsivity, poor impulse control, and aggression, all behaviors that often come with predatory tendencies. These biological factors don't act in isolation; they interact with psychological traits and the environment in ways that further shape a person's behavior.

Speaking of psychology, certain personality traits are strongly associated with predatory behavior. One of the most well-known groupings of these traits is called the "Dark Triad," which includes narcissism, Machiavellianism, and psychopathy. People with narcissism often have an inflated sense of self-worth, while those with Machiavellianism are particularly skilled in manipulation and deceit. Psychopathy, on the other hand, is characterized by a lack of empathy and often a disregard for social rules. All these traits are markers of predatory personalities. For example, someone high in Machiavellianism is skilled at using others for personal gain and may use manipulation as a primary tool for controlling or dominating situations.[89]

Cognitive biases are another factor that influences predatory behavior. One such bias is dehumanization—the tendency to see other people as less than human or as objects to be used rather than individuals with their own rights. This way of thinking makes it easier for someone to exploit or harm others without feeling moral conflict. Dehumanization can stem from early childhood experiences, especially if someone grows up with trauma or neglect. These negative experiences can disrupt the ability to form healthy, trusting relationships, which is crucial for developing empathy. People who are emotionally detached or insecure because of early trauma may resort to exploitative behaviors as a way of coping or protecting themselves.

An individual's sense of entitlement also plays a role in predatory behavior. Many people who engage in exploitation believe they deserve more than others, that their needs come first, and that it's okay to harm others in order to get what they want. This sense of superiority can justify their actions and reinforce their belief that others are merely obstacles to be overcome in their pursuit of power or success. These psychological traits help explain how some people rationalize harmful behavior and believe that their actions are acceptable or even deserved.

The social environment in which someone lives is another major factor in how predatory behavior develops and manifests. Cultural values, societal norms, and economic systems can either discourage or encourage exploitation. In competitive environments where success is the primary goal and ethics take a backseat, people may feel pressured to engage in predatory actions to get ahead. In corporate settings, for instance, aggressive competition, unscrupulous practices, and a focus on profit over integrity can create fertile ground for predatory behavior to thrive. When unethical practices go unpunished or are even rewarded, it sets the stage for exploitation to become normalized.

Social learning theory suggests that people learn behaviors by observing others. If someone is exposed to predatory behavior, like manipulative or exploitative actions from peers or authority figures, they're more likely to adopt similar behaviors themselves. This is especially true if they see those behaviors go unpunished or even get rewarded. Research supports this theory, showing that when unethical behavior is common in a group, like in a workplace, other individuals are more likely to mimic those actions. This cycle of exploitation can continue if no one challenges the behavior or holds people accountable.[90]

Economic inequality also plays a big role in how predatory behavior flourishes. When there's a large gap between the wealthy and the poor, it creates a system where the powerful can exploit the vulnerable. People in positions of power may take advantage of those who don't have the same resources or opportunities, and without adequate legal protections, there may be little risk of punishment. This inequality makes it easier for predatory behavior to go unnoticed or unchecked.[91]

When we combine these biological, psychological, and social factors, it becomes clear that predatory behavior is not simply the result of one thing, but a complex interaction of many influences. A person with brain abnormalities, high testosterone, and low serotonin may be biologically predisposed to aggression and a lack of empathy. If this person also has narcissistic tendencies or a history of trauma, their likelihood of engaging in predatory behavior increases. Add in a competitive, cutthroat environment that rewards unethical behavior, and these tendencies are only further amplified.

To address predatory behavior, we need to look at all of these factors. Biological interventions, like medication to balance hormones or neurotransmitters, can help mitigate some of the biological predispositions. Psychological therapies like CBT can help individuals address harmful thinking patterns and develop more empathy. And socially, we can push for reforms that promote ethical behavior, like stricter regulations and more accountability in corporate environments. By tackling predatory behavior from all angles, we can better understand it and find more effective ways to prevent and stop it.

RED FLAG WARNINGS

Recognizing the early warning signs of predatory behavior is crucial for timely intervention and safeguarding individuals and communities. Predatory behavior often involves a calculated approach where individuals manipulate, deceive, or exploit others for personal gain. These behaviors, while sometimes subtle, can be identified through careful observation and awareness of key indicators.

One of the most common early warning signs is the use of manipulative communication tactics. Predators often employ deceit, flattery, or coercion to achieve their objectives. For instance, they may exaggerate their intentions or fabricate stories to gain trust. Flattery is frequently used to disarm potential targets, making them feel valued and special, while coercion is applied to create pressure or fear, leaving victims feeling cornered and compliant. These tactics are designed to erode boundaries and establish a power dynamic favorable to the predator.

A persistent lack of empathy is another significant red flag. Predators often display an inability or unwillingness to understand or value the emotions of others. This lack of empathy is evident in their disregard for the well-being of others, even when confronted with clear evidence of harm caused by their actions. They may downplay or rationalize the pain they inflict, demonstrating a chilling indifference to human suffering. Empathy, a cornerstone of healthy interpersonal relationships, is notably absent in their interactions.

Control-seeking behavior is also a hallmark of predatory tendencies. Predators use intimidation, charm, or both to dominate others. Intimidation may take the form of overt threats, aggressive posturing, or creating an atmosphere of fear. Conversely, charm is wielded as a weapon to lower defenses and foster dependency. This duality—oscillating between fear and allure—enables predators to maintain control over their targets, effectively manipulating their responses and actions.

Patterns of exploitation further highlight predatory behavior. Exploitation can manifest in various forms, including financial, emotional, or physical abuse. Predators often target individuals who are vulnerable, such as those experiencing loneliness, financial hardship, or emotional distress. By exploiting these vulnerabilities, predators achieve their goals with little regard for the consequences. Their actions reveal a blatant disregard for social norms and ethical standards, emphasizing their focus on self-interest above all else.

A critical aspect of recognizing predatory behavior is vigilance. Awareness of these early warning signs empowers individuals and communities to act proactively, potentially mitigating risks before significant harm occurs. Education and open communication play pivotal roles in fostering this vigilance. By sharing knowledge about predatory behaviors and encouraging dialogue, communities can create environments where individuals feel safe to voice concerns and seek assistance when needed.

Identifying the early warning signs of predatory behavior is essential for protecting individuals and fostering safe communities. Manipulative communication tactics, lack of empathy, control-seeking tendencies, and patterns of exploitation are key indicators that warrant attention. By remaining vigilant and informed, individuals and communities can take proactive steps to address and prevent harm, promoting a culture of safety and mutual respect.

INTERVENTIONS FOR PREDATORY BEHAVIOR

Addressing predatory behavior necessitates a multifaceted approach that incorporates social, psychological, and familial interventions.

Predatory behavior, defined as exploitative and manipulative actions that harm others for personal gain, is a pervasive issue with deep societal roots. Effectively addressing such behavior requires a multifaceted strategy that encompasses education, economic reform, community-based initiatives, and legislative measures. By targeting these areas, society can reduce the prevalence of predatory actions and foster a safer, more equitable environment.

One of the cornerstones of addressing predatory behavior is public education. Awareness campaigns are critical in teaching individuals how to recognize, prevent, and respond to exploitative actions. These programs often focus on empowering potential victims by highlighting warning signs and promoting self-advocacy. Community workshops, school-based curricula, and social media initiatives can effectively disseminate this knowledge.[92] Additionally, by encouraging open conversations about predatory behavior, such programs help reduce stigma and foster a culture of collective responsibility.

Economic reform also plays a vital role in addressing the root causes of predatory behavior. Financial hardship and inequality often create conditions that exacerbate exploitative tendencies, as individuals may turn to unethical means for survival or advancement. Implementing robust economic support systems—such as job training programs, accessible education, and social safety nets—can mitigate these pressures. For example, studies have shown that communities with greater access to job opportunities and financial resources experience lower rates of criminal and predatory behavior.[93] Furthermore, promoting corporate accountability ensures that unethical practices, such as wage theft or fraudulent marketing, are addressed at an institutional level.[94]

Community-based initiatives further enhance societal efforts to combat predatory behavior. Neighborhood watch programs, for instance, encourage collective vigilance, empowering residents to safeguard their communities.[95] These initiatives foster trust among neighbors and serve as a deterrent for potential offenders. Similarly, partnerships between local organizations and law enforcement agencies can provide targeted support to at-risk individuals, helping them build resilience against exploitation. Community centers can also serve as hubs for mentorship, counseling, and skill-building programs that steer individuals away from harmful behaviors.

Legislative measures are another critical component of this multifaceted approach. Strong legal frameworks must be established and enforced to deter predatory behavior and protect victims. Laws addressing cybercrimes, human trafficking, and financial fraud are particularly vital in the modern era, where exploitation often transcends geographical boundaries. Moreover, ensuring that victims have access to legal aid and resources is essential for fostering a sense of justice and preventing re-victimization.[96] Regular reviews and updates to legislation help ensure that legal systems remain effective in addressing emerging forms of predation.

Addressing predatory behavior on a societal level requires a multifaceted approach that integrates education, economic reform, community initiatives, and legislative action. By tackling the issue from multiple angles, society can create a more equitable and secure environment for all individuals. Collaborative efforts across these domains not only mitigate the immediate impacts of predatory behavior but also lay the groundwork for long-term prevention and societal resilience.

Psychological interventions are equally critical. Therapeutic approaches like CBT help individuals identify and modify harmful thought patterns and behaviors. Trauma-informed therapy, which addresses unresolved trauma, can further mitigate its influence on predatory tendencies. Behavioral rehabilitation programs that focus on impulse control and empathy development have also proven effective in reducing recidivism among individuals with predatory inclinations.[97]

Families serve as foundational environments where values and behaviors are shaped. Parenting education programs equip caregivers with effective communication, discipline, and emotional support strategies that promote healthy development. Conflict resolution training reduces the likelihood of modeling aggressive behaviors, while support systems for at-risk youth provide mentorship and positive role models to deter the emergence of harmful tendencies.

Educators are uniquely positioned to intervene during formative years. Integrating social-emotional learning (SEL) into curricula fosters empathy, self-awareness, and interpersonal skills.[98] Anti-bullying campaigns bolstered by clear policies and interventions address behaviors that may escalate into predatory tendencies.[99] Teacher training programs ensure that educators are equipped to recognize and address behavioral red flags, facilitating timely and effective interventions.

Mental health professionals play a pivotal role in prevention and rehabilitation. Early diagnosis of personality disorders or behavioral issues can mitigate long-term consequences. Family therapy strengthens dynamics within households, reducing environmental stressors that contribute to predatory behavior. Specialized programs tailored to high-risk populations ensure that interventions are both targeted and effective.

Faith communities offer unique contributions to prevention. By providing moral guidance and fostering a sense of belonging, these communities help deter predatory behavior. Ethical teachings emphasize empathy, compassion, and integrity, while counseling, mentorship, and support groups address crises within families and individuals. Active participation in charitable and service-oriented initiatives encourages prosocial behavior and reinforces communal bonds.

Preventing predatory behavior requires a comprehensive approach that integrates policy development, collaborative efforts, and public education. Policies aimed at deterring exploitation and promoting equitable opportunities address systemic contributors to harmful behavior. Investment in research further advances understanding and prevention strategies.

Collaborative efforts between schools, healthcare providers, law enforcement, and community organizations create robust support networks that address multiple facets of predatory behavior. Interdisciplinary research fosters innovative approaches to prevention, while media campaigns and educational initiatives raise public awareness about the signs and risks associated with predatory tendencies. By cultivating a culture of accountability and ethical conduct, society can collectively deter exploitative behaviors and promote a safer, more compassionate world. [100]

Addressing the roots of predatory behavior requires a holistic approach that considers psychological, social, and economic dimensions. By recognizing early warning signs and implementing comprehensive intervention programs, society can reduce the risks posed by "wolves in sheep's clothing." Families, educators, mental health professionals, and faith communities each play vital roles in fostering environments that prioritize empathy, integrity, and mutual respect. Through collective efforts, some offenders may have a chance of transforming into constructive members of society, ensuring a safer and more compassionate future for all.

Eliminating predatory behavior from our society is not an unattainable goal, it is a challenge that demands persistence, unity, and a commitment to change at every level. By implementing comprehensive interventions that address psychological, social, economic, and legal factors, we are not only protecting potential victims but also fostering environments where harmful behaviors have no room to thrive. The work of educators, mental health professionals, law enforcement, faith communities, and policymakers must converge in a shared mission: to empower individuals, disrupt cycles of exploitation, and establish stronger safeguards against manipulation and harm. When we commit to cultivating a culture of accountability, integrity, and empathy, we take a crucial step toward dismantling the foundations that allow predatory behavior to persist.

Real change begins with awareness, but it is sustained through action. By strengthening families, providing economic opportunities, enforcing just laws, and ensuring access to mental health resources, we move beyond mere reaction and into the realm of true prevention. Every effort, no matter how small, contributes to a future where individuals are equipped to recognize manipulation, stand against exploitation, and refuse to tolerate predatory behavior in any form. Together, we can forge a society where trust is restored, justice prevails, and every person, regardless of their individual background or circumstance, can exist free from the fear of being preyed upon.

224

Childhood trauma, neglect, and abuse set the stage for maladaptive behaviors, while environmental pressures and cultural norms shape how these tendencies manifest. -MK

Chapter Fourteen

Roots of Predation: Childhood Trauma, Neglect, and Abuse

Criminal behavior has long been a subject of fascination and concern, as society seeks to understand the roots of actions that violate moral and legal codes. Among the many theories and frameworks for understanding crime, the exploration of predatory origins—those behaviors marked by deliberate, premeditated harm—stands out for its complexity. These origins are often shaped by a confluence of childhood experiences, environmental influences, and psychological and neurological factors. By examining these dimensions, we gain valuable insights into the mechanisms that drive predatory tendencies.

Childhood trauma, neglect, and abuse are significant contributors to the development of criminal behavior. Research consistently demonstrates a strong correlation between adverse childhood experiences (ACEs) and later delinquent or violent tendencies. Children who endure physical, emotional, or sexual abuse often develop maladaptive coping mechanisms, such as aggression or withdrawal. These behaviors may later manifest as criminal acts when unaddressed.

Neglect, another form of childhood adversity, deprives children of emotional support, structure, and stability. Without a secure attachment to caregivers, children may fail to develop empathy, impulse control, or an understanding of social norms. For example, studies have shown that individuals with a history of neglect are more likely to engage in antisocial behavior, including theft, assault, and even more serious crimes. The lack of nurturing during critical developmental periods may hinder the formation of healthy brain pathways, particularly those involved in emotional regulation and decision-making.[101]

Moreover, the chronic stress associated with childhood abuse and neglect can alter brain development, decreasing decision-making skills, emotional regulation, and the ability to assess risk, resulting in increased susceptibility to criminal tendencies. In an effort to avoid being too "heady" and relying too much upon quotes from experts, I've decided that the rest of this discussion is going to be in a little more "lay" terminology. I'm going to speak from the heart as if we're just sitting around in a ski lodge chatting about childhood trauma, neglect, and abuse.

Understanding criminal behavior isn't just about childhood experiences—it's also about the environment in which an individual develops. A person raised in an area plagued by poverty, crime, and limited access to quality education or healthcare faces challenges that significantly impact their decision-making. Socioeconomic disadvantage often reduces opportunities for lawful success, and when legitimate means of financial stability are scarce, some individuals turn to illegal activities as a perceived necessity. The correlation between economic inequality and crime rates—particularly in urban settings—is well-documented, with high-crime areas often mirroring stark financial disparities.

Cultural influences further shape behavioral patterns, particularly in environments where aggression, dominance, or retaliation are not only accepted but encouraged. In some subcultures, criminal activity is woven into social expectations, whether through gang affiliations that equate violence with respect or peer groups that normalize deviant behavior. When survival depends on reputation and perceived strength, individuals may adopt predatory behaviors as a means of maintaining status or personal security.

Family dynamics also play a critical role. Individuals raised in homes where criminal behavior, substance abuse, or domestic violence are the norm often internalize these experiences as standard operating procedures for navigating the world. Children who observe aggression, manipulation, or deception within their own household may come to see these behaviors as natural, if not necessary, for self-preservation. In these cases, criminality isn't always a conscious choice but rather a learned response to the environment.

To truly understand the impact of childhood trauma, we must look beyond statistics and theory. The real-life consequences of neglect and abuse unfold in tragic stories that highlight the vulnerabilities of those affected. One recent case exemplifies this all too well: the case of a 14-year-old girl from Long Island whose experiences underscore the devastating reality of unaddressed trauma.

For the sake of anonymity, I will change the victim's name for this text. Although this was a real case and made national headlines, let's call her Jennifer. Jennifer was just fourteen years old when she vanished from her home in Long Island in 2024. Her disappearance didn't make national news right away—she was labeled a runaway, as so many teens in her situation are. But her father knew something was wrong. He sensed it deep in his gut, an unshakable fear that she hadn't just taken off on her own.

For 26 agonizing days, he searched for her himself, knowing that time was slipping away and that, too often, girls like Jennifer are overlooked, dismissed, or written off as troubled youth who bring these situations upon themselves. Then, in a dramatic turn of events, his own determination led him to a 56-foot yacht docked at a marina. What he found inside shattered him—his daughter, shoeless, stripped of her belongings, held captive by multiple adults who had abused and exploited her.

The details that have emerged in the wake of Jennifer's rescue are chilling. Over a dozen arrests have been made so far, revealing a network of predators who had kept her trapped in a nightmare. The yacht's owner, a man in his sixties, has been charged with kidnapping, along with multiple others—including men and women—who played various roles in her abduction, captivity, and abuse.

But here's the part that makes this story even more tragic: Jennifer's situation wasn't random. It was predictable. It was preventable. She wasn't just any kid. She was a girl with a history of struggle, bouncing between juvenile detention centers and substance abuse treatment programs, running away from places that should have been safe but never really were. These behaviors—the running, the instability, the acting out—weren't random, either. They were symptoms of something deeper.

In this chapter, we're talking about childhood trauma a lot, but what does that really mean? It means that kids like Jennifer often grow up without a stable support system, navigating neglect, abuse, or emotional instability from an early age. It means they learn not to trust the people who are supposed to care for them. It means they develop coping mechanisms that make sense in their world, but that the rest of society labels as "problem behaviors."

Jennifer wasn't running away for fun. She was running away because somewhere along the line, the adults in her life had already let her down. And because of that, she became exactly the kind of child that predators look for. We don't like to think about this, but predators are opportunists. They don't usually snatch kids off the street at random. They look for the vulnerable ones—the ones who won't be missed right away, the ones who don't have strong protective systems around them, the ones who've already learned to distrust authority figures.

In this case, Jennifer was the perfect target. Even before she was kidnapped, Jennifer was in the system—a system that recycles trauma instead of healing it. She'd been in facilities meant to help kids with substance abuse, in juvenile detention, in places that were supposed to protect her. But none of those places addressed the root cause of why she was struggling in the first place. They treated her as a problem to be managed, not a child who needed protection. And when she went missing? She was classified as a runaway. That single word changed everything about how seriously her disappearance was taken.

Here's the truth: When a teenage girl from a good home goes missing, people look for her. The media covers it. The police act quickly. But when a girl like Jennifer goes missing—a girl who has a record, a girl who's had trouble at home, a girl who's been in and out of juvenile facilities—the urgency disappears. People assume she left voluntarily. They assume she's out doing something reckless. They don't ask the right questions, questions like; Why did she run? Who was influencing her? And what patterns had been established that made her so susceptible to being taken?

By the time law enforcement really started looking for her, Jennifer had already been missing for weeks. And by that point, she had been through unimaginable horrors. But her story, sadly, isn't that unique. That's what makes it so terrifying. If you look at the statistics, you'll see this same story play out over and over again, kids who experience early trauma are at a significantly higher risk of future victimization, and runaway youth are more likely to fall into the hands of predators. There, they might be trafficked or exploited, but they were first neglected by the systems meant to protect them.

Jennifer didn't become a victim overnight. Her trauma started long before she stepped into that car when she was abducted. Her kidnappers? They weren't lurking in the shadows, waiting to snatch a girl at random. They were part of a much bigger problem, one that thrives in the spaces where childhood neglect and systemic failures intersect.

But to change stories like Jennifer's, we must stop waiting until the worst happens to intervene. We have to start protecting kids before they end up in these situations. That means we figure out a better way to recognize that "at risk" kids might already have traumatized lives. That running away should be taken seriously from the start since they likely are not running "toward something," they are running "away from something."

And predators must be held accountable, not just the ones who get caught, but the entire network that allows this kind of exploitation to thrive. And most importantly, it means changing the way we talk about victims like Jennifer. She wasn't a troubled kid who got mixed up with the wrong people. She was a child who had already been failed multiple times before those predators ever laid eyes on her.

We can be relieved that she is now home after her father most likely saved her life. But she'll never undo those 26 days where she was robbed of so much more. Which leaves us with a probing question, how many more kids like Jennifer will have to go through this before we start paying attention? Regrettably, she won't be the last, unless we start seeing these stories for what they really are—not just horrific crimes, but predictable consequences of childhood trauma, systemic neglect, and a world that too often looks away until it's too late.

This girl's case is a stark reminder of how early adversity shapes behavior and risk exposure. Without intervention, those who experience severe trauma often find themselves caught in cycles of victimization or, in some cases, evolve into the very predators who once exploited them. Understanding this cycle is critical—not just for criminal investigations but for developing proactive strategies that prevent trauma from breeding future harm.

Then there are those who operate on an entirely different psychological level like predatory offenders, often exhibiting traits associated with psychopathy. Unlike those who commit crimes out of necessity or environmental conditioning, these individuals lack empathy, remorse, and impulse control. Their behavior is not a response to hardship but rather a calculated means of achieving personal gain. Many exhibit traits outlined in the Hare Psychopathy Checklist, such as superficial charm, pathological lying, and a complete absence of guilt. These offenders are often highly manipulative, able to blend into society while engaging in predatory acts with little to no internal conflict.

Ultimately, criminal behavior is influenced by a complex interplay of environmental, social, and psychological factors. While some individuals turn to crime due to a lack of opportunity, others do so because it aligns with their worldview, or in the case of psychopathy, because they simply have no emotional deterrents. Understanding these underlying motivations is crucial in both criminal investigations and crime prevention, offering insight into how individuals arrive at the point where law-breaking becomes a way of life.

Researchers have found that people who show predatory or violent behavior often have brains that function a little differently than the average person's. One of the biggest red flags? The prefrontal cortex, or the part of the brain that helps with decision-making, impulse control, and knowing right from wrong. Some studies suggest that it doesn't work as well in some individuals and that can lead to poor impulse control and reckless behavior. On the flip side, the amygdala, which processes emotions like fear and excitement, can be overactive, making these people more reactive to threats or opportunities. Basically, their brains can push them toward aggression without the usual "wait, think this through" response kicking in.

Brain scans of people with psychopathic traits show another eerie pattern suggesting there's weak communication between the prefrontal cortex and the limbic system (the part of the brain that handles emotions). This could explain why some people lack empathy, seem emotionally cold, and have no problem lying, manipulating, or even committing violent crimes without remorse. If their brains aren't making strong connections between logic and emotions, then the emotional weight of their actions just doesn't register the way it does for most of us.

But it's not just the brain's structure that influences us, hormones can be a factor, too. High levels of testosterone are linked to increased aggression and dominance-seeking behavior, while irregular cortisol responses (which help regulate stress) can make it harder for someone to keep their emotions in check. Add a history of stress or trauma into the mix, and the risk of violent behavior climbs even higher.

Then there's the genetic factor. Some people inherit traits that make them more prone to aggression or impulsivity. Perhaps you've heard of the so-called "warrior gene," which has been linked to impulse control issues. While having this gene doesn't automatically make someone a criminal, it can increase the chances of someone developing certain antisocial behaviors, especially if combined with environmental triggers like abuse or neglect.

So, what does all this mean? While not everyone with these brain differences or genetic traits becomes dangerous, understanding these risk factors can help investigators and the true crime enthusiast get inside the minds of criminals. It also opens the door for early intervention, possibly helping prevent violent behavior before it ever starts.

Understanding the origins of criminal and predatory behavior requires a multifaceted approach that considers the interplay of childhood experiences, environmental and cultural influences, and psychological and neurological factors. Childhood trauma, neglect, and abuse set the stage for maladaptive behaviors, while environmental pressures and cultural norms shape how these tendencies manifest. At the same time, psychological and neurological patterns provide a biological framework that influences an individual's capacity for empathy, self-control, and moral reasoning.

By addressing these root causes through early intervention, community support, and mental health treatment, society can work toward mitigating the factors that contribute to criminal behavior. Such efforts not only improve individual lives but also promote safer, more cohesive communities. Policymakers and practitioners must focus on evidence-based strategies to address these factors holistically, fostering resilience and rehabilitation rather than mere punishment.

Empathy, the ability to understand and share the feelings of others, is a fundamental component of moral behavior. It acts as an internal safeguard, preventing individuals from harming others by allowing them to recognize and internalize the suffering they might cause. Without empathy, this moral compass is weakened, making it easier for individuals to justify or ignore the consequences of their actions. Research has consistently shown that deficits in empathy are strongly correlated with criminal behavior, particularly predatory offenses where exploitation and harm are intentional.

Empathy and moral awareness are deeply interconnected. Moral awareness refers to an individual's ability to recognize ethical dilemmas and align their actions with societal values. This development begins in early childhood, influenced by parenting, social experiences, and environmental stability. Empathy can be divided into two areas: cognitive empathy, which is the intellectual ability to understand another person's perspective, and emotional empathy, which is the capacity to feel what someone else is experiencing. These two types work together to guide the behavior, reinforcing the social contract that discourages harmful actions.

For individuals who lack empathy, however, the ability to recognize or care about the suffering of others is impaired. This is particularly evident in those who engage in predatory crimes, such as fraud, violent assault, or exploitation. In many cases, these individuals exhibit not only a lack of remorse but also a pattern of rationalization that allows them to dehumanize their victims. This detachment often stems from a combination of adverse childhood experiences, neurological abnormalities, and social conditioning—all of which contribute to an individual's ability to justify harming others without guilt.

Psychopathy, a personality disorder characterized by emotional callousness, egocentricity, and an absence of guilt, is strongly linked to predatory behavior. Studies have shown that individuals with psychopathic traits display reduced empathy. For instance, a fraudster may justify their deception by viewing victims as gullible rather than as individuals whose financial security is being destroyed. Similarly, violent offenders often dehumanize their victims, stripping them of personhood to make their actions feel justified. These cognitive distortions, facilitated by empathy deficits, allow offenders to suppress moral considerations while pursuing their goals.

Understanding the role of empathy in criminal behavior has led to the development of targeted interventions aimed at fostering emotional and moral awareness in at-risk individuals. Several approaches have been shown to be effective in preventing and rehabilitating those prone to predatory behavior.

One of the most effective ways to address empathy deficits is through early intervention programs that focus on children raised in high-risk environments. Exposure to chronic adversity—such as neglect, abuse, or violence—can disrupt the natural development of empathy. Programs that teach emotional literacy, perspective-taking, and conflict resolution in schools have demonstrated positive effects in reducing aggression and antisocial behavior.

For individuals already engaged in criminal activity, CBT and empathy training have been successful in challenging distorted thinking patterns. These interventions help offenders develop emotional regulation, recognize the real impact of their actions, and reframe their perception of victims. By encouraging offenders to reflect on the harm they cause, these therapies reduce the likelihood of reoffending.

Restorative justice takes rehabilitation a step further by emphasizing accountability and reconciliation. This approach facilitates structured dialogues between offenders and their victims, allowing perpetrators to directly confront the human impact of their actions. Research suggests that these interactions can significantly increase empathy in offenders, leading to lower recidivism rates by humanizing victims and breaking down the psychological barriers that allow for rationalized harm.

Social reintegration is another critical factor in reducing criminal behavior. Mentoring programs and peer support initiatives provide at-risk individuals with positive role models who reinforce prosocial values and interpersonal skills. These programs help offenders develop meaningful relationships and emphasize the role of empathy in maintaining social bonds, which in turn discourages future criminal activity.

Empathy plays a critical role in moral reasoning and good behavior, while its absence is a defining characteristic of predatory actions. Whether it is influenced by environmental means or social conditioning, having empathy helps develop good citizens, while a lack of empathy contributes to the rationalization of hurting others.

By recognizing and addressing these issues through early intervention, therapy, restorative justice, mentorship, and scientific techniques, it is possible to reduce criminal behavior and encourage rehabilitation. While no intervention is guaranteed to "fix" every offender, a deeper understanding of empathy's role in shaping behavior is an invaluable tool in both criminal justice and crime prevention.

Empathy isn't just a feel-good trait—it's a psychological safeguard against crime. The ability to recognize and respect the humanity of others acts as a natural deterrent to predatory behavior. When empathy is absent, individuals are far more likely to justify exploitation, manipulation, or violence without remorse. This is why fostering empathy in at-risk individuals is a crucial strategy in crime prevention. Programs that encourage emotional awareness and moral reasoning don't just help individuals make better choices; they contribute to a more just and compassionate society. Rehabilitation efforts that focus on strengthening empathy have been shown to reduce recidivism, reinforcing the idea that moral awareness isn't simply innate—it can be cultivated.

But what determines whether someone develops a strong moral compass in the first place? Is it something hardwired into their DNA, or is it shaped by experience? This brings us to one of the most enduring questions in criminal psychology: nature versus nurture. Despite the growing body of evidence suggesting that genetics can play a role in criminal tendencies, biology is far from destiny. Genetics may increase a person's susceptibility to impulsivity, aggression, or risk-taking behaviors, but they don't guarantee a life of crime. The question remains: how much of criminal behavior is embedded in an individual's DNA, and how much is a product of their environment? This debate is not just an academic exercise—it has real-world implications for criminal profiling, rehabilitation, and even legal responsibility. Understanding whether criminals are "born" or "made" helps shape everything from sentencing policies to intervention programs aimed at steering individuals away from crime before they ever enter the system. So, how do nature and nurture interact in the making of a predator? Let's break it down.

Despite the compelling evidence for the influence of genetics on criminal behavior, it is important to acknowledge that genetics alone do not determine an individual's path. The presence of certain genetic markers or predispositions may make an individual more vulnerable to certain behaviors, but they do not guarantee that a person will become a criminal. -MK

Chapter Fifteen

Nature vs. Nurture Debate:
Unraveling the Origins of Criminal Behavior

The debate over nature versus nurture is one of the oldest and most enduring discussions in psychology, philosophy, and the social sciences. At the heart of this debate lies the question of whether human behavior is primarily determined by genetic inheritance—our nature—or by the environment in which we are raised—our nurture. While many agree that both genetic predispositions and environmental influences play significant roles in shaping who we become, the balance between the two has been the subject of considerable debate.

Understanding the interplay of nature and nurture is particularly important when examining complex behaviors such as criminality. The question of why some individuals will engage in criminal activities while others do not, has intrigued scholars, policymakers, and practitioners for centuries. We find ourselves asking the question,

"Are individuals born with a predisposition to criminal behavior, or is it their life experiences and environmental factors that drive them to commit crimes?" This question becomes even more compelling when we consider that many individuals who engage in criminal behavior have been shown to have certain genetic traits or familial histories that suggest a predisposition to aggression or antisocial behavior. At the same time, many offenders come from backgrounds characterized by poverty, abuse, and neglect, factors that clearly shape their development and behavior.

Let's explore the nature versus nurture debate in the context of criminal behavior, focusing on how genetic predispositions and environmental influences interact to shape an individual's propensity for crime. Through the examination of case studies of criminal offenders and their developmental histories, we will seek to understand the complex dynamics at play in the formation of criminal tendencies. The objective is not to argue that one factor outweighs the other, but rather to explore how the two factors work together to influence human behavior. By understanding this balance, we can develop more effective strategies for prevention, intervention, and rehabilitation for those at risk of criminal involvement.

THE NATURE SIDE OF THE DEBATE

The question of whether human behavior is determined by nature or nurture begins with the understanding of genetic predispositions—the "nature" side of the debate. Genetic factors, including inherited traits, are believed to influence everything from intelligence and personality to health risks and susceptibility to certain behaviors. In the context of criminality, nature refers to the potential for individuals to inherit certain characteristics that may make them more prone to aggressive behavior, impulsivity, or antisocial tendencies.

Research in the field of behavioral genetics has provided compelling evidence that genes play a significant role in shaping human behavior. Twin studies, for example, have demonstrated that identical twins who share nearly all of their genetic material, tend to have more similar behavioral traits than fraternal twins, who share only 50 percent of their genetic material. These studies suggest that genetic factors contribute to a significant portion of personality traits and behavioral tendencies. In particular, studies have shown that traits such as aggression, impulsivity, and the propensity for violence have a heritable component, meaning they can be passed down from one generation to the next.

In addition to twin studies, adoption studies have been instrumental in showing the impact of genetics on behavior. By comparing the behaviors of adopted children with those of their biological and adoptive parents, researchers have been able to isolate the influence of genetics from the influence of the environment. One of the most notable findings from such studies is that adopted children tend to exhibit behavioral tendencies that are more similar to their biological parents than to their adoptive parents. This suggests that genetic inheritance plays a significant role in shaping an individual's predispositions, even when they are raised in a completely different environment.

Furthermore, genetic disorders and abnormalities have been linked to criminal behavior in some cases. For example, certain genetic conditions, such as the XYY syndrome, have been associated with an increased likelihood of violent behavior. The XYY syndrome occurs when a male has an extra Y chromosome, and research has indicated that individuals with this genetic abnormality may be more prone to aggression and impulsivity. Although this is just one example, it highlights the potential connection between genetic factors and criminal tendencies.

The concept of genetic predispositions is supported by research that shows imbalances in neurotransmitters can affect mood regulation, impulse control, and aggression. These chemical imbalances have been linked to conditions such as ASPD, which is commonly associated with criminal behavior. Individuals with low serotonin levels, for example, may exhibit impulsive aggression, while those with dopamine abnormalities may engage in risky or thrill-seeking behavior. These biological factors may increase the likelihood of engaging in criminal activities, especially in combination with other factors such as environmental stressors.

Despite the compelling evidence for the influence of genetics on criminal behavior, it is important to acknowledge that genetics alone do not determine an individual's path. The presence of certain genetic markers or predispositions may make an individual more vulnerable to certain behaviors, but they do not guarantee that a person will become a criminal. This is where interaction with environmental factors becomes crucial.

THE NURTURE SIDE OF THE DEBATE

While genetic predispositions undoubtedly play a significant role in shaping an individual's behavior, environmental factors are equally influential in determining how these predispositions manifest themselves. The nurture side of the debate focuses on the importance of one's upbringing, experiences, and social environment in molding personality, values, and behavior. In the context of criminal behavior, the environment can include early childhood experiences, family dynamics, education, peer influences, and the socioeconomic conditions in which an individual is raised.

Research has consistently shown that adverse childhood experiences, such as abuse, neglect, and trauma, have a profound impact on an individual's development and behavior. Children who grow up in environments marked by violence, instability, and emotional neglect are more likely to develop behavioral issues that can lead to criminal tendencies later in life. For example, children who witness domestic violence or experience physical or sexual abuse are more likely to struggle with emotional regulation, exhibit aggression, and develop antisocial behaviors. These early experiences can alter brain development and affect how individuals respond to stress, conflict, and social interactions.

One key aspect of environmental influence is the role of parenting. Studies have shown that children raised in environments where parents are neglectful, abusive, or absent are more likely to engage in criminal behavior. Parental supervision, attachment, and discipline are critical factors in shaping a child's behavior. A lack of positive parental involvement can result in a child seeking out negative peer influences, engaging in delinquent behavior, or failing to develop the necessary skills to navigate social norms. On the other hand, children raised in supportive, nurturing environments are more likely to develop prosocial behaviors and emotional resilience.

Socioeconomic factors also play a significant role in shaping behavior. Poverty, limited access to education, and a lack of social mobility can increase the likelihood of individuals engaging in criminal activities. In disadvantaged neighborhoods, individuals may face higher rates of unemployment, crime, and social disintegration, which can create a cycle of deprivation and criminal behavior. The concept of social disorganization theory, which suggests that communities with weak social bonds and high levels of poverty are more likely to experience higher rates of crime, supports the idea that environmental conditions can create an environment conducive to criminal behavior.

Peer influence is another important environmental factor in the development of criminal tendencies. Adolescents, in particular, are highly susceptible to peer pressure and may engage in delinquent behaviors in order to gain acceptance or approval from their social circles. Peer influence is especially strong in environments where criminal behavior is normalized, such as in certain neighborhoods or social groups. The process of social learning, as outlined by criminologist Albert Bandura, suggests that individuals learn behaviors through observation and imitation of others. If a young person is surrounded by peers who engage in criminal activities, they are more likely to adopt similar behaviors themselves.

Case studies of criminal offenders often reveal the powerful influence of environment on behavior. One example is the case of individuals who grow up in foster care systems marked by instability and lack of emotional support. These individuals may face significant challenges in forming healthy relationships and developing self-regulation skills. Research has shown that individuals raised in the foster system are at higher risk of engaging in criminal activities as adults, particularly when they experience multiple placements or suffer neglect within the system.

Another significant environmental factor is exposure to substance abuse. Children raised in households where substance abuse is prevalent are at greater risk of developing behavioral issues themselves, including criminal behavior. The chaotic and unpredictable nature of substance-abusing households creates an environment in which children may learn maladaptive coping strategies, become desensitized to violence or criminal activity, and develop emotional or psychological problems that contribute to later criminal conduct.

In examining the environment's role in criminal behavior, it becomes clear that the impact of adverse experiences during childhood and adolescence can significantly alter the trajectory of an individual's life. While some individuals may be genetically predisposed to aggression or impulsivity, these traits may be magnified or mitigated depending on the environmental factors that shape their development. For instance, a child who experiences abuse and neglect may be more likely to develop violent tendencies, even if they do not have a strong genetic predisposition to aggression. On the other hand, a child with a supportive and stable environment may be able to overcome genetic predispositions toward aggression or impulsivity and develop into a well-adjusted adult.

CRIMIINAL BEHAVIOR AND GENETICS

While environmental factors undoubtedly shape behavior, an increasing body of research suggests that genetics plays a significant role in the predisposition to criminal behavior. The field of behavioral genetics has uncovered evidence of genetic markers and predispositions that may influence the likelihood of individuals engaging in criminal activities. This section explores the genetic factors associated with criminal behavior, including studies of violent offenders, genetic disorders, and the identification of specific genes that may predispose individuals to antisocial tendencies.

One of the central debates in the study of criminal behavior and genetics is whether there are specific genetic markers that predispose individuals to engage in violent or criminal acts. Early research in this area focused on identifying genetic disorders that might be linked to increased aggression or impulsivity. As mentioned briefly in the nature section, the XYY syndrome, in which males have an extra Y chromosome, was one of the first genetic abnormalities to be linked with a higher propensity for violent behavior. Studies in the 1960s and 1970s suggested that males with XYY syndrome were more likely to engage in criminal acts, particularly violent crimes. However, subsequent research has questioned the strength of this link, suggesting that while the syndrome may contribute to certain behavioral traits, it is not a definitive predictor of criminality.

Highlighted in the "Nature vs. Nurture" discussion, studies of twins and adoptees have provided insights into the role of genetics in criminal behavior where identical and fraternal twins are compared.

Identical twins who share 100 percent of their genetic material are more likely to exhibit similar criminal behavior than fraternal twins, who share only 50 percent of their genes. Findings like this suggest that genetic factors play a significant role in the development of criminal tendencies. However, twin studies also indicate that the environment plays an important role in shaping behavior, as identical twins raised apart often exhibit differences in behavior, demonstrating that nurture can influence the expression of genetic predispositions.

One compelling case study that illustrates the role of genetics in criminal behavior is the life history of Richard Ramirez, the "Night Stalker." Ramirez's family history was marked by violence and dysfunction, with his father being abusive and his uncle introducing him to disturbing behaviors at a young age. However, researchers have also noted that Ramirez exhibited certain genetic traits, including impulsivity and a lack of empathy, which may have predisposed him to engage in violent acts. While his upbringing certainly played a significant role in shaping his criminal behavior, his genetic makeup may have contributed to his predisposition toward aggression and violence.

In the case of serial killer, Ted Bundy, his early life was marked by significant emotional turmoil, including being raised by a mother who later lied about his parentage, creating a sense of identity confusion. Bundy displayed certain traits of psychopathy, including a lack of empathy and an ability to manipulate others. While Bundy's upbringing was likely a factor in his criminal behavior, studies have suggested that his genetic predisposition to certain psychopathic traits may have played a role in his development into a violent criminal. Bundy's case highlights the complexity of the relationship between genetic factors, environmental influences, and the manifestation of criminal behavior.

While genetic factors may predispose individuals to certain behavioral tendencies, including aggression and antisocial behavior, it is important to remember that genetics alone do not determine criminality. The interaction between genetic predispositions and environmental influences plays a critical role in shaping behavior. Genetics do not provide a definitive explanation for why some people commit crimes. Instead, it is a combination of genes and environment, childhood experiences, family dynamics, and social influences that ultimately determines whether an individual will engage in criminal behavior.

If Ted Bundy's case teaches us anything, it's that the making of a killer is never as simple as nature or nurture alone, it's a tangled web of both. Bundy's genetic predisposition may have set the stage, but his unstable upbringing added fuel to the fire. But what happens when that disturbing fire ignites much earlier in a person's life, before adulthood, before adolescence, or even before a child understands the weight of life and death decisions?

That brings us to Mary Bell. Unlike Bundy, who didn't start killing until his early twenties, Mary was just ten years old when she took her first life. If Bundy's story raises questions about genetic fate, Mary's case forces us to confront an even more unsettling question: Can a child truly be a born killer?

THE "BAD SEED"

When we think of serial killers, we often imagine calculating adults, hardened criminals, or deranged minds shaped over years of neglect and violence. But what if that murderer is just a child? A little girl who, instead of playing with dolls or skipping rope, strangles toddlers and leaves cryptic, taunting notes at crime scenes? That's the story of Mary Bell,

Britain's youngest female killer, who committed two brutal murders at the age of ten. Her case is a chilling blend of nature versus nurture, wrapped in a tale of severe abuse, emotional detachment, and an unsettling lack of remorse.

If there was ever an argument that upbringing shapes behavior, Mary Bell's life would be Exhibit A. Born in 1957, she was unwanted from the moment she entered the world—literally. Her mother, Betty Bell, a teenage prostitute with a violent streak, reportedly tried to give Mary away multiple times. One story even claims she once sold her daughter to a woman who wanted a child, only for Mary's older sister to track her down and bring her back home.

Mary wasn't just neglected; she was abused in ways that defy comprehension. Relatives believed her mother deliberately harmed her, citing multiple "accidents" where she suffered serious injuries. And then there was the horrific claim that Betty involved her daughter in sadomasochistic acts with clients, making Mary an unwilling participant in the darkest corners of human depravity.

So, was Mary Bell born evil? Or did her monstrous childhood create a monster?

By the time she was in school, Mary's behavior was already disturbingly violent. She strangled classmates for fun, pushed another child off a roof, and even tried to force-feed a girl sand, blocking her trachea. These weren't normal playground scuffles either, they were cold, calculated attacks, always focused on exerting power over smaller, weaker children.

But in 1968, at the age of ten, Mary escalated from assault to murder. On May 25, 1968, just a day before her 11th birthday, Mary Bell strangled four-year-old Martin Brown inside an abandoned house in Newcastle. His body was found later that day, but with no obvious injuries, authorities ruled it an accident. Mary, however, wasn't done with her game. The day after Martin's death, Mary and her friend Norma broke into a nursery, vandalized it, and left eerie, handwritten notes claiming responsibility for the murder. One of them read: "I murder so that I may come back." The police dismissed the notes as a prank. A deadly mistake.

Two months later, on July 31, 1968, Mary struck again—this time targeting three-year-old boy named Brian. This murder was even more sadistic. Mary not only strangled him but also mutilated his body with a pair of scissors, cut off some of his hair, and carved an "M" into his stomach. It was a level of violence and control far beyond her years, and it finally raised enough suspicion for police to start looking her way.

When police began questioning neighborhood children, Mary stood out immediately. Unlike others, who were nervous and shaken by the murders, Mary was cold and detached. She even went to the murdered boys house the day after his death and asked his grieving mother, "Can I see [the boy]? I want to see him in his coffin."

During the police investigation, she gave a self-incriminating statement—casually mentioning details of the crime scene that had never been made public. That was enough to put her under suspicion, and when fibers from her clothing were found on Brian's body, it was game over. On August 7, 1968, Mary Bell was arrested for two counts of manslaughter.

Mary's trial in December 1968 was a legal nightmare—how do you prosecute a child for murder? Was she fully aware of what she was doing? Or was she a victim of her own tragic upbringing? Psychiatrists concluded that Mary was suffering from a psychopathic personality disorder—she lacked empathy, was manipulative, and saw people as objects to be controlled and discarded. The jury ultimately convicted Mary of manslaughter while acquitting her accomplice. Mary was sentenced to detention at Her Majesty's pleasure, a vague ruling that meant she could be locked away indefinitely.

After 12 years in custody, Mary Bell, now 23, was released. She was given a new identity and anonymity. After being released from prison, she reportedly had a child of her own.

In 1998, Mary Bell broke her silence and agreed to an interview with author Gitta Sereny for a book about Bell's life, titled, "Cries Unheard: The Story of Mary Bell." During that interview, Sereny learned that Bell and her accomplice were tried in a small courtroom in 1968, supposedly to be less frightening for the girls. At that time, England operated under a principle that presumed defendants under the age of 14 were incapable of understanding right from wrong. This favored the defense and meant that the prosecution had to convince the court that the young defendants understood the differences between right and wrong and still chose to commit the homicides.

There are indications that Mary was captivated by the courtroom proceedings and despite her young age, showed a great deal of composure. She didn't cry or seek any form of comfort, and some accounts suggest she seemed to revel in certain aspects of the testimony. Her response to the inquiry didn't go unnoticed by the jury.

This case highlights the complex interplay between genetic predispositions and environmental influences in shaping criminal behavior. The study of criminal offenders' developmental histories provides valuable insights into the nature versus nurture debate, illustrating that both genetic and environmental factors must be considered in understanding the causes of criminal behavior. While the influence of genetics is undeniable, the environment remains a powerful force in shaping behavior and determining whether individuals will follow a path of criminality or lead productive lives.

The nature versus nurture debate has been a long-standing discourse in understanding human behavior, particularly criminal behavior. While the question of whether genetics or environment plays a more significant role in shaping an individual's actions is far from settled, current research suggests that it is not an either/or proposition. Instead, it is the dynamic interplay between genetic predispositions and environmental factors that shapes behavior. In the context of criminal behavior, this understanding has profound implications for both criminal justice policies and prevention programs.

In the past, the nature versus nurture debate was often framed as a binary choice: either genetics or environment was the primary determinant of behavior. However, in recent years, scientific advancements have led to a more integrated view of human development, where both nature and nurture are understood to work in tandem. Genetic predispositions may provide certain inclinations or vulnerabilities, but it is the environment in which an individual is raised that often determines whether those genetic traits are expressed or suppressed.

Research into epigenetics has changed the way we look at the whole nature-versus-nurture debate. Epigenetics is all about how things like stress, trauma, or even loving care can influence how our genes work. So, rather than genetics and environment being two independent forces, they actually are interacting and shaping each other in ways we're still trying to fully understand. It's not just about being born with certain traits, it's about how life experiences can turn certain genes "on" or "off," potentially affecting behavior in the long run.

Studies have shown that individuals who are genetically predisposed to high levels of aggression may be more likely to engage in violent behavior if they are raised in an environment characterized by abuse or neglect. Conversely, individuals with similar genetic predispositions may not develop aggressive tendencies if they are raised in a stable and supportive environment. This highlights the importance of understanding the interaction between genes and environment in shaping behavior, rather than focusing solely on one or the other.

When we talk about predators, we expect to find an origin story— a moment where everything went wrong. Childhood abuse, violent parents, head trauma, a genetic predisposition to psychopathy, something that explains how an ordinary baby grows into a murderous predator. But what if that moment never happened? What if a killer had a normal childhood, loving parents, no history of abuse, and still turned into a monster?

These cases are rare, but they exist. And they shake the foundation of everything we think we know about why people kill. To highlight this, let's look at the case of Israel Keyes, the serial killer who shouldn't have been one. Israel Keyes was a methodical, calculated killer who operated across the United States, leaving behind a trail of undiscovered bodies and unanswered questions. When he was finally caught in 2012 after abducting and murdering 18-year-old Samantha Koenig in Alaska, investigators expected to uncover a childhood filled with trauma. But what they found was … nothing.

Keyes was raised in a strict but stable household. There were no

reports of physical or emotional abuse. His parents were religious—not cruel. He wasn't beaten, starved, or neglected. And yet, from a young age, he admitted to feeling different, he called it being "wired differently." As a teenager, he fantasized about murder. His first known violent act was abducting, raping, and planning to kill a teenage girl when he was just out of high school.

FBI investigators were surprised that Keyes didn't fit the mold of the typical serial killer. He wasn't a social outcast, he wasn't abused, and he had no history of head trauma or mental illness. He just … wanted to kill. He enjoyed it. And no one saw it coming.

And then, there's Jeffrey Dahmer, the boy next door who turned into a killer and a cannibal. Dahmer wasn't raised by violent criminals. He wasn't tortured as a child. He didn't experience sexual abuse. In fact, in his early years, he had a stable and loving home. His father, Lionel Dahmer, later wrote a memoir trying to understand how his son had turned into a monster, admitting that he could not pinpoint any moment that might have "made" Jeffrey into what he became.

Yet, by the time he was a teenager, Dahmer was already fantasizing about control, dominance, and murder. By his first kill at 18, the urge was unstoppable. He later admitted that he felt no empathy, no remorse, and no real understanding of why he was driven to kill. He wasn't created by his environment. He wasn't shaped by abuse. He simply was.

When serial predators emerge from normal homes with no history of trauma, it leaves criminologists and psychologists grasping for explanations. If it wasn't abuse, genetics, or neglect—then what? Some experts believe that in these cases, there may be hidden neurological abnormalities—perhaps underdeveloped emotional centers in the brain that prevent feelings of guilt or empathy. Others argue that certain people are just born without the ability to connect to others as human beings—a rare, natural-born psychopath.

In cases like Israel Keyes and Jeffrey Dahmer, there were early warning signs—a lack of empathy, an obsession with control, a growing hunger for violence. But without abuse or extreme hardship to blame, these cases force us to ask a terrifying question: are some people simply born killers? And if the answer is yes that might be the most unsettling reality of all which would take us back to the very question of this chapter—is it nature or nurture?

As our understanding of the nature versus nurture debate continues to evolve, it is essential to consider the implications for criminal justice policies and prevention programs. A more nuanced understanding of the causes of criminal behavior can lead to more effective and individualized approaches to crime prevention, rehabilitation, and sentencing. If both genetic and environmental factors contribute to criminal behavior, then addressing only one aspect—such as focusing solely on punishment without considering the underlying psychological and environmental factors—may be insufficient in reducing crime.

The growing recognition of the role of mental health in criminal behavior underscores the need for a more comprehensive approach to criminal justice. Many individuals who engage in criminal behavior suffer from untreated mental health disorders, such as ASPD, conduct disorder, or substance use disorders. By integrating mental health care into the criminal justice system, we can address the underlying psychological factors contributing to criminal behavior and provide individuals with the tools they need to reintegrate into society successfully.

Changes are required in criminal justice policies and intervention programs, and there is a need for increased public awareness and education regarding the complex causes of criminal behavior. Public perceptions of crime are often shaped by simplistic views of good and evil, where individuals are judged solely by their actions without consideration of the broader context of their development. By promoting a more nuanced understanding of criminal behavior—one that acknowledges the role of both genetics and environment—we can reduce stigmatization and increase empathy for individuals who have committed crimes.

Education about the nature versus nurture debate can play a crucial role in preventing crime before it occurs. By teaching young people about the importance of empathy, emotional regulation, and healthy relationships, we can help create a generation of individuals who are less likely to engage in criminal behavior. Programs in schools that focus on conflict resolution, and mental health awareness can provide students with the skills they need to navigate challenges and avoid destructive behaviors.

Looking ahead, future research will continue to explore the interplay between genetics and environment in the development of criminal behavior. Advances in genomics and neuroscience will likely provide even deeper insights into the biological underpinnings of criminality. However, it is important that future research also considers the broader social and environmental factors that contribute to crime.

The nature versus nurture debate continues to evolve, with a growing recognition of the complex interaction between genetic predispositions and environmental influences in shaping human behavior. In the context of criminal behavior, this understanding has significant implications for both criminal justice policies and prevention efforts. By addressing both genetic and environmental factors, we can create more effective strategies for reducing crime, rehabilitating offenders, and preventing future criminal behavior. The future of the debate lies in further research that explores the dynamic relationship between genes and environment, as well as the continued development of interventions that consider the full complexity of human behavior.

As we move forward, it's important to look at criminal behavior through a lens of understanding rather than just condemnation. People don't just wake up one day and decide to become criminals—there's almost always a mix of factors at play, from genetic predispositions to environmental influences. By addressing both, we can move beyond just punishing crime and actually start preventing it, giving individuals the tools they need to live stable, productive lives instead of getting trapped in a cycle of bad decisions and worse consequences.

But for all the science behind criminal behavior, sometimes the simplest explanations are the most useful. That's where Maslow's Hierarchy of Needs comes in. If we strip away the complexities of psychology, neurology, and sociology, human motivation boils down to a handful of core needs—things like food, security, belonging, and self-worth. And when those needs aren't met? Well, that's when people start bending or breaking the rules to get what they're missing.

So, what if we looked at crime through this framework? What if, instead of asking, "What's wrong with this person?" we asked, "What need is driving this behavior?" It might not excuse crime, but it could help us understand it better—and understanding is the first step toward real solutions. Turn the page and explore this concept with a new set of glasses.

*When people feel invisible, ignored, or undervalued, they seek
ways to stand out. Some do it the right way—through hard
work and perseverance. Others take shortcuts, believing that
if they can just get ahead, the recognition will follow. -MK*

Chapter Sixteen

Cracking the Code:
Understanding Crime Through Human Needs

The Understanding criminal behavior through the lens of
Maslow's Hierarchy of Needs offers a nuanced perspective on the
motivations that drive individuals to commit crimes. By examining
real-world cases corresponding to each level of the hierarchy, we can
gain insight into how unmet needs may lead to unlawful actions. It
doesn't excuse the behavior but may help us understand why the crime
occurred. Let's start by talking about the most basic of all needs, the
need for food, water and shelter.

If you want to understand why people commit crimes, you don't
necessarily need a degree in psychology or criminology. Sometimes,
it helps to go back to the basics, those fundamental needs that drive
human behavior. That's exactly what Maslow's Hierarchy of Needs
does. The theory suggests that every human being is motivated by a
set of core needs, ranging from the most basic necessities like food,
water, and shelter, to higher-level desires like social connection, self-
respect, and personal achievement. When those needs are met in

healthy ways, people thrive. But when they're denied or threatened, people will do whatever it takes to fulfill them, including breaking the law.

For many criminals, their actions aren't just about greed, cruelty, or a thirst for power. Often, they're trying to meet an unmet need, whether it's stealing to survive, joining a gang for a sense of belonging, or committing fraud to gain recognition and success. Even the most ruthless predators are operating within this framework, differentiated by the darker, more extreme routes they take to fulfill their desires.

So, if we really want to understand why predators do what they do, we need to start at the foundation: What need was driving their crime? Let's start by talking about the most fundamental level, the physiological needs or the basics of survival, the essentials like food, water, and shelter. At the very foundation of human existence are the basics of survival, food, water, shelter. Without these, everything else falls apart. It's easy to talk about morality and the law when you have a full stomach and a warm bed to sleep in, but when someone is starving, cold, and desperate, survival instinct takes over. And sometimes, that means breaking the law just to stay alive.

Maslow's first tier of needs demands physiological survival, the most basic and primal human requirement. Without food, water, or shelter, a person isn't worried about their career, social status, or even long-term consequences. They're thinking about getting through the next few hours, the next day, the next week. Just imaging that you haven't eaten in two days. Your stomach is cramping, your body feels weak, and your mind is foggy. You walk past a grocery store, and the sight of food makes your hunger unbearable. You have no money, no resources, and nowhere to turn. What do you do?

For many people in extreme poverty, the answer is simple: they steal. It's not about greed, it's about survival. For example, in Los Angeles, 2019, a homeless man was arrested for stealing food from a grocery store. He wasn't a career criminal; he wasn't trying to make a profit—he was just hungry. No one likes to think of themselves as someone who would steal, but hunger is a powerful force. It can drive even the most law-abiding person to do something they never imagined.

Now, imagine this scenario: You're a single parent. Your children haven't eaten all day. The fridge is empty, the rent is overdue, and there's no money left. You've tried everything including looking for work, asking for help, but you've hit a dead end. And now, your kids are crying from hunger. Do you let them go to bed with empty stomachs? Or do you walk into a convenience store and grab a few items, hoping you don't get caught?

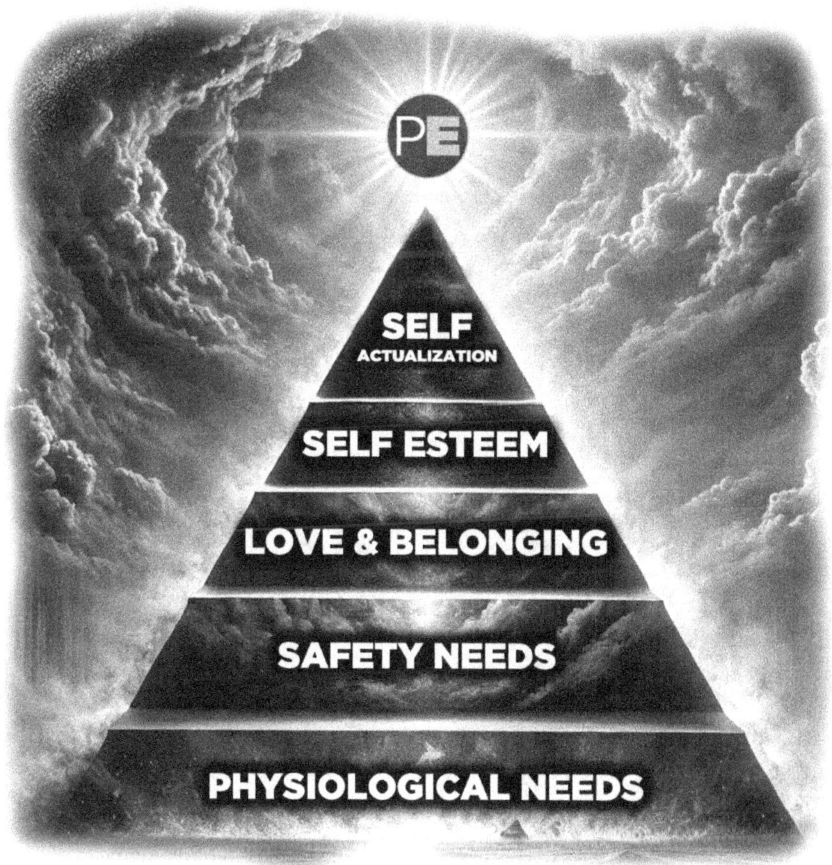

For some, this is just a hypothetical situation. For others, it's reality. Parents, desperate to keep their kids alive, sometimes turn to theft, fraud, or even drug dealing—not because they want to, but because they see no other option. In New York, 2021, a woman was caught shoplifting baby formula and diapers. When confronted, she broke down in tears, saying she had lost her job and had no way to feed her infant. The store owner, rather than pressing charges, decided to help her instead. But not everyone gets that kind of mercy.

On another front, some people break into vacant homes for shelter. Food and water are crucial but so is having a place to sleep. When temperatures drop below freezing, when storms roll in, or when the streets become too dangerous, people without shelter look for any way to find a safe, dry place to rest. That's why many homeless individuals break into vacant homes, abandoned buildings, or even cars. It's illegal, yes. But is it understandable? Think of the homeless man from Chicago in 2023. He was arrested for breaking into a foreclosed house during a snowstorm. He had nowhere else to go and would have frozen to death if he stayed outside. He didn't damage the property; he didn't steal anything; he just wanted a warm place to sleep.

When crimes like theft, trespassing, or even low-level fraud happen, we often ask: Why did they do it? But when you look closer, the answer is usually: Because they had run out of other options. At the end of the day, survival is a powerful force and when people are pushed to their limits, they will do whatever it takes to stay alive.

As we move up the list of needs, ultimately reaching the level of self-actualization, we'll next talk about the safety needs. Once physiological needs are met, the focus shifts to safety, personal security, and financial stability. Perceived threats to these can lead to criminal behavior aimed at establishing security. If there's one thing that motivates people almost as much as food and water, it's safety. Whether it's locking our doors at night, keeping an eye on our bank accounts, or avoiding dark alleys, we all crave security and the assurance that we won't lose what we have, that we won't be harmed, and that tomorrow won't bring disaster. But when people feel constantly unsafe, they may resort to crime as a survival strategy.

Maslow's second level of needs, safety, includes everything from having a stable place to live, feeling protected from violence, and ensuring financial security. If these needs aren't met, people don't just feel uncomfortable. They feel desperate. And desperation can lead to actions that seem criminal on paper but make perfect sense when you look at the circumstances.

Imagine being homeless. Not for a weekend, not because you're between apartments, but because every night, you don't know where you'll sleep. Maybe it's a tent in a park, a space under a bridge, or a bus stop bench. Now imagine it's winter, and the temperature is below freezing. For thousands of people across the country, this isn't a hypothetical, it's their daily reality. And when people are freezing, exhausted, and vulnerable to violence on the streets, what do they do?

Some break into vacant homes. It's called squatting, and while legally it's trespassing or burglary, for those doing it, it's just finding a roof over their head, so they don't freeze to death or get attacked in the middle of the night. In Chicago, 2023, a mother with two young children was found living in an abandoned foreclosed home. She had lost her job, and the shelters were full. So, she took her kids and moved into a house no one was using. She wasn't stealing jewelry or vandalizing the property, she was just trying to keep her kids safe. But when the bank found out, she was arrested for trespassing. Did she break the law? Yes. Was she acting maliciously? No. She was simply doing what any parent would do, trying to protect her children from the elements and the dangers of the street.

And what about those people who are so concerned for their physical safety, they'll do anything, including carrying weapons, regardless of whether it's legal or not. Think about it: If you lived in a dangerous neighborhood, had been robbed before, or worked late-night shifts in an area known for muggings, wouldn't you want some kind of protection? For many, especially in high-crime areas, carrying a knife or an unregistered gun isn't about looking for trouble—it's about making sure they don't become someone else's easy target. In Atlanta, 2022, a man was arrested for carrying a concealed weapon without a permit. He wasn't a criminal mastermind; he was just a construction worker who had been mugged twice walking home from work. When the police asked why he had the gun, he simply said, "I don't trust that if I call 911, help will get there in time." That's a reality many people live with.

Not all safety concerns are about physical danger either, sometimes, it's about financial survival. If you lose your job, your bills pile up, and you have no safety net, what do you do? Some people resort to theft, fraud, or financial crimes to keep themselves afloat. During the COVID-19 pandemic, thousands of people filed fraudulent unemployment claims, not because they were career criminals, but because they were desperate. They had rent due, kids to feed, and no way to make money. Some were caught and charged, but for many, it wasn't about greed, it was about survival.

When people feel unsafe, they make choices they wouldn't normally consider. Breaking into a vacant house, carrying a weapon, or committing financial fraud doesn't necessarily come from a place of malice, it comes from fear. But that doesn't mean laws shouldn't be enforced. It does mean we need to understand the root causes of crime. If people had stable housing, police protection they could trust, and financial security, many crimes wouldn't happen in the first place. Because at the end of the day, when people don't feel safe, they do whatever it takes to survive.

As we build upon the different levels and theories, we need to examine how social need, the pursuit of love and belonging, influences decisions to commit crime. Humans aren't meant to be alone. From the moment we're born, we all crave connection, things like love, friendship, acceptance. It's why we form families, build friendships, and create communities. But what happens when someone doesn't have that? When they feel like an outsider, unwanted, or invisible?

Maslow's third tier of needs, love and belonging is one of the most powerful motivators of human behavior. When people don't find positive connections, they often seek acceptance in places they never imagined and sometimes it leads them straight into criminal behavior. One of the most well-known ways people seek belonging in the wrong places is gang involvement. The logic is simple: If someone feels isolated, rejected, or unsafe, a gang offers brotherhood, loyalty, and protection. It doesn't matter that the price of admission may include violence, drug dealing, or even murder. To some, the trade-off is worth it if it means having a place to belong.

For example, in Chicago, 2011, a 15-year-old boy, feeling invisible at school and ignored at home, was approached by older gang members. They treated him like family, offering a sense of importance and identity he had never felt before. Within months, he was running drugs and committing violent acts, not because he was inherently a criminal, but because he felt accepted for the first time in his life. That acceptance came at a steep price, eventually leading to his arrest and imprisonment. The truth is, many gang members aren't bad people at heart—they're just people who were searching for connection in the only place they could find it.

And that connection includes love, at times, at any cost. Love is a powerful motivator that can lead people to crime. When someone is desperate for affection, they may ignore red flags or go to extreme lengths to keep a relationship intact, even if it means breaking the law. In Texas, 2022, a woman was arrested after helping her boyfriend escape from police custody. She wasn't a criminal, and she had never been in trouble before, but she loved him. He convinced her that if she really cared, she'd help him. She believed him, followed through, and found herself behind bars because her need to feel loved overpowered her judgment.

For many, the fear of rejection is worse than the fear of getting caught. People, especially young adults, will go along with illegal activity just to avoid being seen as weak or uncool. In Los Angeles, 2019, a college freshman was caught shoplifting designer clothes. Did she need the clothes? No. But her new group of friends dared her to do it, and she didn't want to be the odd one out. She took the risk knowingly, not because she wanted the thrill, but because she wanted their approval. It's a familiar story: People don't always commit crimes because they want to, sometimes they do it because they want to belong.

When people lack love, friendship, or community, they often gravitate toward anything that fills that void, even if it's dangerous. It's easy to say, "They should have known better," but when someone feels invisible or unloved, logic takes a backseat to emotion. Addressing this need early on through mentorship, support systems, and strong community connections, can help prevent crime before it ever starts. Because at the end of the day, what most people really want isn't to break the law. They just want to belong.

The pursuit of respect and recognition makes up the fourth level of Maslow's Hierarchy of Needs chart with the Esteem level. At some point, everyone wants to feel respected, valued, and important. Whether it's in our careers, social circles, or personal lives, we crave recognition for our efforts. When we feel overlooked or dismissed, it can eat away at us, leading to frustration, resentment, and, for some, criminal behavior. This level is all about self-worth and validation. People will go to great lengths to earn respect, prove their competence, or gain status. But when they feel like they're constantly being undervalued or ignored, they may bend (or break) the rules to get the recognition they feel they deserve.

It happens in many different ways where success doesn't seem to be enough for a budding predator. For people in high-pressure jobs, status can mean everything. If someone has been working hard for years with little reward, the temptation to cut corners or cheat the system can become too great to resist. For example, in San Francisco, 2015, a mid-level executive felt stuck in his career. Despite his dedication, he was constantly passed over for promotions. He watched as less experienced colleagues climbed the corporate ladder, leaving him in their dust. Frustrated and desperate to prove his worth, he turned to insider trading—using confidential company information to make profitable stock trades. He was caught, fired, and charged with securities fraud.

Did he need the money? Not really. He wanted recognition, power, and the respect of his peers. But instead of getting the admiration he craved; he got a prison sentence.

It's not much different on the streets where respect by any means necessary seems to be the rule of thumb. In some environments, respect isn't just about pride, it's also a weird form of survival. For many in high-crime neighborhoods, being seen as "weak" can make you a target. This is why some individuals turn to violent crime as a way to command respect and establish dominance. In New York, 2022, a young man was involved in a deadly altercation over a social media insult. Someone called him weak online, and instead of ignoring it, he felt he had to "defend his name." To him, backing down meant losing respect in his community and that was something he couldn't afford. The confrontation escalated, and he ended up pulling a gun and killing the other man. It wasn't about money or power. It was about status, reputation, and proving he wasn't someone to mess with.

Sometimes, people are so desperate for status and recognition that they create a false image of success, even if it means breaking the law. That proved out in a 2021 case in Los Angeles where a woman was arrested for posing as a wealthy socialite. She attended elite parties, scammed her way into VIP events, and even convinced banks to loan her money based on fake credentials. She wasn't trying to steal for survival, the woman just wanted to be admired, envied, and respected.

When people feel invisible, ignored, or undervalued, they seek ways to stand out. Some do it the right way through hard work and perseverance. Others take shortcuts, believing that if they can just get ahead, the recognition will follow. But crime for the sake of validation is a losing game. Whether it's an executive committing fraud, a street-level altercation over respect, or someone pretending to be something they're not, the pursuit of status at any cost often leads to disaster instead of admiration. At the end of the day, respect should be earned, not stolen because when people chase recognition the wrong way, it usually comes with a mugshot instead of a medal.

At the very top of Maslow's Hierarchy of Needs sits self-actualization, the ultimate pursuit of becoming the best version of yourself. This is where people chase personal growth, creativity, and their full potential. It's the level where artists create their greatest works, scientists make groundbreaking discoveries, and leaders leave their mark on history.

Sounds noble, right? But here's the catch, when the desire to "be the best" takes over, some people cross ethical lines to get there. Not because they're starving, not because they need money, but because they're obsessed with success. Some of the most infamous intellectual frauds come from people who were already brilliant but that wasn't enough. They wanted to be remembered as legendary, and when reality didn't match their ambitions, they faked their way to greatness.

In Germany, 2006, a respected academic made headlines after fabricating some of his research data, hoping to garner envy and attention. He was desperate to produce groundbreaking findings in his field, something that would put his name in history books. But rather than putting in the work to get there, he faked the results. Why? Because he wanted to be remembered as a genius, not just another professor. His downfall wasn't a lack of intelligence, it was a need to be extraordinary, no matter the cost. It boiled down to a lack of integrity.

It could also be someone who is so driven to be something great, that they are willing to pretend they are something they're not. There have been cases of fake doctors, pilots, and lawyers, all of whom took dangerous risks just to live out their dream careers. In Florida, 2021, an 18-year-old posed as a doctor, and actually saw patients! He dressed the part, used medical jargon, and even managed to fool real healthcare professionals for a while. When he was caught, he didn't seem remorseful. He believed he was meant to be a doctor and thought he was just "skipping a few steps" to get there.

And it doesn't stop with certain professions, for some, self-actualization means being the best in their field but when hard work isn't enough, they turn to cheating. Think about the steroid scandals in professional sports. Athletes who were already world-class competitors risked their careers by using performance-enhancing drugs. Why? Because being great wasn't enough, they wanted to be the greatest of all time. Or take Hollywood, where actors have been caught lying about credentials, stealing scripts, or bribing their way into roles. When you crave legendary status, ethical concerns can feel like minor obstacles in the pursuit of greatness.

When people break the law for basic survival, we get it. But when someone already successful throws it all away just to be more successful, it's harder to understand. The truth is that ambition can be just as dangerous as desperation. Some people don't just want to do well, they want to be iconic, untouchable, and remembered forever. And when their talent or hard work isn't enough to reach that level, they cheat, lie, and manipulate their way to the top.

But history is unforgiving. People who take shortcuts to success rarely stay on top for long. And when they fall, they don't just lose their reputation, they lose everything. These cases demonstrate how unmet needs at various levels of Maslow's Hierarchy can influence individuals toward criminal behavior. Addressing these underlying needs through social support, economic opportunities, and mental health services is crucial in preventing such actions and promoting a more just society.

As we wrap up this exploration of Maslow's Hierarchy of Needs and Crime, it's important to remember that not all crime is committed by people seeking power, revenge, or greed. Sometimes, people break the law for reasons that, at their most basic level, make sense, like needing food, shelter, or security. When someone steals bread because they're starving, or trespasses into an abandoned house because they have nowhere else to go, it's easy to see how desperation, not malice, was the driving force behind their decision.

But as we move up the hierarchy, crime shifts from acts of survival to acts of personal ambition, status, and power. A person committing financial fraud to gain recognition, a gang member committing a violent act to earn respect, or a scientist falsifying data to secure fame have all committed crimes, but they stem from different needs than those at the bottom of the hierarchy. This is where the line between understandable and predatory crime begins to blur.

The further up Maslow's pyramid we climb, the less crime is about immediate survival and the more it's about personal gain. And yet, at every level, the common denominator remains: an unmet need. Some needs are universal and urgent like food, water, shelter, while others are more psychological such as belonging, esteem, or self-fulfillment. When those needs aren't met through legal, ethical means, some people turn to crime as a shortcut.

The takeaway? The more we can ensure people's basic needs are met, the less likely they are to resort to crime. When people have food, shelter, security, and opportunities, the desperation that fuels criminal behavior decreases. That doesn't mean we excuse criminal acts, but if we understand why people commit them, we might just have a better shot at preventing them before they happen.

Now that we've looked at how unmet needs fuel crime, it's time to explore something even darker, the people who don't just commit crimes out of necessity but do so because they want to. Some predators don't kill for money or security. They kill because they like it. In the next chapter, we'll take a closer look at the "wolves in sheep's clothing," those predators who manipulate, deceive, and destroy for their own twisted satisfaction.

We've spent this chapter dissecting why people commit crimes, breaking it down to human needs, and seeing how everything from survival instincts to power-hungry ambition can drive someone to break the law. But while understanding crime is crucial, it's only half the battle. The real question is: How do we protect ourselves from it?

Crime doesn't just exist in news reports or true crime documentaries, it's something that happens in real time, to real people, every day. And often, the difference between becoming a target and staying safe comes down to awareness, preparation, and instinct.

Imagine walking home at night, feeling that gut instinct telling you something is wrong. Maybe it's a shadow lingering too long in your periphery, or the sound of footsteps that weren't there a moment ago. It's easy to dismiss the feeling—to tell yourself you're just being paranoid. But in reality, that instinct might be your best defense.

This is where we shift gears. Crime happens—but you don't have to be helpless against it. In the next chapter, we'll explore practical strategies to stay safe, recognize danger before it strikes, and empower yourself with the tools to reduce the risk of victimization. Because while understanding the mind of a predator is useful, knowing how to stop them in their tracks is even better.

Awareness is most effective when paired with proactive decision-making. Taking deliberate steps to reduce risk can make a significant difference in personal safety. -MK

Chapter Seventeen

Staying Safe: Strategies for Personal Awareness and Protection

The rain came down in sheets as Linda stepped off the bus, her umbrella already fighting against the wind. She had walked this route a hundred times, the well-lit streets and familiar storefronts providing her a sense of security. Yet tonight, something felt off. A shadow loomed longer than usual in her periphery, and her heart quickened. Linda adjusted her grip on her belongings and thought back to the self-defense seminar she had attended months ago. *Be aware of your surroundings*, the instructor had said. That mantra now echoed in her mind as she mentally prepared herself for the possibility of danger.

Linda's story is not unique. In a world where predatory behavior can manifest in various forms, whether it is theft, assault, or scams and awareness and preparedness are key. This chapter will delve into strategies for personal safety, offering empowering guidance to reduce the risk of victimization.

Awareness is the foundation of personal safety, providing individuals with the ability to anticipate and avoid potential dangers. Predators often exploit moments of distraction, targeting individuals who appear preoccupied or unaware of their surroundings. By cultivating a state of heightened awareness, people can significantly reduce their vulnerability to threats and increase their overall sense of security.

Situational awareness is the ability to perceive, understand, and respond to one's environment. It involves staying attuned to surroundings and recognizing potential threats before they materialize. Developing this skill begins with observing one's environment deliberately. As you navigate the world, take note of who and what is around you. Are there people behaving suspiciously or lingering without a clear purpose? Is the area adequately lit and free of hidden spaces? These seemingly simple observations can be the difference between danger and safety.

In another example, Megan pulled her coat tighter around her body as she descended the steps into the subway station. It was late—too late, really, and she regretted staying out past rush hour when the platforms were still crowded. Now, the dim station felt emptier than she liked, the usual hum of the city replaced by the occasional echo of footsteps. It was those footsteps that made her stomach clench.

She had first noticed the man outside the convenience store when she stopped to buy a bottle of water. At first, she thought it was coincidence, after all, people walked the same way all the time. But then she caught his reflection in a storefront window. He wasn't just walking though; he was following her. Megan took a slow, steady breath and reminded herself to stay calm. She had read about this before. Stay aware, trust your instincts, and act before a situation escalates.

Instead of heading straight to her usual platform, she veered toward the station's service counter. The uniformed transit worker behind the glass looked up as she approached. "Excuse me," she said, keeping her voice level, "Can you tell me when the next train to Midtown arrives?"

It wasn't the question that mattered, it was the eye contact, the human connection, the subtle signal that she was alert and not alone.

Out of the corner of her eye, she saw the man hesitate. He had been lingering near the turnstiles, but now, with her standing in plain sight, he seemed uncertain. Megan took another step toward the service window, making a show of adjusting her bag. "Also," she added, lowering her voice just enough for the transit worker to hear, "I think I'm being followed." The worker's gaze sharpened immediately. He nodded, glanced discreetly in the man's direction, and reached for the station's radio. "Stay where you are," he said in a firm, calm voice.

Megan didn't move, keeping herself positioned near the bright fluorescent lights of the counter. A minute later, a uniformed officer from the transit police appeared at the top of the stairs. He surveyed the station, his eyes landing on the loitering man. Just like that, her would-be follower turned on his heel and disappeared back up the steps, swallowed by the night.

The officer watched him go before turning to Megan. "You did the right thing," he told her. She exhaled, realizing how tight her shoulders had been. As the train pulled into the station, Megan stepped on with a newfound sense of control. She had trusted her instincts, stayed in a well-lit area, and sought help when she needed it. Tonight, she had walked away unharmed. And because of that, she knew she would never ignore her gut feeling again.

These incidents underscore how staying alert to one's surroundings can preemptively neutralize threats. A vital aspect of awareness is learning to trust your instincts. Often referred to as a "gut feeling," instinctual reactions are your brain's way of processing subtle cues that may indicate danger. Acting on these feelings without hesitation can be lifesaving. If a situation feels off, it is essential to prioritize your safety over social niceties or fear of overreacting.

Consider the case of a mother in a quiet Dallas, Texas neighborhood. It was a typical day, kids playing outside, parents catching up on chores, and the Texas sun beaming down. But what started as an ordinary afternoon quickly turned into every parent's worst nightmare.

Genna was inside when she heard the sudden, panicked screams of her children and their friends. It wasn't just the usual playground shrieks; it was pure terror. When she ran to her front door, she saw her two sons, Zachary and Jonathan, along with their friends, sprinting toward the house, their faces filled with fear.

According to ABC News, Genna's home security camera captured the terrifying moment. Two vehicles had pulled up near the group of kids, and a man in a white SUV got out, attempting to lure Jonathan inside. He said, "There's a football in the back of the car. We should get in the back of the car," Jonathan later recalled. But this kid wasn't falling for it. Instead, he bolted. "I'm sorry. I don't talk to strangers," he said before running straight to his house.

The video showed the kids running and screaming for help, their instincts kicking in at just the right time. Zachary was the first to reach the door, yelling, "Someone's trying to kidnap us!" By the time Genna got outside, armed with her phone to record the scene, the man noticed her and took off. But he made one crucial mistake, and she managed to snap a picture of his license plate before he disappeared.

Authorities later revealed that just miles away, another attempted abduction had been caught on a neighbor's security camera. This time, a teenage girl was seen hiding behind a car, trying to evade a man who had been following her. The car's owner told Good Morning America (GMA) that the terrified girl knocked on his door for help. "She said that somebody that she didn't know had been following her, staring at her, making her feel uncomfortable."

Both incidents serve as a chilling reminder of how quickly things can take a dangerous turn. Experts say that kidnappers often use vehicles to lure victims, offering things like lost pets, candy, or as in

Jonathan's case, a football. Callahan Walsh, the executive director of the National Center for Missing and Exploited Children, told GMA that parents need to have open conversations with their kids about how to recognize and avoid these situations. "We know that perpetrators are using the same lures," Walsh said. "Children should be very wary of strangers in a car approaching them."

Fortunately, Jonathan and his friends knew exactly what to do. They ran, screamed, and refused to engage with the stranger. It was enough to save them. While authorities are still searching for suspects in both attempted abductions, Genna's family is just grateful their boys made it home safe. Their story is a stark warning, but also proof that teaching kids how to react in dangerous situations can make all the difference.

In today's technology-driven world, distractions are everywhere. Smartphones, headphones, and other devices often monopolize attention, leaving individuals unaware of their immediate surroundings. Unfortunately, this disengagement makes people more attractive targets to predators. Staying alert and minimizing distractions not only helps deter threats but also conveys confidence and awareness, which are deterrents in themselves.

In Kentucky, USA, a routine evening walk turned tragic when 43-year-old man named Jeremy was fatally struck by a car while crossing U.S. Highway 68. According to the Marshall County Sheriff's Office, the accident happened around 6 p.m. when Robinson, reportedly wearing headphones, stepped into the path of an oncoming vehicle. Despite the driver's attempt to avoid him, the impact was unavoidable.

Authorities confirmed that Jeremy frequently listened to music while walking, something many of us do without a second thought. But this heartbreaking incident is a sobering reminder of how distractions, even something as simple as headphones, can significantly reduce awareness of our surroundings.

In today's fast-paced world, we're constantly multitasking. Whether it's listening to music, texting, or checking social media, our attention is often split between what's happening in our ears or hands and what's happening around us. Unfortunately, this distraction can be deadly, especially when navigating areas with vehicle traffic. When we wear headphones or focus on our screens, we lose critical awareness of oncoming cars, horns, sirens, or other warning signs that could prevent an accident.

Jeremy's tragic accident is a heartbreaking lesson in how a simple habit can become dangerous in the wrong setting. While technology enhances our daily lives, it's essential to prioritize safety first. A song or podcast can wait but life can't be rewound.

Awareness is most effective when paired with proactive decision-making. Taking deliberate steps to reduce risk can make a significant difference in personal safety. For instance, choosing well-lit paths, avoiding isolated areas, and informing someone of your whereabouts are small yet impactful actions. Additionally, practicing situational drills, such as identifying escape routes or safe locations in unfamiliar places, can enhance preparedness.

When disaster strikes, the difference between survival and tragedy often comes down to one thing: preparation. That was painfully clear during the Maui wildfires of 2023, where residents who had thought ahead and had supplies ready, including knowing the evacuation routes, were far more likely to escape unharmed, even in the middle of all the chaos. The fire moved so fast that many people had little time to react, and in some cases, official warnings never even came. Roads became gridlocked, communication systems failed, and uncertainty turned deadly. But those who had already mapped out alternate routes and knew what steps to take didn't freeze. They moved. They got out. And they survived.

This kind of proactive decision-making isn't just about wildfires or natural disasters. It applies to personal safety in everyday life. Whether you're walking to your car at night, traveling alone, or in a situation where something just feels off, having a plan before you need it can be the key to staying safe.

Think about how often people get caught off guard in dangerous situations, not because they're reckless, but because they assume nothing bad will happen to them. It's human nature to downplay risk. But when the unexpected does happen, hesitation can be deadly. In personal safety, just like in the Maui fires, knowing what to do before a crisis happens can make all the difference.

A woman walking alone at night who senses someone following her will have a better chance of avoiding danger if she's already considered her escape options. Where's the nearest well-lit area? Is there a store or a gas station nearby where she can step inside? Can she call someone and let them know her location? Someone who has already rehearsed these scenarios in their mind will react faster and with more confidence than someone who hasn't.

The same concept applies to self-defense. People who successfully escape an attack don't always do so because they're physically stronger, they do it because they're mentally prepared. They've trained themselves to stay aware of their surroundings instead of zoning out on their phones. They've thought about what they would do if someone grabbed them. They might even carry a personal safety tool, like pepper spray or an alarm, and know how to use it.

One of the biggest lessons from Maui or from personal safety instruction in general is that denial is dangerous. In moments of crisis, many people freeze, not because they don't care about their safety, but because their brain is struggling to accept that something terrible is happening. That's why thinking ahead is so critical. When you've already mentally prepared for a dangerous situation, you're less likely to hesitate when seconds matter most.

If you're walking alone at night and get that uneasy feeling that something isn't right, would you already have a plan? Would you know where your closest safe location is? Would you be prepared to change your route or act if needed? In Maui, the people who survived weren't necessarily the ones who were the fastest runners or the strongest, they were the ones who anticipated danger before it arrived.

The tragic reality of the Maui fires proves that waiting for help isn't always an option. Sometimes, your survival is entirely up to you. That's not about living in fear; it's about living with awareness. Being prepared, whether for a wildfire, an attack, or any unexpected crisis doesn't mean you're paranoid, it means you're smart enough to think ahead. Because when the worst happens, the best thing you can be is ready.

Awareness is not just an individual responsibility; communities play a crucial role in fostering a culture of vigilance. Programs such as neighborhood watch groups and community safety workshops empower residents to look out for one another. Sharing information about potential threats or suspicious activities enhances collective safety and encourages a sense of solidarity.

As technology evolves, so too do the methods predators use to exploit individuals. Online awareness has become just as critical as situational awareness in physical spaces. Phishing scams, cyberstalking, and data breaches are common threats in the digital realm. Understanding privacy settings, recognizing suspicious links, and safeguarding personal information are essential steps to maintain security.

In the publication, *ScamWatch*, one story of an investment scam summed up how seemingly intelligent people can make critical mistakes. It all started with a phone call from an online trader who

sounded incredibly confident. The caller told the victim his company specialized in binary options, cryptocurrency, and forex trading, claiming they were on the cutting edge of technology and could offer guaranteed returns. It all seemed so professional, the online broker had the right answers, and the victim was intrigued.

At first, the victim invested a few thousand dollars and started using their online trading platform, which appeared to work flawlessly. He could see his trades making profits, and everything looked promising. Encouraged by the results and the scammer's insistence that he could earn even more; he invested more money. They assured him that he was on the fast track to major returns.

Then came the red flags. When he decided to withdraw his money, they suddenly told him he needed to pay taxes on his profits before he could access any of it. This was the first time he had heard anything about paying upfront taxes, but they were adamant—it was a requirement before he could cash out.

Right after he refused to send more money, things took a nosedive. His trades, which had been consistently profitable, started failing, and his accumulated profits began to vanish. That's when the pressure kicked in. They urged him to invest even more, saying it was the only way to recover his losses and boost his "trade volume." According to them, if the victim didn't act fast, he would lose everything.

At that point, the victim started to see the truth. He had fallen for a scam. They made it seem like he was about to be "kicked off the market" because his trades were failing, and his balance had dropped to just 3 percent of his initial investment. But by then, he knew it was all a lie.

After this experience, the victim felt embarrassed and angry. The online predators were incredibly convincing, professional, and strategic in how they manipulated the victim. Everything used in the scam, the "platform," the profits, the urgency, was all designed to lure the victim in and drain him dry. Unfortunately, he learned the hard way that if something sounds too good to be true, it probably is.

Awareness is not a one-time effort but a lifelong practice. It requires continuous learning, adapting to new environments, and reflecting on past experiences. Training programs, self-defense courses, and mindfulness practices can further enhance one's ability to stay alert and respond effectively to threats.

Organizations like the National Crime Prevention Council offer resources and training to help individuals develop situational awareness. Such programs provide practical tools for identifying risks and taking proactive measures, emphasizing the importance of preparation.[102] Similar programs are often available through local police departments.

The power of awareness lies in its ability to transform individuals from passive participants in their environment to active agents of their safety. By cultivating situational awareness, trusting instincts, reducing distractions, and making proactive choices, people can significantly reduce their vulnerability to threats. Furthermore, fostering a culture of awareness within communities and adapting to the challenges of the digital age strengthen collective safety.

The examples of those who have evaded danger through vigilance, from subway stations to wildfire evacuations, demonstrate that awareness is a critical life skill. It empowers individuals to take control of their surroundings, prioritize their safety, and respond effectively to potential risks. In this ever-changing world, staying aware is not just a choice but a necessity that provides you with the power to save lives.

Understanding the psychology of predators is a vital aspect of personal safety and awareness. Predators, whether criminal opportunists or more calculated manipulators, operate based on a clear set of strategies designed to exploit their victims' vulnerabilities. By learning how predators think and operate, individuals can make informed choices to protect themselves from harm.

Predators operate with a focused intent: to achieve their goals with minimal effort and risk to themselves. This intent often involves identifying those they perceive as the weakest or most susceptible to their tactics. In doing so, predators assess potential victims using a combination of environmental, physical, and psychological factors. Their behavior is often driven by an understanding of human nature and a calculated approach to exploiting it.

At the core of the predatory mindset is the principle of opportunity. Much like predators in the animal kingdom, human predators seek out scenarios where their chances of success are highest. They exploit moments of distraction, isolation, or complacency, relying on their ability to remain undetected until they strike. This opportunistic behavior highlights the importance of awareness and preparedness as essential tools in avoiding becoming a target.

Predators typically evaluate three primary factors when selecting their victims: accessibility, vulnerability, and the likelihood of resistance. Each of these plays a critical role in determining who is targeted.

Accessibility refers to how easily a predator can approach or isolate their target. Predators often seek individuals in secluded or poorly lit areas, where the chances of intervention are minimal. Locations such as empty parking lots, quiet streets, or isolated public spaces provide an environment conducive to their plans. Accessibility also extends to situations where a victim is preoccupied—checking a phone, wearing headphones, or carrying multiple items—reducing their ability to notice or react to potential threats.[103]

Vulnerability is another critical factor in victim selection. Predators look for individuals who appear distracted, impaired, or physically weaker. Distraction reduces situational awareness, making it easier for a predator to approach undetected. Impairment, whether due to alcohol, drugs, or fatigue, diminishes a person's ability to respond effectively to danger. Physical weakness, such as a smaller stature or visible injuries, further increases perceived vulnerability. Predators are highly attuned to body language, seeking signs of insecurity, nervousness, or submissiveness in their targets.[104]

The likelihood of resistance is the final consideration for most predators. They prefer victims who seem unlikely to fight back or draw attention. Confidence, on the other hand, can serve as a powerful deterrent. Individuals who walk with purpose, maintain strong posture, and appear aware of their surroundings project an image of strength and preparedness. This reduces their appeal as targets, as predators tend to avoid individuals who might resist or complicate their efforts.[105]

Beyond physical and situational factors, predators often rely on psychological manipulation to achieve their objectives. These tactics are designed to lower their target's defenses, create confusion, or instill a false sense of security. Understanding these methods can help individuals recognize and respond to manipulative behavior before it escalates.

Many predators use charm and flattery as tools to gain trust. By presenting themselves as friendly, helpful, or charismatic, they disarm their target's natural wariness. This tactic is especially effective in situations where a predator's intentions might initially seem benign. For example, helping with groceries or striking up a conversation about a shared interest may appear innocent but can serve as a precursor to manipulation.

Fabricating emergencies or time-sensitive situations is another common strategy. Predators may claim they need immediate help or create a scenario that pressures their target to act quickly. This tactic preys on the human instinct to assist others in distress, diverting attention from potential red flags. For instance, a predator might feign car trouble or pretend to search for a lost pet to lure their victim into a vulnerable position.[106]

Boundary testing involves subtle actions to gauge a person's reaction to inappropriate or invasive behavior. Predators may invade personal space, make overly familiar remarks, or engage in minor physical contact to assess their target's response. If the individual tolerates these behaviors or fails to assert their boundaries, the predator may interpret this as a sign of acquiescence, encouraging them to escalate their actions.

To highlight these complexities, let's look at the author's recollections after he and Greg Cooper interviewed a serial killer inside the Montana State Prison. Meeting inmate Daniel Troyer was an experience neither will forget. They sat across from him in a Montana prison interview room, speaking with a man convicted of two murders but suspected of many more.

What began as a standard conversation about his past quickly took a chilling turn as Troyer confessed to eight murders, all elderly women from Salt Lake City. Law enforcement had long believed there were additional victims, but until that moment, those were just suspicions. Troyer confirmed what investigators had feared.

He didn't see himself as a monster, though. Instead, he likened himself to a lioness stalking prey. "When you look at the lioness sunning herself, playing with her cubs, licking her paws, you have a difficult time understanding how vicious and violent she can be," he told us. "But after a while, the hunger builds up inside of her, and she begins to hunt. When she kills, it is terribly brutal. She then feeds and when full, returns to laying in the sun and rolling on her back. That's how I feel after I kill an old lady."

Troyer's violent history started young. At just 20 years old, he broke into the home of a 70-year-old quadriplegic woman he knew and sexually assaulted her. The woman promised not to tell, but as soon as he fled, she reported him to the police. Troyer was convicted, but his time in prison only solidified his future path—he vowed that from then on, no victim would be left alive to report him.

He followed through on that vow. Within weeks of his release, he committed his first murder. One of his victims, in a particularly twisted act of cruelty, was Mrs. Easthope, the mother of his cellmate, a man already infamous in Utah as the Sugarhouse Rapist. Troyer had no connection to her beyond knowing her son from prison, but that was enough.

His method was simple but effective. He conned his way into his victims' homes by preying on their loneliness. "Old people are lonely and want to talk," he told us with an eerie nonchalance. Troyer would purchase a few magazines from a nearby convenience store and pretend to be selling them, gaining access under the guise of a door-to-door salesman.

Once inside, he killed quickly. In the beginning, he preferred strangulation from behind because that method ensured there would be a minimal struggle. But as his confidence grew, he started killing them while looking into their eyes. For Troyer, though, the murder itself was only part of the experience. Afterward, he would spend time with the victim's body, engaging in necrophilia acts, bathing the victim, dressing them in pajamas, and carefully placing them in bed. Within a day or two, a family member would check in, find their loved one dead in bed, and assume they had simply passed away in their sleep.

Daniel Troyer's strategy worked. For years, his victims were buried as natural deaths, their murders unnoticed. His luck might have continued if not for a single mistake where he left a fingerprint at a crime scene. When detectives questioned him about the crime, Troyer confused the event with one of his murders. In his attempt to explain himself, he confessed to the wrong crime, unintentionally opening the door to his darkest secrets.

Perhaps the most disturbing moment of our interviews came when Troyer explained the way he thought as a psychopath.

"Let's say I hate my brother-in-law, and I want to kill him," he told us. "But my mother loves my brother-in-law, and I love my mother... I know if I kill him, it would hurt her emotionally, so the solution is simple—I'll kill my mother first so that I don't hurt her... and then I can kill my brother-in-law."

His logic was chilling, completely detached from human empathy. To him, murder was simply a means to an end.

As we wrapped up the interview, we asked him one final question: "Daniel, what would you do if you were released from prison today?" Without a moment's hesitation, Troyer smiled slightly and said,

---

"I'd go out and kill an old lady."

There was no remorse. No second thought. Troyer was a hunter who never intended to stop.

The ability to recognize predatory behavior is a crucial step in protecting oneself. Awareness of common tactics and red flags enables individuals to take proactive measures to avoid danger. When encountering potentially manipulative behavior, it is essential to trust one's instincts and act decisively.

Asserting boundaries firmly and confidently can serve as a powerful deterrent. When confronted with intrusive behavior, making clear statements such as "I'm not comfortable with that" or "Please step back" communicates that such actions are unwelcome. Disengaging from situations  that feel unsafe or suspicious is equally important. This may involve leaving the area, seeking help, or contacting authorities. Individuals must prioritize their safety over social niceties, breaking the predator's expectation of passivity.

Ultimately, personal safety is about cultivating a proactive and adaptable mindset. Building a safety network is another valuable strategy. Share travel plans with trusted friends or family members and when possible, use GPS tracking apps. Incorporate safety strategies into your daily life. It doesn't require a lot of effort and consistency, but the payoff is invaluable. By combining awareness, tools, and training, you can take control of your safety and reduce your susceptibility to threats.

When considering your digital footprint, practice these same prevention tactics on your keyboards and mobile devices. Create strong, unique passwords for each online account. In addition to strong passwords, implement two-factor authentication and make sure your privacy settings are where you want them on your social media accounts.

Avoid clicking on suspicious links or downloading attachments from untrusted sources. Hovering over a link to preview the URL can help identify whether it leads to a legitimate website or a malicious one. Downloading attachments should also be limited to files from known and trusted sources to avoid opening potentially harmful content. And use up-to-date security software.

Build a support network you can rely upon. A crucial first step in building your support network is identifying reliable individuals. Family members often form the foundation of this network. These are people who can offer emotional support, provide a sense of security, and help with practical needs. Close friends, too, can be invaluable, providing not just emotional comfort but also a fresh perspective on personal matters. Colleagues, particularly those who understand your work environment, can be allies in both professional and personal contexts. Neighbors are also an important part of your support system.

Having local residents who are familiar with your daily routines can provide a sense of reassurance, as they are often more attuned to any changes or potential concerns in your environment. Additionally, participating in local community activities—whether through clubs, organizations, or volunteer groups—can expand your network and connect you with people who share common interests. These community ties not only broaden your support base but also foster a deeper sense of belonging and collective responsibility. The American Red Cross suggests that older adults, in particular, build a personal support network with several individuals who can check in during emergencies and provide assistance when needed.[107]

Regular communication is essential for maintaining a strong support network. By setting up consistent check-ins with trusted contacts, you ensure that someone is always aware of your whereabouts and well-being. This is particularly important when traveling alone or in high-risk situations. Communicating your plans, such as where you're going and when you expect to return, allows your support network to stay informed and mobilize help quickly if necessary. If you are traveling or living in unfamiliar areas, this step becomes even more critical.

Designating safe spaces and meeting points is another crucial element of your safety strategy. Safe spaces can be well-lit public areas or known establishments—places where you feel comfortable and secure. Identifying these areas in advance allows you to have a fallback plan if you find yourself in a potentially dangerous situation. Additionally, establishing designated meeting points with your support network can provide clear and easy-to-follow instructions in case of an emergency. For example, if you feel unsafe or need assistance, you can agree to meet at a particular café, park, or friend's home. These designated places help reduce confusion during stressful situations and ensure that you have a reliable place to seek shelter.

Engaging in community activities is a great way to build a strong network of support. Participating in local events, joining clubs, or volunteering can help you form meaningful connections with people who share your values. These activities not only help you stay engaged with your local environment but also provide opportunities to make new friends and create a safety net of people who can assist you in times of need. In addition, such involvement can provide important social resources, such as access to local knowledge or connections to emergency services.

Stepping in when something's not right can make a world of difference, and that's where bystander intervention comes into play. If more folks felt empowered to act when they spotted trouble, we'd all be a bit safer. But doing so requires wisdom. Evaluate whether the timing is right for your personal intervention or if you should be dialing 9-1-1.

The organization Right To Be (formerly Hollaback!) has laid out five straightforward strategies known as the 5 D's of Bystander Intervention to guide us in these kinds of situations. They are Direct, Distract, Delegate, Delay, and Document. Each component offers a way to intervene without putting yourself at risk. If it's safe to do so, address the bad behavior you are witnessing head-on. This might deescalate things. A simple, "Hey, that's not okay" might be all that it takes. You might create a diversion, a distraction to defuse the situation. Your unrelated question or harmless commotion may break the flow of a harmful situation.

You don't have to do these measures alone. You can delegate the responsibility to someone else, like a store manager or security guard to address the issue. If intervening isn't possible and you know the person being affected, check in with them and show support. A simple "Hey, are you okay?" can mean a lot. And, when you witness something, record it (discreetly and safely) so that you can provide evidence of the situation later if needed.

But encouraging bystander intervention isn't just about stopping immediate harm; it's about fostering a culture where we all look out for each other. This ties into the concept of watching out for each other. When we watch out for each other, we create environments where harmful behaviors are less likely to go unchecked

Building supportive networks isn't always straightforward. There may be feelings of isolation, past trust issues, or simply not knowing where to start that can get in the way. The good news is there are local groups, community watch organizations and ways to connect with like-minded individuals who can help you overcome these obstacles.

By investing in community-building efforts, you can begin to realize a safer and more resilient lifestyle.

Personal safety is a shared responsibility that can be easier to obtain through a nurturing support network where you not only enhance your own security but contribute to the well-being of your neighbor.

In the example at the beginning of this chapter, Linda made it home safely that night, her unease dissipating as she locked her door behind her. The steps she had taken—both that evening and in her preparation beforehand—illustrated the profound impact of personal safety strategies.

Empowerment comes not from living in fear but from equipping oneself with knowledge, tools, and the confidence to navigate life's uncertainties. By embracing awareness, understanding predator behavior, and taking proactive measures, individuals can significantly reduce their risk of victimization while fostering a greater sense of control.

While Linda's story underscores the power of individual awareness and preparation, personal safety is only one side of the equation. The pursuit of justice—the relentless search for truth, accountability, and answers—often extends beyond law enforcement and into the hands of the public.

Crime has always fascinated society, but in recent years, that fascination has evolved into something far more impactful. What was once a passive interest has now gripped us by compelling headlines and sensationalized retellings which have transformed into a movement where armchair detectives, internet sleuths, and true crime enthusiasts actively engage with unsolved cases. Some analyze police reports, others pore over decades-old evidence, and in rare but remarkable cases, their efforts have led to real breakthroughs.

This is not an entirely new phenomenon. The hunger to understand crime, its perpetrators, and its victims has deep historical roots. From the grisly broadsheets of 16th-century England to the chilling accounts of Jack the Ripper's reign of terror, crime has always captivated the public imagination. But in the modern era, the true crime genre has evolved beyond mere storytelling—it has become a force capable of changing lives, solving mysteries, and, in some cases, even rewriting history.

The modern era has ushered in a digital revolution that has transformed nearly every aspect of society, including criminal investigations. Among the most profound changes has been the rise of the true crime community, a diverse and highly engaged network of amateur sleuths, who share a passion for uncovering the truth about unsolved crimes. -MK

Chapter Eighteen

The Role of the True Crime Community in Solving Cases

The fascination with true crime is not new; its roots can be traced back centuries. From the lurid pamphlets of 16th-century England detailing gruesome murders to the serialized publications of the 19th century, humanity's morbid curiosity about crime has always found an outlet. These early forms of true crime storytelling were both entertaining and instructional.

During the Victorian era, the publication of detailed crime narratives like those of Jack the Ripper in London newspapers captivated audiences and cemented true crime's place in popular culture. These stories were often dramatized to stoke public interest and sell newspapers, establishing a pattern of sensationalism that continues to this day.

The modern true crime movement began to gain traction in the late 20th century, catalyzed by advancements in media and a cultural

shift toward voyeuristic exploration of deviance. Books like Truman Capote's *In Cold Blood* set a precedent for narrative nonfiction that blended literary artistry with meticulous factual reporting, drawing readers into the intimate details of criminal acts and the lives affected by them. Capote's approach was groundbreaking, using deep character studies and a novelistic structure to turn a rural Kansas murder into a universal exploration of crime and punishment. This genre-defining work inspired a wave of writers and journalists to take similar approaches to crime storytelling, elevating the genre into the literary mainstream.

By the late 20th century, television programs such as *America's Most Wanted* further expanded public engagement with real crime stories by presenting cases in an interactive format, calling upon viewers to assist law enforcement by providing tips and leads. Hosted by John Walsh, whose own son had been murdered, the program combined advocacy for victims with a direct call to action, leading to the apprehension of hundreds of fugitives. This formula, which was part storytelling, part public service, proved immensely successful, paving the way for future programs and media forms that involved audience participation.

The 21st century witnessed an explosion of true crime media, largely driven by the advent of digital platforms. Podcasts such as *Serial* and *Crime Junkie* democratized storytelling, allowing creators to delve deeply into unsolved cases and criminal phenomena. These podcasts not only entertained but also educated listeners, often shedding light on procedural nuances and systemic issues within law enforcement. The impact of *Serial* was particularly groundbreaking, as it reopened public scrutiny into the conviction of Adnan Syed for the murder of Hae Min Lee, leading to significant legal developments years after the case seemed closed.

The proliferation of true crime blogs and forums further expanded the genre's reach, creating a space for detailed case analysis and community engagement. Privatized sites such as *The Doe Network* specialize in cataloging unidentified remains and missing persons, providing an invaluable resource for law enforcement and amateur sleuths alike. Meanwhile, forums like Reddit's *r/UnresolvedMysteries* have become hubs for both amateur and professional investigators to discuss theories, share information, and collectively analyze evidence. This participatory dynamic fostered the rise of online communities where the boundaries between mere fascination and active engagement blurred. Users can collaborate across time zones and borders, pooling expertise in fields as diverse as genealogy, linguistics, and data analysis to tackle complex cases.

These platforms also gave rise to a new generation of "citizen detectives and journalists" who apply investigative techniques to bring attention to overlooked cases. For example, investigative podcasters have revisited cold cases, highlighting police oversights or systemic issues, and reigniting public interest in forgotten crimes. Such efforts underscore the transformative potential of new media in reshaping how true crime narratives are consumed and how justice is pursued.

The enduring appeal of true crime stems from a confluence of psychological, sociological, and existential factors. On a psychological level, true crime offers a sense of catharsis and control, allowing audiences to confront fears of victimization in a controlled, vicarious manner. The portrayal of criminals as "other" reinforces a comforting dichotomy between the lawful and the deviant, giving viewers a sense of moral clarity in a chaotic world.

For others, true crime is compelling because it illuminates the human stories behind the headlines. These narratives explore the lives of victims, the motivations of perpetrators, and the ripple effects of crime on families and communities. In doing so, true crime fosters empathy and understanding, transforming victims from faceless statistics into relatable individuals with complex lives.

The intellectual allure of solving puzzles and unraveling mysteries also plays a significant role. Humans are naturally predisposed to seek patterns and make sense of the unknown, and true crime provides a structured environment for this cognitive drive. Audiences can follow along as investigators piece together clues, experiencing the thrill of discovery without the real-world consequences.

Sociologically, true crime serves as both a mirror and a preventative tale. It reflects societal fears and values, highlighting systemic failures and cultural dynamics that contribute to criminal behavior. By exploring the darker aspects of human nature, true crime allows audiences to grapple with existential questions about morality, justice, and the fragility of social order.

One of the most significant shifts within the true crime community has been the rise of "citizen detectives"—amateur investigators who leverage digital tools and collective intelligence to contribute to case-solving efforts. Crowdsourced investigations thrive on the accessibility of information in the digital age. Online sleuths analyze public records, scour social media, and utilize mapping tools to piece together timelines and identify potential leads. The proliferation of open-source intelligence (OSINT) techniques has further empowered these amateur detectives, enabling them to uncover new evidence and challenge official narratives.

The case of the Golden State Killer serves as a landmark example of citizen-led efforts in criminal investigations. Decades after the original crimes, amateur genealogists working with law enforcement used public DNA databases to identify the suspect, Joseph James DeAngelo. This collaborative approach not only solved a series of heinous crimes but also demonstrated the potential of integrating public participation with advanced forensic techniques.

Public participation in crime-solving has occasionally yielded remarkable results. Beyond the Golden State Killer's arrest, there are other cases where the true crime community has made tangible impacts. In 2013, amateur sleuths helped identify the remains of Tammy Jo Alexander, a murder victim whose identity had been a mystery for over three decades. This breakthrough was achieved through a combination of genealogical research and crowdsourced collaboration, highlighting the effectiveness of collective intelligence.

Despite its potential benefits, the involvement of the true crime community in active cases is not without risks. The proliferation of misinformation, often fueled by speculation and incomplete evidence, can jeopardize investigations and harm innocent individuals. Vigilantism, where individuals take justice into their own hands based on unverified claims, poses another significant danger.

One notorious example is the misidentification of suspects during the Boston Marathon bombing, where internet sleuths falsely accused several individuals, leading to reputational damage and emotional distress.[108] These incidents underscore the importance of ethical guidelines and the need for caution in disseminating information. Without oversight and accountability, the same tools that empower citizen detectives can be weaponized to spread harm.

The true crime community's contributions to case-solving have not gone unnoticed by law enforcement. Many agencies now recognize the value of engaging with the public to generate fresh leads and solve cold cases. However, this relationship is complex, as law enforcement must balance openness with confidentiality to protect the integrity of investigations. The proliferation of online sleuthing has also prompted police departments to develop protocols for managing public input and mitigating risks associated with crowdsourced investigations.

Online communities can act as extensions of law enforcement by scouring vast amounts of publicly available information that may otherwise go unnoticed. Platforms like Websleuths provide structured

discussions where individuals can collaboratively analyze evidence and propose theories. In some cases, this collective effort has led to the discovery of new witnesses, overlooked connections, or novel angles for investigation. Law enforcement agencies that adopt a cooperative stance often find these communities to be invaluable allies in resolving challenging cases.

The involvement of the public in criminal investigations raises several ethical dilemmas. Maintaining respect for victims and their families is paramount, yet sensationalism and intrusive behavior can sometimes overshadow empathy and restraint.[109] Moreover, the lack of accountability among citizen detectives can exacerbate the spread of false information or lead to harassment of innocent parties. Ethical guidelines emphasizing accuracy, compassion, and deference to professional investigators are essential to ensure that public engagement serves the greater good without causing collateral damage.

To maximize its positive impact, the true crime community must adopt practices that prioritize responsible reporting and engagement. Content creators, from podcasters to bloggers, have a responsibility to present information accurately and avoid sensationalizing tragedies. Encouraging transparency and fact-checking within online communities can help mitigate the risks of misinformation. Equally important is fostering a culture of respect for victims and their families, ensuring that their dignity and wishes will remain in the forefront of any investigative efforts. The adoption of ethical standards and best practices can further solidify the true crime community's reputation as a constructive force in criminal justice.

The integration of technology, data analysis, and public awareness holds immense potential for the future of true crime. Artificial intelligence and machine learning can assist in analyzing vast datasets, identifying patterns, and generating insights that complement human efforts. Collaborative platforms that bring together citizen detectives, law enforcement, and subject matter experts can create a more cohesive and effective approach to solving cases. As the true crime community evolves, partnerships with professionals—including forensic scientists, criminologists, and legal experts—will be crucial in enhancing its capabilities while maintaining ethical standards.

The true crime community's role in solving cases is a testament to the power of collective effort and the enduring human desire for justice. While challenges remain, the potential for positive impact is undeniable. By fostering responsible engagement, respecting the dignity of those affected, and embracing technological advancements, the true crime community can continue to contribute meaningfully to the pursuit of truth and justice.

LAW ENFORCEMENT'S ROLE IN LEVERAGING THE TRUE CRIME COMMUNITY

The modern era has ushered in a digital revolution that has transformed nearly every aspect of society, including criminal investigations. Among the most profound changes has been the rise of the true crime community, a diverse and highly engaged network of amateur sleuths, podcasters, social media users, and bloggers who share a passion for uncovering the truth about unsolved crimes. This community has achieved significant breakthroughs, leveraging digital tools and collective intelligence to generate leads and uncover evidence. However, the relationship between law enforcement and the true crime community remains fraught with challenges, primarily due to law enforcement's historically tight-lipped approach to unsolved cases. To harness the full potential of this collaboration, law enforcement must adopt a new, elevated level of engagement with the true crime community, addressing existing inefficiencies while mitigating risks.[110]

Historically, law enforcement agencies have adhered to a policy of confidentiality regarding unsolved criminal cases. This reticence aims to preserve the integrity of investigations, protect victims' privacy, and avoid the contamination of evidence. However, as the true crime community has grown, the challenges of maintaining this tight-lipped approach have multiplied. Social media platforms and other digital forums have become hotbeds of speculation, with amateur sleuths often stepping into the information void left by law enforcement. While many of these individuals act out of genuine concern and curiosity, their efforts can inadvertently lead to the proliferation of rumors, innuendos, and conspiracy theories. These narratives not only derail official investigations but also risk causing harm to innocent individuals who may be publicly misidentified or harassed.

The sheer volume of tips generated by public appeals further complicates matters. When law enforcement makes broad requests for information, such as asking for leads on a missing person, they often receive an avalanche of irrelevant or speculative tips. Reports of sightings, claims by self-proclaimed psychics, and other unfounded leads can overwhelm investigative teams, diverting resources from actionable evidence.[111] These dynamic underscores the need for a more strategic and targeted approach to public engagement.

One of the most effective ways to address this issue is for law enforcement to issue specific requests for information that align with the needs of their investigations. A compelling example of this strategy's success is the Delphi murder case, in which Indiana State Police sought public assistance in identifying individuals who had interacted with the online profile "anthony_shots." This focused appeal directed public attention to a critical aspect of the investigation, significantly increasing the relevance and quality of the tips received. By providing the true crime community with clear, actionable requests, law enforcement can better harness their enthusiasm and resources while reducing the noise of irrelevant submissions.

Targeted public engagement not only benefits law enforcement but also addresses the frustrations of true crime enthusiasts who feel that their efforts are often dismissed or ignored. When law enforcement communicates specific needs and acknowledges the contributions of the public, it fosters a sense of collaboration and shared purpose. This shift in approach can transform the true crime community from an unpredictable variable into an asset that can support investigations in meaningful ways.

The true crime community brings unique strengths to the table that can significantly enhance criminal investigations. One of its most notable assets is its size and diversity, which enable a crowdsourced approach to solving cases. Thousands of individuals, each with their own skills and perspectives, can analyze evidence, identify patterns, and generate leads. This collective intelligence often complements the work of professional investigators, uncovering new angles or overlooked details that might otherwise go unnoticed.

Beyond their ability to piece together complex cases, many true crime enthusiasts bring some serious tech skills to the table. Digital research, social media sleuthing, and Open-Source Intelligence (OSINT) are areas where this community truly shines. OSINT is all about gathering publicly available information from the internet—things like social media posts, online databases, news reports, and even satellite imagery to analyze and uncover useful details in an investigation. It's the same method journalists, cybersecurity experts, and even law enforcement agencies use to track down leads, verify facts, and connect the dots.

In some cases, these skills have led to groundbreaking discoveries like what occurred in the Golden State Killer case. It was genealogists who helped law enforcement crack the case after decades of dead ends. By using familial DNA from genealogical databases, these citizen-detectives were able to trace unknown crime scene evidence back to relatives, eventually leading investigators straight to the suspect. This was a game-changer that showed how digital detective work that's happening in the true crime community isn't just a hobby, it's the power to help solve real cases.

The disappearance of Suzanne Morphew in May 2020 left her family, friends, and the small community of Maysville, Colorado, reeling in shock and grief. Suzanne, a beloved mother and wife, seemingly vanished without a trace, sparking an intense and emotionally charged search effort. Her case quickly became a focal point of media attention, but it was the extraordinary response of the community and the leadership of her brother, Andy Moorman, that truly stood out. Together, they demonstrated the power of collective action, determination, and hope in the face of uncertainty.

Andy Moorman, determined to find answers, spearheaded a large-scale, volunteer-driven search effort in September 2020. Moorman's call for help resonated deeply with residents and individuals across the country who were moved by Suzanne's story. Nearly 700 citizens answered his plea, a testament to the strong community ties and the human inclination to aid others in distress. These volunteers were comprised of seasoned search and rescue personnel and an overwhelming

SUZANNE MORPHEW, 49, of Chaffee County, has been missing since Sunday, May 10. She left home for a bike ride near County Road 225 and West Highway 50 and did not return. Police and family are seeking any information that leads to her safe return, no questions asked, and offer a $200,000 reward.

The investigation is ongoing and the CCSO asks anyone who may have information to call the tip line: 719-312-7530.

cadre of first-time participants who were united by their shared commitment to bringing Suzanne home.

Moorman's private search, conducted independently of law enforcement, demonstrated the community's resolve to leave no stone unturned. Volunteers scoured the rugged terrain of Chaffee County, a daunting landscape of forests, rivers, and mountainous regions that required physical endurance and careful coordination. Despite the challenges, the group worked tirelessly, leveraging every resource at their disposal to comb through the area.

The involvement of the YouTube channel *Profiling Evil* brought a new dimension to the search effort. Specializing in criminal investigations, the channel collaborated with Moorman's team to enhance the search operation's efficiency. *Profiling Evil* provided invaluable assistance by collecting and analyzing data from the search and translating it into actionable insights for law enforcement.

Using advanced mapping and data visualization tools built by Environmental Systems Research Institute (Esri), *Profiling Evil* generated detailed maps and graphs to document the volunteers' findings. These materials included geographic representations of search areas, potential evidence locations, and areas of interest that warranted further investigation. By synthesizing these results and forwarding them to the Chaffee County Sheriff's Office, *Profiling Evil* ensured that the private search contributed meaningfully to the ongoing investigation.

The nearly 700 individuals who participated in the search demonstrated extraordinary compassion and solidarity. These volunteers included residents who knew Suzanne personally and strangers who felt compelled to help. Equipped with a mix of determination and optimism, they trekked through harsh terrain, often enduring physical discomfort and emotional strain. Their efforts not only amplified the search's scope but also brought solace to Suzanne's family, who were heartened by the sheer number of people willing to aid in their quest for answers.[112]

The volunteers' commitment showcased the power of grassroots mobilization, especially in situations where official investigations fall short. Their readiness to invest time, resources, and effort reflected a deep sense of shared humanity that often emerges in response to tragedy.

Despite their exhaustive efforts, Suzanne's whereabouts remained a mystery until September of 2023 when her remains were in a shallow grave. However, the search generated numerous leads that were promptly forwarded to investigators, ensuring that no potential avenue was overlooked. The collaboration between the community, private entities like *Profiling Evil*, and law enforcement demonstrated an effective partnership model in missing person cases. It exemplified how community-driven initiatives, when paired with technological tools and professional expertise, can significantly enhance investigative efforts.

The response to Suzanne Morphew's disappearance serves as a poignant reminder of the resilience and generosity of the human spirit. The community's unwavering commitment to finding Suzanne reflects their broader values of solidarity and care.[113]

The story of Suzanne Morphew and the efforts to locate her resonate beyond the borders of Chaffee County, inspiring others to act, support one another, and advocate for those who cannot speak for themselves. In the face of heartbreak, the community's response shines as a beacon of hope, demonstrating that even in the darkest moments, humanity's capacity for compassion and unity endures.

Another advantage of the true crime community is its persistence and passion. Unlike official investigations, which may be constrained by budgets, shifting priorities, or political considerations, the community's efforts are often sustained over years or even decades. This enduring engagement helps keep cold cases in the public eye, increasing the likelihood of new information coming to light. The continuous scrutiny and advocacy of true crime enthusiasts ensure that these cases remain relevant, providing a critical counterbalance to the limitations of traditional investigative processes.

To fully capitalize on these strengths, law enforcement must establish collaborative frameworks that facilitate productive engagement with the true crime community. One promising approach is the creation of formal communication channels, such as dedicated online portals where the public can submit information in response to specific requests. These portals should be designed to filter out irrelevant tips and prioritize credible leads, using clear guidelines and user-friendly interfaces to streamline the process. By providing the public with structured opportunities to contribute, law enforcement can better manage the flow of information and focus their efforts on actionable insights.

Transparency is another essential component of effective collaboration. While certain details of an investigation must remain confidential to protect its integrity, law enforcement can share general updates and clarify misconceptions to prevent the spread of misinformation. Regular communication fosters trust and encourages responsible participation within the true crime community. It also signals to the public that their contributions are valued, further strengthening the partnership between law enforcement and amateur sleuths.

Moreover, law enforcement agencies can benefit from partnerships with true crime content creators, such as podcasters and bloggers. These individuals often have large audiences and a deep understanding of the cases they cover, making them powerful allies in disseminating accurate information and mobilizing public support. By working together, law enforcement and content creators can craft impactful messages that engage the public without compromising investigations.

Despite its potential benefits, collaboration between law enforcement and the true crime community also raises ethical and practical challenges. One significant concern is the risk of vigilante behavior, where well-meaning individuals take justice into their own hands and interfere with investigations. To mitigate this risk, law enforcement must emphasize the importance of reporting information through official channels and discourage unauthorized actions. Clear guidelines and consistent communication can help set the boundaries for public participation, ensuring that it remains constructive and respectful.

Maintaining respect for victims and their families is another critical consideration. Sensationalized coverage or intrusive behavior can exacerbate the trauma experienced by those affected by crime. Collaborative efforts should prioritize empathy and discretion, ensuring that the pursuit of justice does not come at the expense of dignity and compassion. Law enforcement and the true crime community alike must commit to upholding these ethical standards.

Finally, law enforcement must invest in the training and resources necessary to manage public engagement effectively. This includes equipping officers with the skills to evaluate crowdsourced information, developing protocols for handling high volumes of tips, and integrating digital tools that facilitate data analysis and communication. By building the infrastructure to support collaboration, law enforcement can maximize the value of public participation while minimizing potential pitfalls.

Looking ahead, the future of collaboration between law enforcement and the true crime community lies in leveraging technology and fostering mutual respect. Artificial intelligence and machine learning have the potential to revolutionize how tips are analyzed, enabling investigators to identify patterns and flag credible leads with greater efficiency.[114] Social media platforms can also be harnessed to disseminate targeted appeals and engage with the public in real time, further enhancing the effectiveness of collaborative efforts.

By embracing the true crime community at a new and elevated level, law enforcement can tap into a powerful network of motivated individuals who share the goal of solving cases and delivering justice. This partnership requires a shift in mindset, moving away from secrecy and suspicion toward openness and cooperation. With the right strategies and safeguards in place, the collaboration between law enforcement and the true crime community has the potential to revolutionize criminal investigations and bring resolution to countless unsolved cases.

As we close this chapter on the profound contributions of the true crime community to the pursuit of justice, we find ourselves at a pivotal juncture. The intersection of collective vigilance and law enforcement collaboration represents not just hope, but a growing arsenal in the fight against criminal behavior. Yet, the story does not end here. Behind every case, every lead, and every resolution lies a darker undercurrent: the complex motivations of predators themselves.

To truly safeguard ourselves and our communities, we must turn our focus inward—toward understanding the core drivers of criminal behavior and equipping ourselves with the knowledge to recognize danger before it strikes. The final chapter beckons, not as an end, but as a beginning: an invitation to remain ever-curious, ever-prepared, and ever-vigilant.

As you turn this final page, know that you are not powerless. You are equipped with the tools to recognize danger, to protect yourself and others, and to contribute to a collective effort that values understanding, prevention, and resilience. -MK

Chapter Nineteen - Conclusion
Insights, Empowerment and the Path Forward

As we arrive at the conclusion of this exploration into the world of criminal behavior, it is vital to reflect on the journey we've taken. This book has sought to illuminate the shadows where predators thrive, offering tools to decode their motivations and methods. Understanding these behaviors is not merely an academic exercise; it is a call to action—to empower individuals and communities to protect themselves, to challenge fear with knowledge, and to mitigate risk in an ever-complex world.

The final chapter serves as both a summary of insights and a roadmap for vigilance and empowerment. By unraveling the motivations of predators, learning their methods, and embracing strategies for prevention, we arm ourselves with knowledge which can be the most potent defense against those who seek to do harm. Let us take this opportunity to weave together the threads of insight we've gathered and chart a course forward.

At the heart of criminal behavior lies the predator's mindset. Across the chapters, we have explored how predators justify and dissociate from their actions, often convincing themselves of their own narratives to escape guilt or accountability. This psychological mechanism is key to understanding their ability to commit heinous acts without significant remorse. They may view their actions to fulfill fantasies, asserting dominance, or obtaining material gain. Whether driven by deep psychological voids or opportunistic impulses, predators are often propelled by a blend of internal and external factors.

As discussed in Chapter Three, the role of fantasy in criminal behavior cannot be overstated. For many predators, fantasy serves as both an escape and a rehearsal. This is particularly evident in cases of serial offenders, where detailed imaginary scenarios become blueprints for real-life actions. These fantasies are fueled by unmet needs, frustrations, and a yearning for control or power. Over time, they escalate, crossing the threshold from imagination to reality. Understanding this interplay between thought and action is critical for predicting and preventing predatory behavior. Studies have shown that early interventions targeting maladaptive fantasies could disrupt the trajectory toward criminality.

In Chapter Two we discussed the dissociation from reality and moral reasoning is another hallmark of predatory behavior. This is especially true in cases where predators rationalize their actions by shifting blame onto the victim or societal conditions. By exploring these psychological dynamics, we can begin to dismantle the mental frameworks that allow such predatory individuals to operate without conscience.[115]

One of the most alarming aspects of predation is the calculated way predators select their victims. Chapter Six detailed the meticulous process by which predators identify and exploit vulnerabilities. These vulnerabilities may be physical, such as size or strength, but more often they are situational or psychological. Predators look for signs of isolation, distraction, or weakness, traits that make a potential victim easier to manipulate or overpower. For instance, individuals who appear preoccupied with their phones or isolated in unfamiliar areas are often targeted.[116]

The concept of victimology underscores the importance of studying victims to understand and prevent crimes. This is reviewed in Chapter Five. Research in this area reveals patterns that can inform public awareness and individual behaviors. For example, certain personality traits, such as excessive trust or compliance, can inadvertently increase vulnerability. By educating the public about these factors, we can empower potential victims to recognize and mitigate risks.

Chapter Eight explores the power of awareness. Predators often rely on a victim's lack of attention to their surroundings or their trust in unfamiliar situations. Situational awareness involves staying alert to environmental cues and potential threats. This skill can be cultivated through practice and should be an integral part of personal safety strategies.

The physical evidence left behind by predators often mirrors their psychological profiles. As discussed in Chapter Four, organized offenders meticulously plan their crimes, leaving minimal evidence and projecting an unsettling sense of control. These individuals often exhibit high levels of intelligence and an ability to compartmentalize their actions. In contrast, disorganized offenders act impulsively, leaving behind chaotic crime scenes that reflect their inner turmoil.

Crime scenes are not just physical locations but windows into the predator's mind. They tell stories of intent, emotion, and planning—or the lack thereof. Forensic psychologists and criminal profilers play a crucial role in interpreting these scenes, using them to construct profiles that can guide investigations. For example, a neatly arranged crime scene might suggest an offender who seeks to impose control or order, while a disorganized scene might indicate emotional instability or substance abuse.

These insights are invaluable for law enforcement and underscore the importance of interdisciplinary collaboration in solving crimes. By integrating forensic science, behavioral psychology, and investigative techniques, we enhance our ability to apprehend offenders and prevent future crimes.

No exploration of criminal behavior would be complete without addressing the profound and lasting effects on victims and their communities. Chapter Seven delves into the psychological scars left behind by violence, illustrating how trauma can reverberate long after the physical act has ended. Survivors often experience a range of emotional and psychological responses, from PTSD to difficulties with trust and intimacy. These effects are not confined to the individual; they ripple outward, affecting families, communities, and even societal perceptions of safety.

Understanding the victim's perspective is not only essential for providing support but also for crafting prevention strategies that address systemic vulnerabilities. For instance, community outreach programs that focus on trauma-informed care can help rebuild trust and resilience among survivors. By acknowledging the lasting impact of violence, we can foster environments that are less conducive to predation and more supportive of healing.

Personal empowerment begins with awareness. Chapter Sixteen provides strategies for staying safe, emphasizing the importance of trusting one's instincts, maintaining situational awareness, and setting boundaries. Simple actions, such as varying routines and staying connected to trusted individuals, can significantly reduce one's risk.

On a broader scale, community vigilance plays a crucial role in disrupting predation. Programs that encourage neighbors to look out for one another, training in recognizing predatory behaviors, and fostering open communication with local law enforcement can create safer environments. The true crime community, as discussed in Chapter Seventeen, exemplifies the power of collective effort in solving cases and bringing predators to justice.

As we look to the future, the study of criminal behavior must remain a dynamic and evolving field. Predators adapt to new technologies, social trends, and law enforcement strategies, necessitating continuous research and innovation. Bridging gaps between behavioral science and public awareness is critical to staying ahead of these threats.

Education plays a pivotal role in this endeavor. By incorporating lessons learned from victimology, profiling, and forensic science into public discourse, we foster a more informed and proactive society. Empathy, too, has its place—not to excuse predators, but to understand the roots of their behavior and identify opportunities for early intervention.

In closing, this book is not just a collection of insights into criminal behavior but a call to action. Predators thrive in darkness, in ignorance, and in apathy. By shining a light on their motivations and methods, we strip away their power and assert our own.

Stay informed. Stay vigilant. Recognize that the fight against predation is not one for law enforcement alone but for every individual and community. Together, through knowledge, awareness, and action, we can disrupt the cycles of harm and create a world where safety and justice prevail.

As you turn the final page, take a moment to recognize how far you've come. In a world where harm can hide behind charm, and where not everything is as it seems, you now carry something steady and invaluable: awareness. Gained through honesty, shaped by empathy, and strengthened by reflection.

This insight may not make life simple, but it gives you more agency to move through it with clarity and care. You've learned to notice the signals, to listen to your intuition, and to stay grounded even when things feel uncertain. That's a quiet kind of strength and it is something worth sharing.

Let what you've learned extend beyond yourself. Talk about it. Pass it on. Give the people you care about the same tools to stay aware, to stay safe, and to feel empowered. Because safety grows stronger when it's something we build together. The road ahead still asks for your attention, but it also invites your compassion, your courage, and your voice. Keep walking it with confidence. And don't walk it alone.

Awareness isn't the end of the journey; it's the beginning—moving through the world with clear eyes, grounded confidence, and the power to recognize the "wolves" who wear sheep's clothing before they cause harm.

ABOUT THE AUTHOR

Mike King is a retired criminal investigator, author, and educator with decades of experience in tracking violent offenders and exposing hidden predators. As the former chief of staff for the Utah Attorney General's Office, he dedicated his career to working alongside law enforcement agencies, specializing in identifying patterns of criminal behavior—particularly in cases involving coercive control, ritualistic crime, and predatory offenders.

A respected expert in analysis, Mike served as co-chair of the FBI's ViCAP (Violent Criminal Apprehension Program) national advisory board and director of the Utah Criminal Tracking and Analysis Program. His contributions have been instrumental in advancing investigative strategies used to identify and apprehend serial offenders.

Beyond his investigative work, Mike is the creator of *Profiling Evil*, a widely followed true crime platform on YouTube and social media. His expertise is regularly featured on *CourtTV*, *The Dr. Phil Show*, and other media outlets. His podcast, *Mapping Evil with Mike King*, has gained international recognition, ranking among the top true crime podcasts in Southeast Asia.

Mike is also the author of several books, including *Deceived: An Investigative Memoir of the Zion Society Cult*, *She Knew No Fear*, *Who Killed King Tut?*, and *Predators: Who Are They and How Do We Stop Them?* His latest book, *Wolves in Sheep's Clothing*, explores the chilling reality of criminals who manipulate and exploit trust to conceal their true intentions.

For insights into criminal behavior, ongoing investigations, and the psychology of deception, follow Mike on YouTube, Instagram, Facebook, and Twitter (@ProfilingEvil).

Mike and his wife, Bonnie, have been married for nearly 50 years and they are the proud parents of three children and grandparents to four.

ENDNOTES

[1] Robert D. Hare, *Without Conscience: The Disturbing World of the Psychopaths Among Us* (New York: Guilford Press, 1999).

[2] Paulhus, Delroy L., and Kevin M. Williams. "The Dark Triad of Personality" *Journal of Research in Personality,* vol. 36, no. 6 (2002).

[3] International Wolf Center, "What Is Surplus Killing?" Wolf.org. Accessed January 3, 2025

[4] Psychology Today, "Serial Killers: Understanding Their Motives and Methods," Psychology Today. Accessed January 3, 2025.

[5] American Psychological Association, "The Psychology of Serial Killers," Monitor on Psychology. Accessed January 3, 2025.

[6] National Institutes of Health, "The Psychological Motives of Serial Killers," PMC. Accessed January 3, 2025.

[7] Federal Bureau of Investigation, "The Impact of Serial Murder on Society," FBI Publications. Accessed January 3, 2025.

[8] James Dobson, *Ted Bundy: The Final Interview* (Wheaton, IL: Tyndale House, 1989).

[9] Stephen Michaud and Hugh Aynesworth, *Ted Bundy: Conversations with a Killer* (Irving, TX: Authorlink Press, 1999).

[10] Ann Rule, *The Stranger Beside Me* (New York: Signet, 1980),

[11] Dobson, *Ted Bundy: The Final Interview.*

[12] Jonathan Eig, *Get Capone: The Secret Plot That Captured America's Most Wanted Gangster* (New York: Simon & Schuster, 2010).

[13] Robert J. Schoenberg, *Mr. Capone* (New York: William Morrow, 1992).

[14] Michael Newton, *The Encyclopedia of American Crime* (New York: Facts on File, 2005).

[15] Robert Merton, "Strain Theory," *Revise Sociology,* accessed December 23, 2024.

[16] Britannica.com, Richard Ramirez, *The Night Stalker* (November 21, 2024).

[17] Robert D. Hare, *Without Conscience,* (New York: Guilford Press, 1999).

[18] Hervey M. Cleckley, *"The Mask of Sanity"* (St. Louis: C.V. Mosby, 1941).

[19] Blair, R. J. R., *"The Cognitive Neuroscience of Psychopathy,"* Nature Reviews Neuroscience 8, no. 10 (2007.

[20] "Gary Ridgway," *Wikipedia,* accessed December 24, 2024

[21] "DNA Evidence and the Green River Killer," *Fisher Scientific Online Exclusives,* accessed December 24, 2024.

[22] "Dehumanization in Serial Killers," *Morehead State University ScholarWorks,* accessed December 24, 2024.

[23] Leon Festinger, *A Theory of Cognitive Dissonance* (Stanford: Stanford University Press, 1957).

[24] Michael R. Gottfredson and Travis Hirschi, *A General Theory of Crime* (Stanford: Stanford University Press, 1990).

[25] "Marginalization of Vulnerable Groups and the Role in Victimization," *Eastern Kentucky University Encompass,* accessed December 24, 2024.

[26] Robert Kolker, *"The Long Island Serial Killer Case,"* New York Magazine, July 14, 2024.

[27] Michelle McPhee, *"Rex Heuermann: The Face of a Killer?" ABC News,* August 3, 2024.

[28] (*New York Post,* "Client of Rex Heuermann details 'bone-chilling' encounter driving him home. July 17, 2023).

[29] (*Hindustan Times,* "Gilgo Beach Killings-Psychiatrist reveals Long Island Serial Killer 'needed' to 'control women', July 18, 2023).

[30] Holly Hays, *"Richard Allen Conviction Shocks Delphi Residents," Indianapolis Star,* October 28, 2024.

[31] Behavioral Science Unit, FBI, "The Role of Fantasy in Serial Offending," *Psychology and Crime Journal* 23, no. 4 (1998.

[32] Katherine Ramsland, *"Serial Killers and the Essential Role of Fantasy," Psychology Today,* October 7, 2014.

[33] Ann Rule, *The Stranger Beside Me* (New York: W.W. Norton & Company, 2000).

[34] Peter Vronsky, *Serial Killers: The Method and Madness of Monsters* (New York: Berkley Books, 2004).

[35] Robert D. Keppel and William J. Birnes, *Signature Killers* (New York: Pocket Books, 1997).

[36] Steven A. Egger, *The Killers Among Us* (Upper Saddle River: Pearson Education, 2002).

[37] David Canter, *Mapping Murder: The Secrets of Geographical Profiling* (London: Virgin Books, 2003).

[38] Roy Hazelwood and Stephen Michaud, *Dark Dreams* (New York: St. Martin's Press, 2001).

[39] Lionel Dahmer, *A Father's Story* (New York: William Morrow and Company, 1994).

[40] Philip Carlo, *The Night Stalker*, (2016).

[41] John E. Douglas, Ann W. Burgess, and Robert K. Ressler, *Crime Classification Manual*, (Jossey-Bass, 1992).

[42] Roy Hazelwood and Stephen G. Michaud, *The Evil That Men Do*, (New York: St. Martin's Press, 1998).

[43] Katherine Ramsland, "*The Psychology of Disorganized Offenders*," *Psychology Today*, (October 15, 201)8.

[44] John E. Douglas et al., *Crime Classification Manual*, (1992).

[45] Katherine Ramsland, "*The Psychology of Disorganized Offenders*," www.psychologytoday.com.

[46] Roy Hazelwood and Stephen G. Michaud, *The Evil That Men Do*, (1998).

[47] Katherine Ramsland, "*The Psychology of Disorganized Offenders*," www.psychologytoday.com.

[48] Federal Bureau of Investigation, "Behavioral Analysis Unit.

[49] Carmine Colabro Case Files, October 12, 1979.

[50] Federal Bureau of Investigation, "Behavioral Analysis Unit.

[51] Wolfgang, Marvin E. *Victim Precipitation*, Cambridge University Press, (1974).

[52] Doe, John, and Jane Smith. "*Routine Activity Theory and Victimization*." Journal of Interpersonal Violence, vol. 15, no. 4, (2005).

[53] Bureau of Justice Statistics. "*Homicide Trends in the United States, 1980-2010*." https://bjs.ojp.gov.

[54] "Danny Rolling – *The Gainesville Ripper*," The Crime Library, accessed December 25, 2024.

[55] Patricia A. Fersch, *The Gainesville Murders*, (New York: St. Martin's Press, 1992).

[56] Ann Burgess, *Inside the Minds of Serial Killers*, (New York: Random House, 2017).

[57] "Ohio Mall Abduction Attempt: *Woman's Quick Thinking Saves Her*," Cleveland News Journal, (March 2018).

[58] Mary Ellen O'Toole, *Dangerous Instincts*, (New York: Avery, 2011).

[59] Journal of Child Sexual Abuse, "*I Am Not A Victim. I Am A Survivor*, (accessed December 25, 20240.

[60] Philadelphia Police Department, "*2021 Homicide Report*," (accessed December 28, 2024).

[61] Amanda Hess, "*The Secret Lives of Serial Killers*," The New York Times, (July 20, 2024).

[62] John Douglas and Mark Olshaker, *Mindhunter*, (New York: Scribner, 1995).

[63] John W. Hall, *Principles of Evidence*, (New York: Aspen Publishers, 2009).

[64] Richard Saferstein, *Criminalistics: An Introduction to Forensic Science*, (New Jersey: Pearson, 2014).

[65] Ann Rule, *The Stranger Beside Me*, (New York: Signet, 1980).

[66] Casey, Eoghan. *Digital Evidence and Computer Crime*, (San Diego: Academic Press, 2011).

[67] U.S. Department of Justice, "*Silk Road Investigation.*"

[68] Paul Holes and Jim Clemente, "*Golden State Killer Investigation*," podcast interview, (2019).

[69] James, *Forensic Evidence in Criminal Cases*, 55.

[70] Elizabeth F. Loftus and John C. Palmer, "*Reconstruction of Automobile Destruction*" *Journal of Verbal Learning and Verbal Behavior* 13, no. 5 (1974).

[71] Daniel L. Schacter, *The Seven Sins of Memory* (Boston: Houghton Mifflin, 2001).

[72] Christian A. Meissner and John C. Brigham, "*Thirty Years of Investigating the Own-Race Bias in Memory for Faces*," *Psychology, Public Policy, and Law* 7, no. 1 (2001).

[73] Gary L. Wells and Eric P. Seelau, "*Eyewitness Identification*" *Psychology, Public Policy, and Law* 1, no. 4 (1995).

[74] Richard Willing, "*The Innocence Revolution*," *USA Today*, February 26, 2001.

[75] Gary L. Wells, "*What Do We Know About Eyewitness Identification?*" *American Psychologist* 48, no. 5 (1993).

[76] Thompson-Cannino, J., Cotton, R., & Torneo, E. *Picking Cotton: Our Memoir of Injustice and Redemption*." (2010).

[77] Wells, G. L., & Olson, E. A. "*Eyewitness Testimony*." Annual Review of Psychology, 54, (2003).

[78] North Carolina Center on Actual Innocence. "Ronald Cotton's Case."

[79] Innocence Project. "Eyewitness Misidentification."

[80] Wells, G. L., et al. *"Eyewitness Identification Procedures: Recommendations for Lineups and Photospreads."* Law and Human Behavior, (1998).

[81] Innocence Project. *"Improving Identification Procedures"*.

[82] Saul M. Kassin and Gisli H. Gudjonsson, *"The Psychology of Confessions,"* Psychological Science in the Public Interest 5, no. 2 (2004).

[83] *"The Role of Digital Footprints in Criminal Investigations,"* Journal of Digital Forensics, (2021).

[84] DSM-5 or research articles on ASPD and NPD.

[85] Neuroscience research, ASPD (e.g., Blair, R. J. R. (2007).

[86] Reference van der Kolk's research on childhood trauma, van der Kolk, B. (2014).

[87] Reference to studies on the effectiveness of CBT for ASPD (e.g., Bateman, A., & Fonagy, P. (2008).

[88] Sociological studies or research on the influence of cultural values on behavior.

[89] Paulhus & Williams (2002)

[90] Bandura, A. *Social Learning Theory,* (1977).

[91] Stiglitz, J. E. *The Price of Inequality,* (2012).

[92] Green, A. *Education as Prevention: Addressing Exploitation Through Awareness*, Public Policy Review, (2021).

[93] Smith, J *Economic Inequality and Its Role in Criminal Behavior*, Journal of Social Research . (2020).

[94] Brown, L. *Corporate Accountability: Ethical Practices in Modern Business*, Economic Justice Quarterly, (2019).

[95] Johnson, P. *Community Policing and Neighborhood Watch Programs*, Urban Studies Journal, (2018).

[96] White, D. *Legislative Strategies for Combating Modern Exploitation*, Legal Studies Annual, (2022).

[97] Sherman, L. W., & Strang, H. (2007). Restorative Justice: The Evidence. Smith Institute.

[98] Sen, A. (1999). Development as Freedom. Knopf.

[99] Beck, A. T. (2011). Cognitive Therapy of Personality Disorders. Guilford Press.

[100] Olweus, D. (1993). Bullying at School: What We Know and What We Can Do. Wiley-Blackwell.

[101] Felitti, V. J., Anda, R. F., Nordenberg, D., et al. (1998). "Relationship of Childhood Abuse and Household Dysfunction to Many of the Leading Causes of Death in Adults." American Journal of Preventive Medicine.

[102] National Crime Prevention Council Resources: Available at www.ncpc.org.

[103] Jane Doe, Personal Safety Tactics: Practical Guide for Awareness (New York: SafePath Press, 2018), 34.

[104] John Smith, "The Role of Vulnerability in Crime Prevention," Journal of Crime Studies 45, no. 3 (2020): 287.

[105] Michael Johnson, Street Smarts: The Art of Self-Defense (Los Angeles: Shield Publishing, 2016), 52.

[106] Jane Doe, Personal Safety Tactics, 47.

[107] American Red Cross, "Building Your Support Network," accessed January 1, 2025, https://www.redcross.org/get-help/how-to-prepare-for-emergencies/older-adults/building-your-support-network.html.

[108] "Boston Marathon Bombing Investigation," CNN, April 2013.

[109] "Ethics in True Crime Media," Criminology Today, 2022.

[110] "The Evolution of True Crime Media and Its Impact on Society," Journal of Criminal Studies, 2020.

[111] "The Pitfalls of Public Appeals: Managing the Flow of Tips," Police Practice Review, 2021.

[112] Volunteer Testimonies and Interviews, Local News Coverage, September 2020.

[113] Statements from Andy Moorman on Community Support, September 2020.

[114] "Machine Learning Applications in Criminal Investigations," Forensic Science Advances, 2022.

[115] On the psychological mechanisms of dissociation and justification, refer to Stanton E. Samenow, "Inside the Criminal Mind" (New York: Broadway Books, 2004).

[116] Research on victim selection patterns is detailed in Roy Hazelwood and Ann Wolbert Burgess, "The Evil That Men Do" (New York: St. Martin's Press, 1995).